Instructor's Manual with Test Bank and T
Masters to accompany

THE LITIGATION PARALEGAL

A Systems Approach
Fourth Edition

James W. H. McCord
Sandra L. McCord

WEST
★
THOMSON LEARNING ™

Australia Canada Mexico Singapore Spain United Kingdom United States

WEST LEGAL STUDIES

Instructor's Manual with Test Bank and Transparency Masters to accompany
The Litigation Paralegal: A Systems Approach 4E
James W.H. McCord and Sandra L. McCord

Copyright © 2002 Delmar
West Legal Studies is an imprint of
Delmar, a division of Thomson
Learning, Inc. Thomson Learning is a
trademark used herein under li-
cense.

Printed in the United States of
America
    5 XXX 05

For more information contact
Delmar, 3 Columbia Circle, PO Box
15015,
Albany, NY 12212-5015.

Or find us on the World Wide Web
at http://www.westlegalstudies.com.

For permission to use material from
this text or product, contact us by
Tel (800) 730-2214
Fax (800) 730-2215
www.thomsonrights.com

Library of Congress Card Catalog
Number: — 2001046527

ISBN 0-7668-4056-5

NOTICE TO THE READER

Publisher does not warrant or guarantee any of hte products described herein or perform any independent analysis in con-
nection with any of the product information contained herein. Publisher does not assume, and expressly disclaims, any
obligation to obtain and include information other than that provided to it by the manufacturer.

The reader is notified that this text is an educational tool, not a practice book. Since the law is in constant change, no rule
or statement of law in this book should be relied upon for any service to any client. The reader should always refer to standard legal sources for the current rule or law. If legal advice or other expert assistance is required, the services of the appropriate professional should be sought.

The Publisher makes no representation or warranties of any kind, including but not limited to, the warranties of fitness for
particular purpose or merchantability, nor are any such representations implied with respect to the material set forth herein,
and the publisher takes no responsiblity with respect to such material. The publisher shall not be liable for any special, conse-
quential, or exemplary damages resulting, in whole or part, from the readers' use of, or reliance upon, this material.

CONTENTS

Introduction   v

Chapter 1   Welcome to the Law Office   1

Chapter 2   The Initial Interview   11

Chapter 3   Evidence and Investigation   19

Chapter 4   Drafting the Complaint   34

Chapter 5   Filing the Lawsuit, Service of Process, and Obtaining a Default Judgment   41

Chapter 6   Defending and Testing the Lawsuit: Motions, Answers, and other Responsive Pleadings   46

Chapter 7   Discovery   Overview and Interrogatories   56

Chapter 8   Discovery: Depositions   64

Chapter 9   Discovery   Document Production and Control, Medical Exams, Admissions, and Compelling Discovery   71

Chapter 10   Settlement and Other Alternative Dispute Resolutions   80

Chapter 11   Trial Preparation and Trial   86

Chapter 12   Post-Trial Practice from Motions to Appeal   92

Test Bank   97

Transparency Masters   191

INTRODUCTION

A COURSE PLAN

This instructor's manual is a resource of teaching ideas and materials to accompany the classroom text *The Litigation Paralegal: A Systems Approach, Fourth Edition*, by James W. H. McCord, published by West Legal Studies. The text and instructor's manual form a course plan consisting of substantive text, exercises in paralegal skills (competencies), a variety of classroom activities, assignments, review questions, tests, and answer keys.

The approach of the text places the student in a law office setting where the instructor assumes the role of the paralegals' supervising attorney. This office training procedure uses a systems approach in which the student incrementally develops a litigation system folder compete with forms, documents, checklists, rules, and practice tips. The system is complete at the end of the course and should provide the student with a valuable resource.

The text and instructor's manual, however, are designed to provide the instructor with maximum flexibility to accommodate a more traditional, or other, approach.

THE SYSTEM FOLDER

A system folder is a detailed procedure manual providing direction, forms, and checklists for tasks regularly performed by a paralegal. As a resource for the paralegal, it provides obvious advantages in efficiency, uniformity, accuracy, and quality. It can also be regularly updated. See the section in this introduction on computer assignments for a suggestion on computerizing the system folder.

Use of the system has proven valuable in both teaching and learning litigation paralegal skills. Because a good system folder helps the student on the job, and perhaps in securing a job, the system folder provides an extra incentive to do the assignments thoroughly and accurately. It helps the student learn the benefits of being organized and develop the confidence to create a system in any are of law. Utilization of the systems approach also reinforces the skills presented in the text.

While this approach can be useful to both the instructor and the students, it is not necessary to the productive use of the text and manual. The key is flexibility; use a process with which you are comfortable.

Appendix A at the end of the text provides an outline of the contents of a completed systems folder.

THE TEXT

The Litigation Paralegal: A Systems Approach, Fourth Edition introduces students to the law office and takes them chronologically through the steps and tasks involved in litigation, from fact situations of cases they will be working on to judgment enforcement. Chapter by chapter, they build proficiency in the specific tasks or competencies required of them as paralegals.

In each chapter the student is given the following:

1. One or more specific litigation tasks.
2. Substantive and procedural background on the task.
3. Guidelines and directions on how to perform the task.
4. Examples from a sample case on how to perform the task.
5. Key terms and definitions.
6. System folder assignments to develop understanding of procedures and to compile a working system folder.
7. Application assignments to promote analytical thinking and the application of skills learned to actual paralegal task in the context of one or more of the provided cases.
8. Helpful Web sites related to chapter materials.
9. Internet exercises for substantive research and to develop familiarity with law-related Web sites.
10. Extensive study guide questions to review and reinforce learning.

THE INSTRUCTOR'S MANUAL

For each chapter this manual provides the following:

1. Chapter objective.
2. Suggestions for instructional supplements.
3. Suggestions for class activities.
4. Chapter outline, including placement of key terms, exhibits, and assignments.
5. Learning exercises with suggested answers or approaches. These exercises include system folder assignments, application assignments, and Internet exercises from the text as well as a section of additional exercises found only in the instructor's manual.
6. Chapter tests and answers. These are a combination of objective questions, short answer, and take-home projects. *In addition, testing material can easily be drawn from study guide questions at the end of each chapter in the text and from the Additional Exercises section of the instructor's manual.*

COMPUTERIZED TEST BANK

The Test Bank in the Instructor's Lounge is also available in computerized format on CD-ROM. Platforms supported include Microsoft Windows 3.1™ and Windows 95™, Windows NT™, and Macintosh®.

Features include the following:

- multiple methods of question selection
- multiple outputs (print, ASCII, and RTF)
- graphic support (black and white)
- random questioning output
- special character support

COMPUTER ASSIGNMENTS AND A COMPUTERIZED SYSTEM FOLDER

Besides the Internet Exercises, a number of assignments are either specifically suggested as computer assignments or can be easily adapted as computer assignments.

Assignments such as document drafting, form creation, research, deposition summaries, time keeping, billing, data storage, damage calculations, and so on, can be computerized. This can be done in a computer classroom on a network system using litigation and other software. Students can do individual assignments in a computer lab, if one is available. If some basic background information, pleadings, depositions, and so on, can be entered on the network or on disks and copied for each student, they can get valuable experience retrieving the basic information as they need it for various projects. A secretary could do the initial data entry that would form the basis for all future computer assignments. Some schools are using optical scanners for this purpose.

The entire system folder can be done on computer, allowing students to leave the course with their own system diskettes. Forms, examples, checklists, and references would be in an easily portable form, ready to be adapted and updated in a particular law office.

MOCK TRIAL

This activity captures student interest and heightens motivation toward the conclusion of the course when the attention of some students begins to wane.

Many of the assignments in the text and workbook may be used as building blocks for the mock trial. Any of the Chapter 1 cases can be used, or another case that you might choose. If the *Forrester* or *Ameche* case is used, there are numerous assignments throughout the text that are particularly appropriate for dividing the class into teams representing the plaintiff(s) or defendant(s). The trial can be held over two to three class periods or at a longer special evening or weekend session. This session might be held in a local courtroom to lend an aura of reality. The instructor, a local attorney, or a judge can serve as trial judge. (It is best to ask someone else to serve as judge so you are free to evaluate each student's work.) Background information, pleadings, depositions, and so on, will have been accumulated by the end of the course to provide the grist for the trial.

Procedure

Divide the class into legal teams for the plaintiff and defendant. Each team can have as many as six or seven members responsible for various aspects of the case, such as opening, direct of witness A, cross of defendant's witness C, closing, and so forth. When not actually playing the lawyer's role, students can sere as supporting paralegals keeping track of documents and making suggestions when needed.

Some of the class will be assigned to be key witnesses for each side. Although the witnesses may have the benefit of material covered previously in the text and workbook assignments, all witnesses will need some general parameters for their testimony. To keep workloads as even as possible, witnesses could also be assigned some of the trial preparation tasks to ease the burden of the legal teams. Remaining students can be assigned as jurors. Students from outside class can be used as jurors if you have a small class. (Students from an Introduction to Law class make good jurors. This is a valuable learning experience for them, too.) If the class is particularly large, you could have two juries.

Each juror is responsible for a critique of their jury's decision process and why they decided the way they did. Several students could be asked to read their critiques as a concluding activity focusing on jury dynamics. For those schools so equipped, a closed circuit video may be arranged so the student legal teams and witnesses could watch the deliberation process.

The following witnesses could be used for the *Forrester* case:*

Ms. Forrester
Mr. Hart
Mr. or Ms. _____, officer at Mercury Parcel
Ms. Schnabel
Ms. Forrester's physician(s)
First police officer on scene
Physician for Mercury Parcel
Mechanic at Mercury Parcel
Mr. Forrester

For the *Ameche* case:*

Mr. and Ms. Ameche
Mr. and Ms. Congden
Robert Warren
Electrical expert (saying fire is possible if conditions were right; it is possible that moving the extension cord may or may not have increased the likelihood of fire)
Physician for Mr. Ameche
Physician for Congdens
First police officer or firefighter on the scene

The time for opening arguments, direct and cross examination, and other matters will have to be calculated and strictly enforced. The maximum time for jury deliberation will have to be determined according to how much class time remains.

The jury should also be given guidelines such as: choose a foreperson, discuss the most critical aspects of evidence, the plaintiff's burden of proof, whether all elements are proved to their satisfaction, whether defendant is negligent and, if so, how much in damages should be awarded.

Critiquing

This class project can be assessed in several ways. Evaluation can be on the basis of a written analysis by each student of their role or task and what they learned overall from the experience. Another method is based on the individual performance of each student's assigned task.

---

*A small team of students could be assigned early in the course the task of drafting the witness background information sheets so the case is close but slightly tilted in one direction. They could be told to draft it both ways so you have the choice and can prevent leaks on which direction the testimony will lean. This is a valuable assignment because it forces the students to focus on elements and needed evidence to support those elements.

Further Suggestions

Opening and closing arguments should be kept brief, possibly no more than five minutes for each side. Most of the time should be allotted to witness testimony through direct examination and cross examination. Judges should deal with objections quickly, giving some latitude to questions and evidence to speed the trial along. Demonstrative evidence can be permitted but needs to be approved ahead of time by the instructor to see that common sense applies and that such evidence does not impair the speed and fairness of the trial. Some instructions may be read to the jury by the judge, but they should be kept brief and go to the heart of the elements in the case. Unless there is a lot of time, jury deliberation should be kept to 30 minutes. It will be the foreperson's job to see that a decision is made in that time.

STUDENT FAIR

Fellow educator Faith O'Reilly has developed a student fair that provides another focus to the course. At the end of the litigation course, the students display their system folders to a team of judges and lawyers. Based on some criteria established by the instructor, the judges evaluate the systems and ask the students questions. They decide on several top places and some honorable mentions. This provides an extra incentive for each student to be conscientious in the preparation of the system, especially near the end of the course. A further benefit is getting prospective employers to see and appreciate the ability of the students and the quality of their instruction.

ASSIGNMENTS AND GRADING

If this text is to be covered in one semester, it is not realistic to expect students to complete all the assignments provided in the text and instructor's manual. The purpose of some assignments is simply to provide more practice for those who need it in an area that has already been covered; others repeat an area, but from a different angle. Many assignments are flexible, allowing you to insert material or cases form your own experience or additional student research. *Select the assignments that best fit the needs of your students and your time frame.*

The learning exercises require the student to prepare a variety of documents. Every student ought to be able to do many of these assignments accurately and completely, leaving little if any differentiation between a grade of A and a grade of C on the assignment. In such instances, it is the drafting and familiarity with the documents that are paramount. Therefore, you may wish to consider using S (satisfactory) or U (unsatisfactory—to be redone) as a more practical system for grading such assignments. It might be added that eventually all such assignments must be completed satisfactorily to receive a passing grade in the course. This procedure will avoid the problem of watering down your A, which should be reserved for those assignments where the difference in student learning or abilities will be more apparent and measurable.

James W. H. McCord
Sandra L. McCord

CHAPTER 1

WELCOME TO THE LAW OFFICE

CHAPTER OBJECTIVE

The purpose of this chapter is to give the students a feeling that they are starting work in a law office. The first section provides case "stories" that demonstrate the kinds of events that may lead to litigation. The stories give the necessary factual settings for many of the assignments and examples in the text, and bring them to life.

The Paralegal Handbook section is "the firm's" introduction to the office, its personnel, the role of the paralegal, important procedures, professional ethics, and professional development. It also introduces the systems approach. The section following the handbook provides an introduction to (or review of) court structure, jurisdiction, and venue.

PREPARING FOR CLASS: INSTRUCTIONAL SUPPLEMENTS

1. A diagram of your state court structure and a detailed description of the jurisdiction of each court.
2. Names, addresses, and phone numbers of the clerk of court for the federal district court in your state and for any appropriate state courts.
3. A list of local paralegal associations, officers, addresses, and phone numbers.
4. Any provision of your state's code of professional responsibility or rules of court that complement the chapter material on ethics for paralegals.
5. Pertinent Web sites.

SUGGESTED CLASS ACTIVITIES

1. Have a carefully chosen attorney or paralegal law office manager speak to the class about the typical structure and procedures of the law office.
2. Invite a local judge to lecture on the state and federal courts and their jurisdictions.
3. Have officers of local, state, or national paralegal associations speak on their associations, the importance of professional ethics, and personal professional development.

OUTLINE

I. Introduction
   Key term: Civil litigation
   Exhibit 1:1, Office Organization Chart
   A. Case I
   B. Case II
   C. Case III
   D. Case IV
   E Case V
II. Office Manual
III. A Paralegal Handbook: Office Orientation
   A. Structure and Personnel
      1. Titles
      2. The Changing Law Office
      3. The Work of the Firm
      4. The Role of the Paralegal
   B. Important Law Office Procedures
      1. Introduction
      2. Timekeeping and billing
         Key terms: billable hours, task-based billing
         Exhibit 1:2, Permanent Time Log
         Application Assignment 1
      3. Disbursement (Expense) Entry
         Exhibit 1:3, Permanent Disbursement Record
      4. Deadline (Docket) Control
         Exhibit 1:4, Deadline Slip
         Application Assignment 2
      5. Technology Management
      6. E-Mail
   C. Techniques for Thriving in the Law Office
   D. The Training Procedure
      1. Procedure, Task Information, Assignments
      2. Developing a Litigation System
         Key term: litigation system
         System Folder Assignment 1
   E. Ethical and other Professional Responsibilities
      1. Introduction

Key term: professional ethics
System Folder Assignment 2
Application Assignment 3
Internet Exercise 1
2. What a Paralegal May Not Do
Key term: legal advice
3. What a Paralegal May Do
4. Confidentiality, Honesty, Conflict of Interest, and Other Ethical Considerations
Key term: pro bono
5. Other Professional Considerations
F. Your Professional Development
System Folder Assignment 3
Internet Exercises 2, 3, and 4
IV. The Court Systems
A. Introduction
B. Basic Components of a Court System
1. The Trial Court
2. The Appellate Court
3. The Intermediate Appellate Court
C. Jurisdiction
Key terms: jurisdiction, jurisdictional amount, supplemental jurisdiction
D. Federal Courts and Their Jurisdiction
1. Introduction
2. United States District Court
Key terms: federal questions, diversity of citizenship, domicile, alienage jurisdiction
3. United States Court of Appeals
Exhibit 1:5, U.S. Courts of Appeals and U.S. District Courts
4. United States Supreme Court
Key term: writ of certiorari
5. Specialized Federal Courts
Exhibit 1:6, The Federal Court System
E. State Courts and Their Jurisdiction
Exhibit 1:7, The State Court System
System Folder Assignment 4
Internet Exercise 5
F. Venue
Key term: venue
G. Choosing a Court: The Relationship between Jurisdiction and Venue, and Other Considerations
System Folder Assignment 5
Application Assignment 4
H. Transfer of Cases
V. A Case Roadmap
Exhibit 1:8, Case Roadmap
VI. Summary

SYSTEM FOLDER ASSIGNMENTS

Assignment 1

Set up a three-ring binder with the tab dividers arranged as described. Copies of the office structure and forms previously discussed should be placed in the system folder as indicated in Appendix A. Begin a table of contents for your system folder and add any information assigned by your instructor.

ANSWER: This assignment starts the use of the system. If you decide to have the students develop a system folder, the setting up of the folder needs considerable emphasis now and throughout the course. You many choose to have the folder turned in periodically for evaluation. unannounced and random spot checks or turn-ins for a grade might help fight inevitable procrastination.

Assignment 2

Look up your state's ethical rules that govern confidentiality, conflict of interest, attorney supervision of lay persons and legal assistants, professional integrity, and others. Record the rule numbers in an ethics section of your system folder. Look up your state's unauthorized practice of law statute; note the wording and the possible penalties. You might want to add this to your folder. As you read further in this text and in other sources, insert in your folder the citations for key ethical rules and guidelines.

ANSWER: What a paralegal may not do:

- Provide legal services directly to the public without the supervision of an attorney.
- Give legal advice or counsel a client.
- Represent a client in court or act as an advocate.
- Accept or reject cases for the firm.
- Set any fee for representation of a client.
- Split legal fees with an attorney.
- Be a partner with a lawyer in practice of law (Except in Washington, D.C.).
- Solicit cases for a lawyer.

Limits to what a paralegal may do:

- The task must be delegated by an attorney.
- It must be performed under an attorney's supervision.
- Paralegals must clearly designate their status.
- The attorney must retain a direct relationship with the client.
- The task must involve information gathering or be ministerial and cannot involve the rendering of legal advice or judgment.
- The work must be given final approval by the attorney.
- The work must merge with the attorney's final work product.

Also:

- A paralegal shall hold inviolate the confidences of a client
- A paralegal must maintain the highest standards of professional integrity and avoid any dishonesty, fraud, deceit, or misrepresentation.
- A paralegal should avoid and reveal any conflicts of interest.
- A paralegal must strive to be competent and current in the field.
- A paralegal should be loyal to the employer and to the legal profession and its standards.

Assignment 3

Locate the names, addresses, and phone numbers of your local and state paralegal associations. If you need help obtaining this information, try the director of a local paralegal program or any experienced paralegal in the firm or elsewhere in the state. The headquarters of the state bar association might also have such information. For future reference, you may choose to place your expanded lists of sources for professional development in your system folder.

ANSWER: You may choose to provide these as a handout. if placed in the system folder, they will provide a handy future resource.

State Paralegal Association	Local Paralegal Association
Name:	Name:
Address:	Address:
Phone:	Phone:
E-mail:	E-mail:
Contact Person:	Contact Person:
Meeting Dates and Times:	Meeting Dates and Times:

Assignment 4

Make a copy of the federal court structure diagram found in this chapter and add any explanatory notes you feel will be useful to you in the future. Include in your diagram the names of U.S. district courts that sit in your state and the U.S. Court of Appeals that covers the circuit in which your state is situated.

Make a similar explanatory diagram for the court system of your state. Research the material to be placed in the diagram, including any jurisdictional amounts, by looking under "courts," "judiciary," and "jurisdiction" in the index of your state statutes or constitution, usually located in the law library, or search your state court Web site. Some states have an administrative office of the courts at the capitol that may provide preprinted state court diagrams.

Place both diagrams and the state court Web site address in the court section of your litigation system folder.

ANSWER: You may decide to provide the state court diagram addressed in this assignment. If so, include the jurisdiction of each court.

Assignment 5

Consult the state's legal directory in the library or online sites to obtain all court addresses, names of clerks of court, important telephone numbers, and so on. Research state statutes for the subject matter jurisdiction in your state's highest, intermediate, and trial courts. Also find the venue requirements for your state courts. Place this data on separate sheets in the court structure portion of your system folder.

ANSWER: You may choose to provide this information, but it would be good for students to locate it so they become familiar with the state legal directory.

Federal Court System   Address:
Highest Court   Clerk:
Name: U.S. Supreme Court   Phone:
Jurisdiction: 1. Appeals from U.S. Court of Appeals and highest state courts
     2. State v. state
     3. Cases involving ambassadors and other foreign representatives
     4. U.S. v. state
     5. State v. citizens of another state or country

Intermediate Appellate Court Address:
Name: U.S. Court of Appeals   Clerk:
Jurisdiction: Appeals from district courts Phone:
Trial Courts   Address:
Name: U.S. District Courts   Clerk:
Jurisdiction: 1. Federal questions Phone:
     2. Diversity of citizenship
     3. $50,000 amount in controversy

State Court System
Highest Court   Address:
Name: Clerk:
Jurisdiction: Phone:
Intermediate Appellate Court Address:
Name: Clerk:
Jurisdiction: Phone:
Trial Courts   Address:
Name: Clerk:
Jurisdiction: Phone

APPLICATION ASSIGNMENTS
Assignment 1

To develop a timekeeping habit during this training period, keep track of your time spent on assignments in the following time log, similar to that in Exhibit 1:2. Use a separate notebook or loose-leaf paper that can be placed at the back of your system folder. Keep track of your time in an electronic timekeeping program, if one is available.

ANSWER: The students may need occasional reminders to keep up their time logs. If you have timekeeping software available, students could keep track of their time by computer.

BG	Budgeting	DM	Document	M	Memorandum	SE	Settlement
C	Conference		Management	MO	Motion	T	Telephone
CT	Court	DS	Discovery	P	Preparation	TR	Travel
D	Document	I	Investigation	PL	Planning	O	Other
	Drafting	L	Letter	R	Research		

TIME LOG Name_____.

Case no.	Service	Comment	Date	Hours by 10ths

Assignment 2

Set up a simple deadline calendar for this training period. Use any type of standard calendar. Enter all important deadlines such as assignment due dates and exam dates. Use a system o advance reminder dates prior to the actual deadline and post-deadline reminders for necessary corrective action.

ANSWER: This should instill a deadline calendaring habit. Use of post-deadline reminders should be emphasized. If your program has access to deadline control computer software, you might require students to use it for the various deadlines in the course.

Assignment 3

Using the ethical standards and rules cited in this section, answer the following questions on ethics.

1. One of our clients asks you what judge will be hearing the client's case. You answer, "Judge Arnow." Are you guilty of the unauthorized practice of law?

ANSWER: No. Especially if this is the local judge that hears all cases of the particular nature in question and there is no question of the attorney deciding on a different judge. No independent professional judgment is being exercised.

2. (a) You have just researched an issue and have found that inattentive driving is a breach of the duty of care that a driver owes to others. In a phone conversation the client asks you,

"If the driver of the vehicle that struck was inattentive, is he in the wrong?" You answer yes. Is this the unauthorized practice of law?

ANSWER: Yes. It calls for independent professional judgment based on knowledge of law given for the benefit of the client.

   (b) What if the paralegal can honestly say, "I just spoke with Mr. White [client's attorney] and he said, 'Yes, the driver would be in the wrong'"?

ANSWER: No, since the judgment is the attorney's , and the paralegal is simply acting as a conduit for that judgment.

3. Ms. Pearlman asks you to draft a release of medical information form for a client. This form is drafted and signed by the client and given to the hospital. Under what conditions can you do this and avoid the unauthorized practice of law?

ANSWER: The task must be delegated by an attorney; the attorney will have to review it for accuracy; the paralegal will have to identify himself or herself as a paralegal in any dealings with the client; and the attorney will have to maintain control over the client's case. This task must not involve the giving of any legal advice, and must merge with the overall final work product of the attorney on behalf of the client.

4. You are working on a client's case for Ms. Pearlman. She is gone, so you want to consult with Mr. White, another attorney in the firm. To do so, however, you must reveal to Mr. White some confi-

dential information about the client. Would this be a breach of confidentiality?

ANSWER: No. the authorization for this disclosure is implied under Rule 1.6(a).

5. Is leaving an open file on your desk in the presence of another client a breach of confidentiality?

ANSWER: Yes, if left in a position that the other client can see it or quickly gain access to it. Rule 1.6(a).

6. In interviewing a client, you and your attorney are convinced that some information provided by the client is false. What consequences can result from the presentation of such information to the court? What model rule of professional conduct applies?

ANSWER: The finding that the lawyer is in a serious ethical breach as defined in Rule 3.3(4) could lead to disbarment. The paralegal could be removed from membership in local or national paralegal associations.

7. Your supervising attorney asks you to release to the press a letter from a third party. The attorney says, "I'll finally get even by truly embarrassing the s.o.b." What should you do?

ANSWER: The attorney's conduct is unethical under Rule 4.4 ("a lawyer shall not use means that have no substantial purpose other than to embarrass"). It is the professional duty of a paralegal to point this out to the attorney. There may be a satisfactory explanation. if not, the paralegal must refuse to commit the act or be a part y to the unethical breach. This is an example where loyalty to the profession and its ethics may supersede loyalty to the attorney.

Assignment 4

Determine in which courts subject matter jurisdiction, personal jurisdiction, and venue exist in the following problems.

1. A, a resident of Florida, sues B, a resident of Washington, who is also the Secretary of the Interior, in a First Amendment freedom of speech issue arising in southeast Georgia.

ANSWER: Subject matter jurisdiction rests in the federal district courts (federal question cases) and all state courts (general jurisdiction).

State venue rests with the residence of the defendant (Washington) or where the cause arose (Georgia). Federal venue where the defendant is an officer of the United States, regardless of the fact that this is a federal question case, exists under §1391(e) in the district where defendant resides (Washington), or where a substantial part of the event or omission arose (Southeastern District of Georgia), or where the plaintiff resides if there is no real property involved (Florida).

The courts with personal jurisdiction, however, include only Washington state courts or the District Court for Washington, absent any long-arm provisions. Therefore, the action can be brought in the District of Washington or in a Washington state court. Section 1391(e), however, suggests that personal jurisdiction can be gained by mail and therefore, the action could be filed in the appropriate district in Florida or southeast Georgia.

2. M, a resident of Wisconsin, and O, a resident of Minnesota, sue Corporations X and Y for industrial injuries amounting to $40,000 for each plaintiff resulting from an accident that occurred in Illinois. X is incorporated in Delaware and Ohio, and Y is incorporated in North Carolina with its principal place of business in Ohio.

ANSWER: No federal jurisdiction because plaintiffs cannot aggregate claims to make the jurisdictional amount. All states mentioned have general jurisdiction. State venue exists in at least Delaware and Ohio for X, in North Carolina and Ohio for Y, and in Illinois for both X and Y because that is where the action arose. Personal jurisdiction, however, can be gained only in Ohio over both defendants. The action must be brought in Ohio state court or as two separate actions in any of their resident states.

3. J and K reside in Oregon and sue R, who resides in Kentucky, and S, who resides in Washington, for a tort (libel) amounting to injuries exceeding $75,000 each, which occurred in Washington.

ANSWER: All state and federal courts have subject matter jurisdiction (there is diversity). Venue rests in state courts in Kentucky (for R) and in Washington (for S), and in Washington, where the claim arose.

Federal venue for a diversity action against R exists in the district in Kentucky where R resides. Venue for an action against S exists in Washington, where S resides. Venue for an action against both R and S exists in Washington where the substantial event arose. Personal jurisdiction for a state action exists in Kentucky for R only and in Washington for S only. Personal jurisdiction for a federal action exists in Kentucky for R and in Washington for S. Unless Washington has a long-arm statute that reaches tort feasors, separate action must be brought against R and S in both states and in their respective federal districts. If Washington has an appropriate long-arm statute, both a joint state and federal action can be brought in the state of Washington.

4. What happens in problem (3) if S is a Canadian citizen living in Louisiana?

ANSWER: Only Louisiana can get personal jurisdiction and venue for a state suit against S. Under federal law (§1391) federal venue exists in any district, but personal jurisdiction exists only in the appropriate district in Louisiana. Therefore, separate state and federal actions would be necessary in Kentucky and in Louisiana. Again, a long-arm statue in Washington could lead to combined state or federal actions in Washington.

5. E sues Great Britain for damages exceeding $500,000 for the illegal impounding of E's commercial plane.

ANSWER: The United States District Court for the District of Columbia [§1391(f)(4)].

INTERNET EXERCISES

1. Visit www.abanet.org/cpr/e2k-intro_and_ summary_changes.html, make a brief list of the substantive changes proposed for the American Bar Association's *Model Rules of Professional Conduct*, and place it in your system folder.
2. Ask your instructor for the name of your state and local paralegal association. Using a general search engine, see if that association has a Web site. If so, note the Web address in your system folder.
3. Go to both the NALA and NFPA Web sites and note the variety of career information available.
4. Go to www.americounsel.com and see what the starting legal fee is for specified services.
5. Using your own search strategy, locate the Web site for your state courts. Note what general categories of information are available and enter this information in your system folder.

ADDITIONAL EXERCISES

1. Without trying to use legal terminology or technical theories, answer the following questions for each of the five hypothetical cases presented in this chapter.
   a. Who is suing and what basis might they have?
   b. Against whom is the suit brought and what defenses might they have?
   c. Who do you think will win and why?

ANSWER:

Case I
   a. Ann Forrester is suing because Richard Hart was not driving carefully (failed to stop), and because the Mercury Parcel van was poorly maintained (no brakes).
   b. Mercury Parcel, that Ms. Forrester was not watching for traffic; that Hart was at fault, not the van. Richard Hart, that Ms. Forrester was not watching traffic and that the van was poorly maintained by Mercury Parcel.
   c. Subjective.

Case II
   a. Carl Ameche, because his injuries were caused by unsafe electrical conditions at the campground.
   b. The Congdens, that Ameche had moved the cord.
   c. Subjective.

Case III
   a. Sam and Emma Coleman for Sean Coleman, because the vehicle was unsafe to be operated as advertised.
   b. Make Tracks, that the vehicle was operated in a reckless manner.
   c. Subjective.

Case IV
   a. Briar Patch Dolls, because unfilled contract orders caused massive business losses.
   b. Teeny Tiny Manufacturing, that unfilled orders were unavoidable because of Ms. Meyers' death.
   c. Subjective.

Case V
   a. Darlene Rakowski, because unpleasant working conditions (sexual harassment) forced her to leave her job.
   b. Montez Construction, that Ms. Rakowski was unable to perform her job.
   c. Subjective.

2. Apply the directions for preparing a time slip to enter these activities. Assume your hourly rate is $40 an hour and the date is today. Round to the nearest tenth of an hour. Use copies of the computer window in Exhibit 1:2 in the text or use a form provided by your instructor.
   6-minute phone call to client A. Forrester, Case I.
   16 minutes to draft letter on behalf of client Heinz, Case IV.
   1 hour and 18 minutes to research cause of action for client Ameche, Case II.
   1 hour and 20 minutes to attend continuing education luncheon to improve general knowledge, but which may be useful on Cases III and IV. Cost: $5. (Should this be charged to the client?

   Delete answers from Exhibit 1:2 in the text or from the following form and copy for student use.

ANSWER:

3. Fill out disbursement records based on this information. Use copies of the computer window in Exhibit 1:3 in the text or use a form provided by the instructor.
   100 photocopies at 10¢ per copy, business records for Heinz, Case IV.

Permanent Time Log

Service Codes

BG	Budgeting	DM	Document	M	Memorandum	SE	Settlement
C	Conference		Management	MO	Motion	T	Telephone
CT	Court	DS	Discovery	P	Preparation	TR	Travel
D	Document	I	Investigation	PL	Planning	O	Other
	Drafting	L	Letter	R	Research		

No Charge Items

NC	No Charge	CE	Continuing Education	PS	Public Service
B	Bar Function	CR	Client Relations		

Date	File No.	Client	Att/Plgl	Serv Code	Hrs	10th	Rate/Hr	Amt
	1	A. Forrester		T		1	40	4.00
	4	Heinz, Briar Patch		L		3	40	12.00
	2	C. Ameche		R	1	3	40	52.00
				CE*	1	3		NC

Comments:

*Out-of-pocket expenseof $5 to be reimbursed by firm

Trip to investigate accident scene for client McVay, Case X: $60, motel; $5, lunch; $11, dinner; 100 miles at .25 per mile.
Computer research time, 10 minutes at $5 per minute for Montez Construction, Case V.

ANSWER:

4. Assume that you have just opened the morning mail and received a copy of a complaint alleging a cause of action against Mr. Holton, who is represented by your firm. His file number is 92-1000. You know that you have 20 days, starting tomorrow, to file an answer and that it is your job to draft an answer for your supervising attorney's review. You have received the complaint on September 5. Using Exhibit 1:1 for the names you need, prepare the following deadline control slip so the document will be ready to mail on the 20th day. Ignore the fact that some days may be weekend days for purposes of this assignment only. Assume it will take a half day to research and draft the answer, one hour for the attorney to review it, a half hour for you to make revisions, and a half hour for the secretary to type it and have it ready for mailing. Complete all sections of the slip. Use copies of the computer window in Exhibit 1:4 in the text or use a form provided by your instructor.

ANSWER: Check that appropriate places are filled in on the slip and that the time sequence is logical and reasonable, as in the example on page 8.

5. Of all the techniques mentioned for thriving in the law office, which two are most important? Explain.

ANSWER: Subjective.

6. Describe a paralegal litigation system folder and its advantages.

ANSWER: A detailed procedure manual that is a collection of directions, forms, and checklists for tasks regularly performed by the paralegal.

Advantages include efficiency, uniformity, accuracy, quality, and currentness. Can be a learning device, a factor in securing employment, and an aid on the job.

7. Read thoroughly the *Model Rules of Professional Conduct* or your state rules of conduct to gain a fuller understanding of your ethical responsibilities. Why is confidentiality so important?

ANSWER: If there is no confidentiality, clients will not confide essential details or will not consult a lawyer at

Permanent Disbursement Record

Expense Codes:

C	Photocopies	L	Lodging	P	Postage	T	Telephone
CT	On-line Computer	M	Meals	$	Cash	TR	Travel
F	Filing & Other Fees	O	Overnight Express	TG	Telegrams	O	Other

Date	File No.	Client	Atty/Plgl	Exp. Code	Amt.
	4	Heinz, Briar Patch		C	10.00
	10	McVay		L	60.00
	10	McVay		M	16.00
	10	McVay		TR*	25.00
	5	Montez Construction		CT	50.00

Comments: *Note destination and mileage.

Deadline Slip

Client: Holton   File Number: 92-1000

Atty: I.P.	Start: 9/20	Due: 9/22	Plgl:	Start: 9/15	Due: 9/17	Staff: M.D.	Start: 9/23	Due 9/24
Task: Review, review amendments,			Task: Draft answer			Task: Prepare Answer sign answer for review, signature, then mail.		
Remarks:			Remarks:			Remarks:		
Reminder: 1 2 Final Done:			Reminder: 1 2 Final Done:			Reminder: 1 2 Final Done:		

all. Consequently, this could result in less use of the system, more self-help, and possibly chaotic results in disputes—and ultimately system failure. Lack of confidentiality could also allow information, and advantage, to leak to the opponent, endangering the adversary system.

8. Paraphrase the goals or statements of policy of your local and state paralegal associations. Do you feel the statement of policy or the goals are adequate? Explain.

ANSWER: Local research. Subjective.

9. Glitter is a corporation that rents expensive jewelry to businesses and individuals. it is incorporated in Delaware and has its principal place of business in northern Indiana. It is licensed to do business in every state except Alaska and Hawaii. Flick, Inc., is a movie company incorporated in Idaho with its principal place of business in Utah. It does no business to speak of in any other state.

During Flick's filming in Nevada, an expensive necklace rented from Glitter falls into a piece of machinery on the set and is destroyed. Glitter wants to sue Flick for negligently destroying the jewelry (worth $700,000). Flick decides to sue Glitter, blaming the loss of a week's filming on the loss of the necklace, which they claim was caused by a faulty clasp made by Glitter. After using the charting method described in this section, answer the following questions:

GLITTER V. FLICK FOR NECKLACE

Court	Subj. Matter	Juris.	Venue	Pers. Juris.
Delaware State	Yes		No	No
Indiana State	Yes		No	No
Idaho State	Yes		Yes	Yes
Utah State	Yes		Yes	Yes
Nevada State	yes	(diversity)	Yes	?*
Delaware Federal	Yes	(diversity)	No	No
Indiana Federal	Yes	(diversity)	No	No
Idaho Federal	yes	(diversity)	Yes	Yes
Utah Federal	Yes	(diversity)	Yes	Yes
Nevada Federal	Yes	(diversity)	Yes	?*

*ISSUE: Is filming a movie in a state a sufficient contact to allow personal service? (May depend on state statutes and overall degree of contacts.)

FLICK V. GLITTER FOR LOSS OF WEEK OF FILMING

Court	Subj. Matter	Juris.	Venue	Pers. Juris.
Delaware State	Yes		Yes	Yes
Indiana State	Yes		Yes	Yes
Idaho State	Yes		No	No
Utah State	Yes		No	No
Nevada State	Yes		Yes	?
Delaware Federal	Yes	(diversity)	Yes	yes
Indiana Federal	Yes	(diversity)	Yes	Yes
Idaho Federal	Yes	(diversity)	No	No
Utah Federal	Yes	(diversity)	No	No
Nevada Federal	Yes	(diversity)	Yes	?

a. If Glitter sues Flick, is there subject matter jurisdiction in federal district court?

ANSWER: Yes.

b. What, if any, kind of subject matter jurisdiction exists in federal district court?

ANSWER: Diversity.

c. What issue concerning personal jurisdiction exists when considering suit by Glitter against Flick in Nevada state and federal court?

ANSWER: Whether the state has a long arm statute that will permit personal jurisdiction on Flick for having filmed one movie in Nevada, where the action arose.

d. Aside from Nevada, in what state and federal courts can Glitter sue Flick?

ANSWER: State courts: Idaho and Utah. Federal courts: District of Idaho and District of Utah.

e. If Flick sues Glitter, does venue exist in the state courts of Idaho and Utah? Why or why not?

ANSWER: No. State court venue normally rests in the state of the defendant and where the action arose.

f. Assume for purposes of this question that Glitter is licensed to do business in Utah and, thus, is subject to personal jurisdiction in Utah.

(1) What impact would this have on jurisdictional considerations?

ANSWER: Federal diversity jurisdiction would not exist, but Flick could sue Glitter in its headquarter site.

(2) With the same facts, assume diversity jurisdiction still exists. Could Utah's federal court have venue, considering that the action did not arise in Utah?

ANSWER: Yes. Since licensing is adequate for personal jurisdiction and since the federal venue statute 28 U.S.C. §1391(c) establishes venue in the case of a *defendant* corporation in all districts where personal jurisdiction is available, both personal jurisdiction and venue exist in the federal district court for Utah.

g. What facts are missing in the Flick v. Glitter scenario that affect jurisdiction?

ANSWER: No jurisdictional amount is given, so we cannot be sure that federal diversity jurisdiction exists.

h. In what state and federal courts can Flick sue Glitter?

ANSWER: State courts: Delaware, Indiana, and possibly Nevada. Federal district courts: Delaware, Northern District of Indiana, and possibly Nevada.

10. Review the Case Roadmap in Chapter 1 and do a sequential list of stages in the litigation process as stated in the roadmap.

ANSWER: Initial Steps
1. event
2. hiring firm
3. client interview
4. informal investigation

Pleadings
1. draft and file complaint
2. service of complaint
3. attack on complaint, request for dismissal
4. draft and serve answer

Preparation
1. discovery
2. motion for summary judgment
3. further preparation

Resolution
1. settlement
2. pretrial hearing
3. trial

Post Trial
   1. request for new trial
   2. appeal
   3. judgment enforcement

11. Work through the questions for study and review
    to test your understanding of the chapter.

ANSWER: Strongly encourage students to use these questions in the text as a study guide at the completion of each chapter. if students can answer these questions, they should do well on an exam. you may choose to draw some of your exam questions from this list.

CHAPTER 2

THE INITIAL INTERVIEW

CHAPTER OBJECTIVE

The purpose of this chapter is to help students understand the purpose of an initial client interview and to develop a systematic way of preparing for, conducting, and summarizing an interview.

PREPARING FOR CLASS: INSTRUCTIONAL SUPPLEMENTS

1. If your students have not studied torts and contracts in previous courses or need a review of those topics, you may choose to assign Appendices B and C.
2. You may choose to supplement the chapter material with comments on interview preparation and interview techniques that have been particularly helpful to you.
3. The chapter lends itself to some expansion on the substantive law of negligence. You will need to tell the class whether their jurisdiction is a contributory or a comparative negligence jurisdiction, and how this aspect of negligence law works in the jurisdiction. For example, if the state is a comparative negligence state, does it have the 51 percent rule barring plaintiff's recovery?
4. You may choose to use different cases in Chapter 1, such as the contract case, or cases from your own research or experience for examples or practice exercises. If so, it will be necessary to give the class some background on the substantive law of your state pertinent to the example used.
5. You may choose to provide samples of interview forms from a variety of contexts. They could be added to the interview section of the system folder.
6. A prepared list of the state's statutes of limitations for common types of lawsuits would be a useful handout.

7. Any additional forms, preferred forms, checklists, etc., that you prefer may be useful supplements to this chapter.
8. Pertinent Web sites.

SUGGESTED CLASS ACTIVITIES

1. Probably the most significant activity that could be used for this chapter is the students' preparing for and conducting an interview. A number of class hours could be set aside for this activity. See Application Assignment 3 in this chapter of the manual.
2. Some class time could be devoted to a brainstorming session by students with your assistance to develop possible areas of inquiry or questions for the interview related to one or more of the needed elements. This activity could be done in small groups, with a general session for groups to report their ideas.
3. You might conduct an example "how to" interview for students to follow. If this interview is well-planned, it could be videotaped and used for each new class of students or put in the video library for review as an out-of-class assignment.
4. Have a psychologist from the college or community come to class to discuss the following:
   a. interview techniques
   b. interview settings and arrangements
   c. lie detection techniques
   d. problematic situations
   e. body language
   f. effective self-desensitization techniques that would allow an interviewer to deal comfortably with people having repulsive injuries or disabilities
5. Have a business communications teacher discuss effective phone and letter-writing techniques.

OUTLINE

I. Introduction
   System Folder Assignment 1
II. The Interview Plan
   A. Interview Plan Checklist
      System Folder Assignment 2
   B. The Interview Plan in Detail
      Key terms: substantive law, procedural law, duty, proximate cause leading question, contingent fee
      Exhibit 2:1(a), Checklist Form: Client Background Information
      Exhibit 2:1(b), Checklist Form: Automobile Accident
      Exhibit 2:2, Confirmation of Appointment Letter
      Exhibit 2:3, Fee Agreement
      Exhibit 2:4, Contingent Fee Agreement
      Exhibit 2:5, Standardized Release Form
      System Folder Assignments 3 through 10
      Application Assignments 1 and 2
      Internet Exercise 1
III. The Interview
   Application Assignment 3
   A. The Introduction
   B. Questions on Circumstances of the Accident
   C. The Issue of Comparative or Contributory Negligence
   D. The Extent of Injury and Sensitive Inquiry
   E. Dealing with Difficult Clients
      Internet Exercise 2
   F. Concluding the Interview
   G. Confirming the Statute of Limitations
      Key term: statute of limitations
      System Folder Assignment 11
IV. Summarizing the Interview
   Exhibit 2:6, Summary Sheet: Initial Interview of Client
   Exhibit 2:7, Summary Sheet: Initial Interview of Client (Completed)
   Application Assignment 4
V. Keeping the Client Informed
VI. Summary
   Application Assignment 5

SYSTEM FOLDER ASSIGNMENTS

Assignment 1

List the task and the purpose(s) of the task at the beginning of the interview section in your system folder.

ANSWER:

1. Sets the tone for firm-client and paralegal-client relationship.
2. Builds client's confidence in the relationship
3. Begins investigation.
4. Determines basis of or defense to lawsuit.
5. Establishes firm's acceptance of case.
6. Sets fee.

Assignment 2

Place a copy of the Interview Plan Checklist in your system folder. Add to this section any forms, techniques, examples, or other material that you or your instructor deem useful.

Assignment 3

Review the interview forms, noting the type of information requested. Place a copy of these interview forms or similar forms into this section of your system folder.

Assignment 4

Review the interview forms in Exhibit 2:1(a) and Exhibit 2:1(b) and compile a list of the names, addresses, phone numbers, medical records, insurance information, and so on that you would like Ms. Forrester to bring to the interview. Make a copy of the list and place it in the system folder. This list will be useful when you call or write the client and will serve as a checklist for future cases.

ANSWER: This assignment can be applied to any case and interview form.

- Social Security Number
- Family addresses and phones
- Employment of spouse
- Information on any divorce
- Address and phone of other close relatives
- Employment information
  - Employer, address, phone, dates, salary, position
  - Self-employment
- Education information
- Income
  - Current gross income, tax forms for last three years
- Time lost
- Real estate owned
- Personal property owned
  - Bank accounts
  - Stocks
  - Bonds
  - Autos
  - Furniture
  - Jewelry
- Prior legal actions: dates, nature
- General background information on other parties

WHITE, WILSON & McDUFF
Attorneys at Law
Federal Plaza Building Suite 700
Third and Market Streets
Legalville, Columbia 00000

Address: Date
                                                                                             Case File No.

This is to remind you of your appointment on _____, at _____ at our office. The purpose of the appointment will be to _____. The appointment is for an hour, or more if necessary.

Please bring the items checked in the following list, if they are available:

( )   Social Security number
( )   Insurance carrier, policy limits, address, and phone number
( )   Name(s) of the other party or parties and any information you have about them, including insurance carrier
( )   Photos of accident, injuries, or other damage
( )   Photos of accident scene
( )   Diagram of accident and location
( )   News clippings regarding accident
( )   Names, ages, birthdates of spouse and dependents
( )   Description of vehicle(s) in accident, license number, owner, damage
( )   Medical bills, treating physicians, medical insurance, medical history
( )   Occupation and salary information, time lost
( )   Accident or injuries subsequent to this incident
( )   Any correspondence regarding accident
( )   Names, addresses, and phone numbers of other witnesses
( )   Be prepared to describe accident
( )   Other _____.

We appreciate your gathering as much of the information as you can. I look forward to meeting you. In the meantime, I can be reached at _____.

- Insurance coverage: deductible, amounts of coverage
- Accident
  - Date, time, location, diagrams, photos, news clippings
  - Automobile information (if applicable): location, photos, owners
- Any statements to others about accident
- Witnesses: addresses, phone numbers, ages
- Parties' previous accidents
- Medical reports
  - Bills
  - Ambulance service
  - Treating and consulting physicians and addresses
  - Pharmacy

- Prior medical history: physicians, hospitals, etc.
- Damages
- Property damage

Assignment 5

Make the letter in Exhibit 2:2 into a form letter for your system folder. Redraft the letter to suit your style and needs, leaving blank those areas of the letter that will contain the variable information (names, addresses, date, and so on) for each new client. Once your form is set up, it can be placed in your system folder and computerized, requiring the entry of only the variable information for each repeated use. Throughout this training period, follow this form-making procedure for letters and other documents that will be used repeatedly from one case to the next.

Note: Keep track of your time by filling out the time log.

Assignment 6

List the pertinent ethical considerations for interviewing a client. Place them in your system folder.

ANSWER:
Unauthorized practice of law
Confidentiality
Honesty

Assignment 7

Prepare a list of the interview techniques in step 8 for your system folder. Add any techniques suggested by your instructor.

ANSWER: Add to this list any suggestions from your own experience.
1. Have the client meet with the attorney first.
2. Make the client comfortable.
3. Be friendly and respectful.
4. Create a private environment free of interruptions.
5. Explain the purpose of the interview.
6. Explain the importance of confidentiality and honesty.
7. Express confidence about what you are doing.
8. Avoid being condescending.
9. Take accurate, detailed, and legible notes.
10. Be a good listener.
11. Be mindful of how a jury might react to the client's body language or mannerisms.
12. Let clients tell their stories; pick up details later.
13. Use open narrative questions.
14. Avoid questions that suggest an answer.
15. Avoid "why" or confrontational questions.
16. Probe the accuracy of judgments.
17. Be prepared to deal with sensitive matters.
18. Deal tactfully but directly with suspected dishonesty.
19. Restate the client's information to ensure understanding.
20. Get thorough details on accident and damages.

Assignment 8

Your supervising attorney has asked you to develop a draft of a brochure for clients with information the client should receive at the initial interview. Include any additions to the brochure suggested by your instructor. Place the brochure in your system folder.

ANSWER: The brochure should contain items in the step 9 list of "information to be given to the client at the initial interview." Offer the students any helpful additions from your own experience.

Assignment 9

Note in your system folder what forms you should have ready for the client at the initial interview. Include samples of those forms or references to where they can be located quickly, such as the page number in this book or the form number in a form file or a computer file.

Assignment 10

Develop your own checklist of the items you will need at the interview site. Such a checklist will be a quick reference for preparing your office or a conference room for the interview. Include the necessary forms and directions. Place this material in the system folder.

ANSWER: A checklist should include the following:
1. A clear desk
2. Writing materials
3. Diagrams or photographs
4. Forms for signature
5. Refreshments
6. Comfortable setting
7. No interruptions/hold calls
8. Emergency preparations

Assignment 11

Locate the common statutes of limitations through the index to the state's statutes. Compile a list of the statute numbers and time limits for cases involving personal injury, property damage, wrongful death, contracts oral and written), and any others requested by your instructor. Place the list into the system folder.

ANSWER: You may choose to photocopy a list of statute of limitation deadlines from the state. It should be stressed to students that such a list should be regularly updated.

Personal injury	_____	years
statute number	_____	
Property damage	_____	years
statute number	_____	
Wrongful death	_____	years
statute number	_____ .	
Contracts		
oral	_____	years
statute number	_____ .	
written	_____	years
statute number	_____ .	
Others		
_____	_____	years
statute number	_____ .	
_____	_____	years
statute number	_____ .	

APPLICATION ASSIGNMENTS

Assignment 1

Test your research skills and learn about your state law by researching the terms *negligence, contributory negligence, comparative negligence, pure negligence,* and *modified negligence* in your state's jury instruction book, statutes, or digest. For additional understanding of these concepts, look in a legal encyclopedia, *Am Jur's Proof of Facts,* or other national reference sources. Note what must be proved, as well as defenses to such actions.

ANSWER: This assignment is designed to reinforce research skills and to give the students a chance to see what kind of research is necessary to isolate the key elements of an area of law that makes up the legal foundation for a cause of action.

Assignment 2

Adapting the methods you have learned to a variety of circumstances is an important process and an invaluable ability in the law office and should give you confidence. Test your understanding of the methodology described in this section by creating an interview form for a breach of implied warranty or other type of case. If needed, see the appendix on contracts to review the elements for an implied warranty case. If each student or group of students is to prepare interview forms for different types of lawsuits, it would be good to exchange copies of these forms to expand the interview section of your system folder.

ANSWER: The student should prepare at least one interview form. The class may be divided to locate or write interview forms in four or five areas to be shared and placed in system folders. you may choose to provide interview forms from various areas of law. These forms may also be used to evaluate the student's forms.

Assignment 3

Conduct an interview of Mr. Ameche (Case II). Do this in class in a role-playing setting unless told to do otherwise by your instructor. Divide the interview into various segments (introduction, personal information, events leading up to accident, the accident, injuries, etc.). Different students should take the responsibility of interviewee and interviewer for each segment. The class should critique each segment of the interview according to the following criteria:

1. Friendly and effective introduction
2. Clarity of questions
3. Application of specific interview techniques
4. Willingness to probe
5. Attitude toward client
6. Effective conclusion of interview
7. Overall preparation
8. Sincerity of interviewer

Data Sheet for Mr. Ameche (pronounced A-mee-chee), Case II

If you are assigned the role of Mr. Ameche:

1. Study the data sheet so that you can respond to questions without having to refer repeatedly to the data sheet. Pay particular attention to the description of the accident.
2. It would be normal to have to refer to documents to get the names of doctors, hospitals, bills, insurance companies, etc.
3. Provide your own answers when asked a question for which the data sheet has not provided information. (MU = make up information)

Has not contacted other attorney
Referred to firm by neighbor
Carl Evan Ameche, Soc. Sec. No. 000-00-0000
2222 2nd St., Thorp, Ohio 10000, Meade County, Phone: MU
Date of Birth: MU Age: 35 Nationality, Race, Religion: MU
Accountant with Miller & Miller 3000 Third St., Thorp $38,000
Married to Zoe Elaine (Jeffers), part-time day care aide and homemaker, Soc. Sec. No. 000-10-0000 Phone: MU Married Oct. 1, 8 years ago
Child: Zachary Nathan (6)
Employment History: 8 years with Miller & Miller, MU other employment
Education: B.S. degree in accounting, Ohio University, 13 years ago
No prior lawsuits

Incident date: Aug. 21, three months ago
Beginning two-week vacation. Stopped first day at maple Meadows Campground, site 36. While setting up camper, saw black electrical cord near where Zach was playing. Moved cord away from campsite. Cord was worn and rubber casing was broken in several spots. Plugged camper into extension cord which was taped to regular outlet. Noticed camper light and radio increasingly flickering off and on. Static on radio became quite loud. Heard son yell and emerged from camper to see son trapped by grass and brush fire. I grabbed old brown army blanket from camper and threw it around me. I ran through some flames to get to my son. I wrapped him in the blanket and carried him on my shoulder through the flames. I wore a short sleeved shirt and khaki shorts, jogging shoes, no socks. Son was OK but my clothes were burning in several places. Zoe and I used another blanket to extinguish the flames burning my clothes and hair. I was obviously burned on my legs and arms. A maintenance worker at the camp took me to the hospital. Zoe and Zach followed in our car. Don't know worker's name.

Defendants: Camp owners Leroy and Margie Congden, Highway 60, Star route 2, Legalville, Columbia. Their insurance carrier is Citizens Insurance Company of Hartford, Connecticut. They have not paid me anything, nor have I signed anything or made nay statements to them.

Weather Conditions: dry and windy.

Description of Campsite: MU

Statements: I told the doctor and nurses what happened. I have also told friends that I thought fire was caused by extension cord.

Witnesses: Mr. Robert Warren (in campsite 34) who is from Legalville and goes to campground occasionally on weekends. I do not have his address. I had spoken to him in the afternoon after arrival. Told him of having electrical problems.

Medical: I suffered first degree burns on my legs, hands, and left side of my face as well as numerous second and third degree burns. About twelve percent of my body was burned. inhaled smoke but no serious damage to lungs. Felt nauseous and the burns were very painful. Hospitalized for two months. Had several skin graft operations. Doctors say I have significant permanent scars on face, hands, and legs.

Restrictions: Restricted movement of right (writing) hand. Some difficulty holding pencil. Overall movement still restricted. Doctors unsure whether restriction permanent or not. hair beginning to grow back in most places. The pain is less now, but it was severe for the first month. I still find the burn damage repulsive.

Hospital: Capitol County General Hospital, 400 Ridge Boulevard, Legalville.

Treatment: Emergency treatment for burns Aug. 21, hospitalized 8/21–10/1

Surgery: Skin grafts to left cheek and left ankle by Albert Find, M.D., plastic surgeon, 313 Broad Street, Legalville.

Prior Medical History: Healthy; broken ankle playing softball six years ago; normal childhood diseases.

Damages: Employment (out of work since accident). May begin in approximately one month, but burn scars will make it hard to face clients.

Pain and Suffering (past-present-future)	Estimate
First month—terrible	$300/day
Second month	$200/day
Third month	$150/day

Rest of life because of scarring (embarrassment), some limitation in movement and use of hand—$40/day

Loss of consortium (love and affection): 3 months at $50/day

Loss of Earnings: Out of work for 3 months

Scarring could cost 10 percent of my clients

Medical:	
Hospital Emergency Room	$3,000
61 days × $400/day	$24,000
Dr., surgery	$10,000
Prescriptions	4700
Other Property: Camper and equipment	$2,000
Other: Loss of vacation	$1,000

ANSWER: *This assignment is probably the highlight of the chapter for most students.* It works best if every student has the opportunity to do an interview, but time may not permit this. You might do an example interview for the entire class. Groups of three students might then alternate the roles of interviewer, client, and evaluator. This could be done in or out of class. If this is still too time-consuming, the interviewer may have to prepare for and conduct one specific phase of the interview. You will need to provide copies of the data sheet for Mr. Ameche. Be sure that students take notes of the interview for use in Application Assignment 4.

Assignment 4

Enter into a computer the notes from your interview with Mr. Ameche. using a duplicate of these notes, delete extraneous material and organize the remaining important information into a summary according to the format in Exhibit 2:6.

ANSWER: Based on Application Assignment 3. Encourage students to use computers to enter notes and edit to summary form.

Assignment 5

Your firm is handling a wrongful death case for the plaintiff. Since the deceased is not available to testify, how can you introduce the human factor into the case? Who would you interview and what information would you want to gather? What information would you gather in other ways?

Now, assume you work for the defense. What information would you gather and how would you gather it? (See *Legal Assistant Today*, Jan./Feb. 1995, at 54.)

ANSWER:

Students should suggest things that show impact of deceased on family before death, what life is like in the family after loss of deceased. Impact on friends.

For defense, friends, neighbors, coworkers might have insights into the "real person," such as a history of abusing others and serious vices that impacted the family negatively.

INTERNET EXERCISES

1. Go to www.atanet.org, click on "find a translator," and locate the name of an ATA certified translator for Japanese to English translation.
2. Go to the sites listed for the Institute for Conflict Prevention. Compare the articles on difficult clients from the sites.

ADDITIONAL EXERCISES

1. List the essential elements and defenses to a cause of action for breach of contract.

ANSWER:

Elements
- Valid contract
   a. Competent parties bargaining at arm's length
   b. Mutual assent including offer and acceptance

```
┌─────────────────────────────────────────────────────────────────┐
│                    Interview Summary Sheet                         │
│  File No.         Date opened:              Interviewer:           │
│  Client: C. Ameche      Spouse: Z. Ameche Children, ages: Zachary, 6│
│  Phone:                                                            │
│  Date of injury: Aug. 21, ____     Statute of limitations:        │
│  Type of action: personal injury                                  │
│  Summary of facts of action:                                      │
│       Set up camp, site 36, Maple Meadows Campground              │
│       Moved damaged electrical cord from where son was playing    │
│       Noticed electrical problems with light and radio            │
│       Son's yell alerted him to fire                              │
│       Ameche suffered burns                                        │
│  Facts related to elements of action: Damaged cord, injuries      │
│  Facts related to possible defenses: Moving the cord              │
│  Witnesses: Robert Warren of Legalville                           │
│  Summary of injury and treatment to date:                        │
│       1st degree burns on legs, hands, left side of face         │
│       Numerous 2nd and 3rd degree burns                          │
│       Two months hospitalization and several sin grafts          │
│       Permanent scars                                             │
│       Restricted movement, particularly in use of hand           │
│  Total medical bills to date: $37,700                            │
│  Summary of business or wage loss: Make up                        │
│  Evaluation of client as witness: Good—scars will elicit sympathy │
│  Other comments:                                                   │
│  Things to do:                                                     │
└─────────────────────────────────────────────────────────────────┘
```

   c. Reciprocal consideration
   d. Lawful and enforceable purpose
   e. In a form required by law
   f. Absence of fraud, duress, undue influence, mistake of fact
 • Breach—failure to comply with terms
 • Damages
 • Damages were caused by breach

Defenses
 • Lack of capacity
 • Undue influence
 • Duress
 • Mistake known to other party
 • Mutual mistake
 • Misrepresentation
 • Fraud
 • Unconscionability
 • Statute of limitations
 • Death or impossibility

2. Using the information following the sample interview form in the text, list the procedural stages for creating your own interview form and place it in your system folder.

ANSWER:
 • Review file.
 • Have attorney identify likely cause of action.
 • Research cause of action to identify needed elements and defenses.
 • Draft interview questions that will elicit information to help prove or disprove cause or defenses to the cause (brainstorm ideas and write out questions).
 • Add name and standard background questions.
 • Have attorney review proposed form, make corrections and additions.

3. Review the Ameche case (Case II). Prepare at least five interview questions that will elicit specific details of this non-automobile accident.

ANSWER: Responses will vary, but may include the following areas:

 • Were you told about the electrical problem before you moved into campsite 36?
 • Describe the condition of the extension cord supplying electricity to your campsite.
 • Describe the area where the cord was lying (any-

thing flammable?) and the area where you threw the cord.

- How hard did you throw the cord? Could the throw have damaged the cord further or loosened connections?
- Did your son have access to matches or anything else that may have caused a fire?
- When you first saw your son trapped by the flames, how far was he from where you threw the cord?
- Can you think of any way you could have rescued your son without injury to this extent?

4. Review the checklist of information to be given at the initial interview. Which three items do you think are most important? Explain.

ANSWER: Subjective. Good class discussion question.

5. Read the fee agreements in Exhibit 2:3 and Exhibit 2:4. Briefly discuss the strengths and weaknesses of these agreements from the point of view of the firm, then from the point of view of the client.

ANSWER:

Exhibit 2:3
   Firm will be paid regardless of outcome of case
   Might not be as much as a percentage if the case is won.
   Client has better idea of required payment, but must pay, win or lose

Exhibit 2:4
   Firm has chance of large payment—or no payment at all.
   Except for costs, client pays only if case is won, but might lose a large chunk of award to firm.
   Client might overlook the need to pay costs.

6. How does the interviewer in the text example interview of Ms. Forrester demonstrate the criteria listed in Application Assignment 3?

ANSWER: Subjective; however, the student should demonstrate ability to recognize the following areas:

   Have attorney meet client.
   Make client comfortable.
   Thank client for gathering requested material.
   Start with easy questions.
   Follow form as a guide.
   Listen carefully.
   Be detailed.
   Check witness information in phone book.
   Catch slang or unclear words.
   Explore implication of evidence (restriction of coat).
   Get precise information (not "I guess").
   Soften the approach when the client is upset.
   Face sensitive issues head-on.
   Avoid euphemisms.
   Ad lib by listening.
   Keeping elements and defenses in mind.

7. One of the most common client complaints is, "My attorney never lets me know what is going on— and she (or he) is never available." Drawing from your text, in what specific ways can a paralegal assist the client in this regard?

ANSWER:

- Assume primary responsibility for communication with client.
- Schedule regular client report letters.
- Promptly respond to all client inquiries.
- Acknowledge receipt of information and material sent to you from client.

8. Work through the questions for study and review to test your understanding of the chapter.

CHAPTER 3

Evidence and Investigation

CHAPTER OBJECTIVE

The purpose of this chapter is to provide the background information and techniques for conducting a sound investigation, as well as the opportunity to practice those techniques.

PREPARING FOR CLASS: INSTRUCTIONAL SUPPLEMENTS

1. A summary of the evidentiary rules for your state. Judges often have quick reference works on the rules of evidence. Copies of these obtained for the class or placed on reserve could be helpful.
2. A description of the local rule on the attorney's work product (trial preparation materials) and what is protected and what is not.
3. Any unique aspects of the state bar's ethical code that address investigation conduct.
4. Any unique aspects of your state law on requesting medical records or other documents.
5. A list of resources on evidence and investigation, including Internet resources, that you have found useful.

SUGGESTED CLASS ACTIVITIES

1. Have a local, state, or federal judge lecture on the most significant rules of evidence.
2. Have experienced law office investigator/paralegals discuss their most successful investigation techniques and how they preserve and organize evidence.
3. Have a local hospital medical records librarian discuss medical records and how to request such records.
4. Set up a mock interview of a witness in Case I, Case II, or any of the other factual situations in the prologue or some other case of your choice. Plan it well and videotape it for future classes.
5. See the test for this chapter and Application

Assignment 5. Have the students role-play to plan and conduct interviews of a witness and take statements. You may want to divide the interview into parts or subject areas. You may use the prepared witness background sheet on Robert Warren (Case II) included in Application Assignment 5 to help selected persons prepare as witnesses. Have students critique interviewers. Students should then fill out the Witness Information Cover Sheet for this witness.
6. Have a law librarian familiar with law-related databases and other computer databases discuss searches, costs, methodology, and so on. Provide the students with the opportunity to do such database and Internet searches if facilities permit.

OUTLINE

I. Introduction
   System Folder Assignment 1
II. The Relationship of Evidence Law to Investigation
   A. Introduction
   B. Evidence in General
      Key terms: testimonial evidence, documentary evidence, real evidence, demonstrative evidence, direct evidence, circumstantial evidence
      System Folder Assignment 2
      Internet Exercise 1
   C. Admissible Evidence
      Key terms: admissible evidence, relevant, material
   D. Inadmissibility of Some Types of Relevant Evidence
      1. Evidence Based on Prejudice, Confusion, or Delay
         Key term: probative value of evidence
      2. Character Evidence
      3. Evidence of Habit or Routine Practice

Key terms: habit, routine
4. Evidence of Offers to Compromise, Insurance, and Remedial Measures
5. Evidence of Past Sexual Conduct, Past Sexual Crimes
6. Illegally Obtained Evidence
E. Privileges
F. Evidence Admissible from a Party
G. Rules Regarding the Testimony of a Witness
1. Requirement of Firsthand Knowledge
2. Opinion
3. Expert Opinion
4. Evidence of Character and Conduct of a Witness
5. Prior Statements of a Witness
6. Capacity to Observe, Record, Recollect, or Narrate
7. Hearsay
Key term: res gestae statements
H. Rules Regarding Physical Evidence and Authentication
Key term: chain of custody, best evidence rule
I. Other Evidentiary Concepts
1. Judicial Notice
Key term: judicial notice
2. Stipulations
Key term: stipulation
3. Burden of Proof
Key terms: burden of proof, affirmative defense, preponderance of the evidence, clear and convincing evidence, proof beyond a reasonable doubt
4. Presumption
Key term: presumption
J. Sources for Evidentiary Research
Application Assignment 1
III. Planning the Investigation
A. Introduction
B. Review the File and Other Available Information
C. Identify the Essential Elements of Proof
D. Identify What Facts Will Be Needed
E. Determine What Sources, Including Witnesses, May Provide Facts
1. Sources of Information and Evidence
Exhibit 3:1, Checklist of Evidentiary Soruces
2. Electronic Investigation and the Internet: Law and General Topic Research
Exhibit 3:2, General Resource Guide for Investigation on the Web
Internet Exercises 2 and 3
F. Methods for Gathering Information or Evidence

G. Record the Investigation Plan
Exhibit 3:3, Investigative Plan
System Folder Assignment 3
Application Assignment 2
H. Consult with the Supervising Attorney
IV. Ethical and Related Considerations
A. Ethics
System Folder Assignment 4
Application Assignment 3
B. Attorney's Work Product (Trial Preparation Materials)
Key term: attorney's work product (trial preparation materials)
C. Revealing Information to a Witness
V. Gathering the Evidence
A. Introduction
B. Gathering Reports, Records, and Other Documents
1. Medical Records
Exhibit 3:4, Request for Medical Records
Exhibit 3:5, Authorization to Release Medical Information
Exhibit 3:6, Request for Physician's Narrative Medical Summary
Exhibit 3:7, Request for Medical Update
Application Assignment 4
2. Employment Records
3. Other Records
4. Check Documents
C. Investigating the Scene of the Accident
Exhibit 3:8, Accident Scene Checklist
System Folder Assignment 5
D. Acquiring the Statements of Witnesses
1. Locating the Witnesses
2. Locating Expert Witnesses
System Folder Assignment 6
3. Planning the Interview
Exhibit 3:9, Witness Information Cover Sheet
Exhibit 3:10, Checklist for Witness Interview
System Folder Assignment 7
4. Conducting the Witness Interview
System Folder Assignment 8
5. Illustrative Interview: Case I
6. Drafting the Statement
7. Tips for Taking and Drafting an Effective Statement
System Folder Assignment 9
8. Concluding the Interview
Application Assignment 5
VI. Preserving Evidence
System Folder Assignment 10
A. Identification
Exhibit 3:11, Photograph Index Sketch

Exhibit 3:12, Witness Location Sketch
Exhibit 3:13, Basic Scene Sketch
  B. Physical Evidence
  C. Control and Retrieval
  D. Storage
     Exhibit 3:14, Evidence Log
  E. Testing and Examination
  F. Surveillance and Activity Checks
  G. Demonstrative Evidence
    1. Sketches and Drawings
    2. Photography
  H. Preserving Recorded Statements
VII. Reviewing the Informal Investigation
VIII. Summary

SYSTEM FOLDER ASSIGNMENTS

Assignment 1

List the purposes of investigation at the beginning of the investigation section of your system folder.

ANSWER:

1. To identify and locate the factual evidence that may be used by both sides to support or defeat each element of a cause of action
2. To locate persons and property
3. To establish expert opinion evidence
4. To develop evidence to discredit (impeach) a witness or opponent
5. To determine if there is sufficient factual evidence to support or defend the cause of action at trial or to form the basis for a settlement
6. To find additional evidence, if necessary
7. To preserve evidence for trial
8. To organize the evidence for trial

Assignment 2

Locate a copy of the Federal Rules of Evidence. Note how a photocopy of the table of contents for these rules can serve as a quick reference guide to evidence. you may choose to photocopy the table of contents to the rules of evidence and write the state equivalent next to each rule. Record whether evidence is admissible (A) or inadmissible (I). Place the reference guide in the investigation section of your system folder.

ANSWER: This assignment will give the student a quick reference chart on evidence. To save time, the rule sections could be divided among groups in the class who would be responsible to supply the rest of the class with copies of their sections. This would give each student a complete guide.

Assignment 3

Place an example of an investigation plan into your system folder.

Assignment 4

Read those Model Rules of Professional Conduct that cover the ethical questions raised in this chapter. Also read Rule 26 of the Federal Rules of Civil Procedure and the state equivalent. Draft a sheet titled "Ethical Applications to Investigation," and write out a one-or two-word topic head for each applicable rule and cite it. Then place this in your system folder.

ANSWER: State rules
Rule 26 of Federal Rules of Civil Procedure
Model Rules of Professional Conduct
    1.1—Competence, 1.2—Scope of representation,
    1.3—Diligence, 1.4—Communication
    2.1—Advisor
    3.3—(a)(d)—Candor toward the tribunal,
    3.4—(a)(b)(f)—Fairness to opposition,
    3.6—Trial publicity.
    4.1(a)—Truthfulness to others,
    4.2—Communication with represented person,
    4.3—Dealing with unpresented person,
    4.4—Rights of third persons.
    5.3—Nonlawyer assistants

Assignment 5

Subsequent to any class discussion in which other items may arise to add to the checklist in Exhibit 3:8, draft your own accident scene checklist and place it in the system folder.

ANSWER: Subjective, based on class discussion and Exhibit 3:8 in text.

Assignment 6

Adding suggestions made by your instructor, create a list of suggestions for locating witnesses and experts and place it in your system folder.

ANSWER: Lists are available in this section of the text.

Assignment 7

Place these items in your system folder: Checklist for Witness Interview, Witness Information Cover Sheet, and a brief description of how to create interview questions.

ANSWER: Creating interview questions:

- Determine key issues based on elements and defenses.
- Word questions to elicit detailed information on these issues.

Assignment 8

Drawing on the section on conducting an interview, draft a checklist of considerations for conducting a witness interview and place it in your system folder.

ANSWER: Checklist of considerations for conducting a witness interview:

1. Courtesy.
   a. call ahead, except hostile witness
   b. time convenient to witness
2. Identify yourself.
   a. position
   b. party represented
   c. purpose
3. Evoke sympathy for client.
4. Seek cooperation.
   a. help could bring case to a quicker, more just end
   b. help preserve evidence that could be lost or forgotten
   c. avoid subpoena
   d. withdraw until formal deposition
5. Complete witness information cover sheet.
6. Focus witness on relevant information.
7. Take notes.
8. Listen carefully, restate for clarification.

Assignment 9

After class discussion, draft your own list of tips for taking and drafting an effective statement, and place it in your system folder.

ANSWER: Include class discussion items as well as the following:

1. Previous visit to scene of accident (occurrence).
2. Note facts as opposed to beliefs.
3. Avoid references to insurance.
4. Take statements from witnesses who say they didn't see anything (impeachment).
5. Note but don't include names of other witnesses.
6. Do not pay witness without attorney approval.
7. Don't probe after favorable answer. (Converse opinion: Get all information at once.)
8. Do not give the witness a copy of the statement.
9. Use diagrams.
10. Avoid qualifiers such as "I think."

Assignment 10

The Preserving Evidence section of this chapter provides a good opportunity for you to test your ability to create a checklist. Draft a detailed checklist for preserving evidence and file it in your system folder.

ANSWER: Checklist for Preserving Evidence

A. Identification
   1. Photography
      a. Witness point of view
      b. Significant features of scene
   2. Sketches
      a. Witness point of view
      b. Graph paper
      c. Composite sketch
      d. Significant features, relationships of scene
B. Physical Evidence
   1. Leave a receipt for items taken from scene.
   2. Evidence must be preserved in its discovered state.
   3. Use standard control and retrieval procedures:
      a. Chain of evidence
         (1) Marking tool
         (2) Sealing tool
         (3) Cable ties
         (4) Sealed bags
         (5) Custody record documents
            (a) Do not mark or alter.
            (b) Keep in labeled transparent bags.
            (c) Photocopy for use, mark as copy.
      b. Storage: Protect from
         (1) Access
         (2) Removal
         (3) Alteration
         (4) Damage
      c. Maintain a check-out log with a statement that material will be safeguarded.
C. Testing and Examination
   1. Notify adversary of examination method, scenario.
   2. Photograph or videotape process.
   3. Record identity of witnesses, experts.
D. Surveillance and Activity Checks
   1. Conducted by trained investigators
   2. Videotape
   3. Talking with neighbors
   4. Best done as the last or later part of investigation
E. Demonstrative Evidence
   1. Scale, date, artist
   2. Means of measurement
   3. Date of examination and measurement
   4. Support drawings with photographs
   5. Models: expensive, accuracy subject to question; consult attorney
   6. Sketches and Drawings
   7. Medical illustrations at times clearer and better than x-rays
   8. Colored drawings: easier to understand, may be idealized
   9. Photography
      a. Subject to question
      b. Simple snapshot doesn't change perspective like wide-angle, telephoto, etc.
      c. Keep photo log
         (1) f stop
         (2) film speed
         (3) film type

(4) filters (arguable at best)
(5) lighting
(6) relate to sketch
d. Judgment required
   (1) Each photo must be explained
   (2) Destruction of photo must be explained
e. Film types may be sensitive to certain colors
   (1) Incandescent light: warm, red-toned
   (2) Fluorescent: yellow-green
   (3) Infra-red: vegetation, heat
f. Other sources: police, fire department, media, neighborhood
g. Professional photographer
   (1) Expensive
   (2) Professionals can usually qualify photos for evidence
   (3) Be specific in request and purpose
h. Overheads
   (1) U.S. Coast and Geologic Survey
   (2) U.S. Department of Agriculture
   (3) U.S. Department of the Interior
   (4) Local governments

   (5) Private sources
i. Distinguish between photos for trial and those to provide insight in planning case
10. Preserving Recorded Statements
a. Special storage facility
b. Numbering system log, cross reference to file
c. Disposal of recording following resolution
d. Last two digits of year, investigator's initials, and number of tape affixed to tape

APPLICATION ASSIGNMENTS

Assignment 1

The following is a list of possible evidence in Case I. Based on your understanding of the necessary elements in a negligence case from Chapter 2, the information in this chapter, and the rules of evidence for both the federal (F) and your state courts (S), indicate whether the listed items of evidence are admissible (A) or inadmissible (I). State any applicable reason and rule number.

Evidence	Fed	State	Reason	Rule(s)
Witness: "Mr. Hart is a good baseball player."	I	I	irrelevant	F401 S
1. Witness: "Mr. Hart smelled of beer."	A		relevant, personal knowledge	F401, 602 S
2. Bloody video of Ms. Forrester's hip repair.	I		prejudicial	F403 S
3. Witness: "Mr. Hart is a cautious person."	I		character not allowed	F404 S
4. Routine practice of Mercury to check all brakes of vehicles.	A		habit or routine allowed	F406 S
5. Forrester's offer to Mercury to settle for $50,000.	I		can't use offers to compromise	F408 S
6. Hart told wife he was too tired to be driving.	I		privileged	F501 S
7. Forrester's letter to friend stating she didn't look for traffic.	A		admission by party opponent	F801(d)(2) S
8. Friend's opinion that signature on letter is Forrester's.	A		lay opinion	F701 S
9. Doctor's testimony that van caused Forrester's injuries.	A		expert opinion	F702 S
10. Independent evidence that van caused Forrester's injuries.	I		needless cumulative evidence	F403(b) S
11. Testimony from Hart's minister that Hart is honest.	A		only after credibility attacked	F608(a) S
12. Independent evidence that doctor previously said falling on the ice was cause of injury.	A		if given a chance to explain inconsistency	F613(b) S
13. Witness: "Mr. Forrester said, "Hart was going fast.""	I		hearsay	F801(c) S
14. Witness at scene: "That van driver didn't even try to stop."	A		present sense impression	F803(1) A
15. Nearby service station attendant: "Hart said before accident, 'I'm going to scrape off that windshield.'"	A		state of mind showing vision could be problem	F803(3) S
16. Mercury vehicle service log.	A		to show inconsistency with previously admitted hearsay	F806(b) S
17. Relevant former testimony of unavailable witness.	I		unless opponent had chance to cross at time	F804(b)(1) S
18. Duplicate photograph of left front fender of van where authenticity of original in question.	I		original evidence rule	F1002, 1003 S
19. Witness identification of bald tires from Hart's van with proper chain of custody.	A		authenticated and identified by witness with knowledge	F901(b)(1) S
20. A one-time computer printout showing a comment: "Hart's truck checked for brake problems—OK" with date entered two days before accident. This entry was made by one of Mercury's mechanics.	I		hearsay	802

ANSWER: This is an important assignment. To complete the assignment the student must understand the rules of evidence sufficiently to apply them to specific types of evidence that might arise in Case I. Please provide answers for your state's rules.

Assignment 2

Following the steps and examples of planning an investigation as presented in this chapter, create an investigation plan for Case II. Develop the elements and facts to be proved, the sources, and the methods to be used in a format similar to that in Exhibit 3:3.

ANSWER: You may choose any case on which to base the investigation plan. Results will vary but should be in a format similar to the following:

Assignment 3

Citing the relevant Model Rules of Professional Conduct, what should you do under the following circumstances?

ANSWER: You may choose to have the students do research on other special issues raised by investigation.

a. You need to see one last critical witness who you are fairly sure will not speak with you if you tell the witness you are representing Ann Forrester.

Possible to Prove or Acquire	Possible Source of Information	Method Cost
Defendant Margie and LeroyCongden Financial status	Midwest Campgrounds Assoc. Dun's	Letter Modem
Breach of Duty Weather conditions Electrical defect/cord Conditions at scene	Certified copy of weather conditions from National Climatic Center Electrician Fire marshal's report Inspection of cord remains Statement of camp employees Mr. Warren (witness) Scene of accident	Mail Phone Mail Hire fire expert Interview/deposition Interview Visit/photos
Plaintiff's Injuries Immediate injuries, burns, etc. Immediate and long-term disabilities Pain	Doctors' reports Emergency room records Hospital records X-rays Doctors' testimony Doctors' reports (follow-up visits) Doctors' testimony Mr. Ameche Ms. Ameche Nurse Friends Mr. Ameche's testimony (pain log) Ms. Ameche Nurse Hospital and doctors' reports Doctor's testimony Ambulance assistants Mr. Warren (witness)	Mail Mail Mail Mail Interview/letter Mail Interview Interview Interview Phone Phone Interview Interview Phone Mail Interview Phone Interview
Comparative Negligence Cord was moved to dry grass Child played with cord	Mr. Warren (witness) Fire marshal's report Mr. Ameche Mr. Warren Mr. Ameche Ms. Ameche	Interview Mail Interview Interview Interview Interview

You arrive at the witness's apartment and she answers the door. What should you do?

ANSWER: Paralegal should identify self and client represented (Rule 4.3).

b. You are investigating a low profit case where your elderly client is trying to hang onto the only house and property she has ever had. yet, to interview the key witness in the case will cost more than the case will bring to the firm. What should you do?

ANSWER: Consult with attorney; see if the work can be done pro bono (Rule 6.1).

c. Your firm is representing a federal judge in a civil suit. You have come to admire this judge and know that the firm believes he is a very valuable client. One night you are working with the judge on his case. There is a letter in the file that the judge received from a third party. The judge asks you to change one word in the letter because he knows that is what the party said he meant in the first place. The judge has offered you a terrific federal job at the close of this case. What would you do?

ANSWER: Refuse to change the letter. Tactfully explain why. Get third party to attest to original meaning. Consult supervising attorney [Rule 3.4(a)(b)].

d. As you are preparing a legal memo on a case for your supervising attorney, your fellow paralegal tells you not to deal with or cite two of the strongest cases against you because that is likely to help the other side—especially if they failed to find these cases. What should you do?

ANSWER: Include the two cases [Rule 3.3(a)(d)].

Assignment 4

Assume that you have received the hospital reports for the treatment of Mr. Ameche in Case II, and these reports confirm the injuries described by him in his initial interview (Chapter 2 instructor's manual). Draft a letter to Mr. Ameche's physician requesting a medical report. Use the letter in Exhibit 3:6 as a guide. Remember, however, to keep the letter specific to Mr. Ameche's injuries. Place your letter into your system folder.

ANSWER: This is a good assignment for students to use the editing functions of computers, if they are available. An interview background sheet for Mr. Ameche is in the instructor's manual, Chapter 2. The students could use this or their own interview of Mr. Ameche, if that was done as an assignment for Chapter 2.

WHITE, WILSON & McDUFF
Attorneys at Law
Federal Plaza Building Suite 700
Third and Market Streets
Legalville, Columbia 00000

Albert Find, M.D.
313 Broad St.
Legalville, Columbia 00000
Re: Carl Ameche, Soc. Sec. No. 000-00-0000
Dear Dr. Find:
Mr. Ameche has retain this office to represent him regarding injuries he sustained in a fire on Aug. 21, _____ Mr. Ameche suffered numerous burns and received skin grafts. As a result of these injuries Mr. Ameche has not been able to return to work.
To assist Mr. Ameche we would appreciate it if you would send us a report on the following:
1. Your diagnosis of Mr. Ameche's mental, emotional, and physical injuries.
2. Your opinion as to the cause of Mr. Ameche's injuries.
3. A description of the treatment given Mr. Ameche.
4. Likely degree of pain and discomfort related to such injuries.
5. Mental, physical, and emotional limitations as they relate to employment, recreational activities, enjoyment of life.
6. Future treatment needed.
7. Prognosis.
8. Likelihood of Mr. Ameche being able to return to work. If so, when?
In addition, please send an itemized bill for all your services related to these injuries. The necessary authorization is enclosed. Upon receipt of your report, this office will promptly pay an preparation fee.
Please keep us informed regarding Mr. Ameche's future visits to your office and nay change in condition or prognosis.
Thank you for your cooperation.

_____,
Paralegal
Enclosed: Authorization to Release Medical Information
cc: Mr. Carl Ameche

Assignment 5

Following the directions of your instructor and the procedure set out in this chapter of the text and Chapter 2 on interviewing, conduct an interview with Robert Warren, a witness to the incident in Case II. After the interview, prepare a witness statement according to the recommended procedures and tips covered in this chapter.

ANSWER: The students have the opportunity in this assignment to apply what they have learned to a live witness, Robert Warren in Case II, played by selected members of the class or volunteers from outside the class. These witnesses can prepare for the interview by using the following data sheet on Robert Warren. The data sheet may be photocopied for distribution. The students should follow the procedure and techniques listed in this chapter and Chapter 2. A good written and signed statement is the ultimate goal of this assignment. The statement could also be used as a take-home exam for this chapter. The results will vary but should accurately reflect the information provided by Robert Warren.

The following is background material on Robert Warren. Read the material so you will know enough about what Robert Warren saw to respond to the questions of a student playing the role of an investigative paralegal. During the interview, if you are asked a question o which you have not been supplied the necessary information, please try to create an answer somewhat consistent with the information supplied below. Also when answering, let the sudden draw out much of the information through questions.

Background Information on Robert Warren:

You will be asked your full name, phone number, social security number, marital status, etc. Please make up any response to these questions consistent with being a reliable witness and a grandparent. You reside in Legalville, Columbia, Capitol County, and come to the campground to get away from the city.

Factual Information from Robert Warren:

I arrived at Maple Meadows Campground on August 21 around 1:00 P.M.

There were few other campers present.

I chose campsite 34. Found conditions to be warm, dry, and windy.

I observed a young family arrive about 2:00. I checked my watch. They set up in campsite 36.

I was sitting in my chair relaxing and happened to watch some of the activities in the neighboring campsite.

I observed a man set up the camper-tent while a woman unloaded something from the car to bring to the camper.

Their little boy, about 6 or 7, got very busy exploring, picking up things, etc. I enjoyed watching him because he reminded me of my grandson.

After awhile I heard the man ask his wife something to the effect that he wondered why they had placed an electrical cord, and not a very good one, that near a campsite where children might be playing. I saw him pick up what I assume was the cord and throw it back into the grass and brush away from where his son was playing.

They were having difficulty with their electrical hook-up. He came over to see me and asked if I was hav-

ing difficulty with the electricity. I told him that I was not. He said the light in their camper kept flickering on and off as did their radio. I remember the comment about the radio because I don't like radios in campgrounds. After that I knew the man as Carl Ameche.

Later I noticed the Ameche boy playing further back in the grass and bushes. I saw light flicker briefly and assumed the boy was playing with a sparkler like they do on the Fourth of July. It did not occur to me that it might be the cord. Anyway, the Ameches seemed to be distracted and were not watching their child very closely.

I went into my camper and lay down. I was awakened by a child's screams. When I looked over I saw the brush behind the Ameche's campsite ablaze and the wind was spreading the fire. Then I was shocked to see the boy in the middle of the fire. Mr. Ameche threw a blanket over himself and ran into the fire to get his son.

When Mr. Ameche emerged, his son was wrapped in a blanket that was on fire. Mrs. Ameche pulled the blanket from her son and used another blanket to smother the flames on Mr. Ameche's clothes.

I came over with my small fire extinguisher, but it was nearly useless. Mr. Ameche's face was obviously burned on the left side as were his arms and legs.

By this time, a couple other campers came to help as did the manager of the campground. A camp maintenance worker offered to take Mr. Ameche to the hospital in nearby Thedford. Mrs. Ameche and her son followed in their car.

It wasn't long before we realized the fire was completely out of control. We hurried to our vehicle and retreated to the entrance of the camp. About 20 minutes later fire trucks arrived and eventually gained control of the fire. Several small buildings and a lot of the campground burned.

Thinking back, I would say the cause of the fire must have been the electricity problem. The brief flashes I saw were apparently some sort of electrical short circuit. This seems probable because the Ameches were having trouble with their light and radio—also because of where the fire started, which was in the area where the cord had been tossed.

INTERNET EXERCISES

1. Using www.law.cornell.edu or www.lawresearch.com/v2/caserule.htm locate the changes in the Federal Rules of Evidence that were effective December 1, 2000. Find the Advisory Committee Notes for the change to Rule 701. In those notes, what article is quoted, saying, ". . . the court should be vigilant to preclude manipulative conduct designed to thwart the expert disclosure and discovery process"?

ANSWER: Joseph, *Emerging Expert Issues Under the 1993 Disclosure Amendments to the Federal Rules of Civil Procedure*, 164 F.R.D. 97, 108 (1996).

2. Go to www.cpsc.gov. Assume your client was badly burned after raising and lowering the hood on her White (brand name) lawn and garden tractor. Determine if any of these tractors were recalled for fuel leaks and, if recalled, in what months of what years the recalled tractors were sold.

ANSWER: 11/99–12/00

3. Using at least three different Web sites for locating people listed in Exhibit 3:2, see if you can locate your phone number by entering your name. Next, try to find a friend's name by entering only the phone number.

ADDITIONAL EXERCISES

1. Make a list of three possible items of relevant evidence in the Ameche case (Case II) and in the Briar Patch Doll case (Case IV). Indicate the fact of consequence for each item, whether that item would be direct or circumstantial evidence, and whether it would be testimonial, documentary, real, or demonstrative.

ANSWER: You may choose to give students the facts and let them provide the evidence and type. Examples may include the following or others:

Ameche:
EVIDENCE: Statement by Mr. Congden that the electric cord was damaged
FACT: That the damaged cord caused the fire
TYPE: Circumstantial, testimonial

EVIDENCE: Statement by witness that Mr. Ameche moved the cord
FACT: That Mr. Ameche moved the cord
TYPE: Direct, testimonial

EVIDENCE: Before and after photos of the campsite
FACT: That damage was done to campground
TYPE: Direct, demonstrative

EVIDENCE: Statement by witnesses that Zach Ameche played near the cord just before the fire started

FACT: That the cord caused the fire
TYPE Circumstantial, testimonial

EVIDENCE: Electrician's appointment book showing September date to do electrical work at campground
FACT: That there was an electrical problem at the campground
TYPE: Circumstantial, documentary

Briar Patch Dolls
EVIDENCE: Business Records of Briar Patch that show losses
FACT: That breach of contract caused losses
TYPE: Circumstantial, documentary
FACT: That there were losses
TYPE: direct, documentary

EVIDENCE: The contract itself
FACT: That Teeny Tiny was obligated to produce certain numbers of items at certain times
TYPE: Direct, documentary

EVIDENCE: Examples of defective product
FACT: That some products were defective
TYPE: Direct, real
FACT: That defective products caused losses
TYPE: Circumstantial, real

EVIDENCE: Invoices of delivery from Teeny Tiny to Briar Patch
FACT: That deliveries were in deficient numbers
TYPE: Direct, documentary

EVIDENCE: Survey of first-grade children showing that interest in Briar Patch dolls has waned.
FACT: That breach of contract caused loss of business
TYPE: Circumstantial, testimonial or documentary, depending on how it is presented

2. What are the major requirements and limits of relevancy?

ANSWER:

> Must be material (of consequence).
> Must tend to prove or refute fact of consequence.
> Probative value must outweigh:
> > unfair prejudice
> > confusion of issues
> > misleading jury
> > undue delay
> > needless cumulative evidence
> Must not be based on character trait, except as element of claim.
> Must not include privileged communications.
> Testimony must be firsthand.
> Physical evidence must be authenticated.

3. Using Exhibit 3:4, draft a form letter Request for Medical Records, then fill it in to request records on Mr. Ameche, Case II. Use the data sheet in Chapter 2 of this study guide. If a computer is available, use its editing functions for this assignment.

ANSWER:

WHITE, WILSON & McDUFF
Attorneys at Law
Federal Plaza Building Suite 700
Third and Market Streets
Legalville, Columbia 0000

Medical Records Librarian

Re:
     Address:
     Soc. Sec. No.
     Birthdate:
     Dates of Care:
Dear _____:

The firm of white, Wilson & McDuff has been retained to represent the above named individual.

Enclosed is a current Authorization to Release Medical Information executed by our client.

Would you please send copies of the following records to me:

( )   Discharge summary
( )   ER and outpatient reports
( )   Patient's chart
( )   History and physical
( )   Operative and pathology reports
( )   X-ray reports
( )   Lab reports
( )   Progress notes by physicians and nurses
( )   Doctors' orders
( )   Consultation reports
( )   Nurses' notes
( )   Alcohol and drug treatment notes
( )   Others _____.

On receipt of the records, our firm will promptly submit payment for any preparation fee.

Thank you for your assistance.
Sincerely,

_____.
Paralegal

Enclosure: Authorization for Release of Medical Information

WHITE, WILSON & McDUFF
Attorneys at Law
Federal Plaza Building Suite 700
Third and Market Streets
Legalville, Columbia 00000

Ms. Sarah Ohm
Medical Records Librarian
Capitol County General Hospital
400 Ridge Blvd.
Legalville, Columbia 00000

Re: Medical Records of
     Mr. Carl Ameche   2222 2nd St., Thorp, Ohio 10000
     Soc. Sec. No. 000-00-0000
     Birthdate: make up
     Dates of Care: 8/21/__ –10/21/__

Dear Ms. Ohm:

The firm of White, Wilson & McDuff has been retained to represent the above named individual.

Enclosed is a current Authorization to Release Medical Information executed by our client.

Would you please send copies of the following records to me:

(X)   Discharge summary
(X)   ER and outpatient reports
(X)   Patient's chart
(X)   History and physical
(X)   Operative and pathology reports
(X)   X-ray reports
(X)   Lab reports
(X)   Progress notes by physicians and nurses
(X)   Doctors' orders
(X)   Consultation reports
(X)   Nurses' notes
( )   Alcohol and drug treatment notes
( )   Others _____.

On receipt of the records, our firm will promptly submit payment for any preparation fee.

Thank you for your assistance,
Sincerely,

_____,
Paralegal

Enclosure: Authorization for Release of Medical Information

4. What tools would you need—and for what purposes—to investigate the accident scene in Case II?

ANSWER: A variety of answers are possible, including the following:

Tool	Purpose	Evidence
camera/ video camera	record damage	extent of fire scene in general any pertinent details
magnifying glass, tweezers, zip bags	find pick up store	possible bits of cord or other evidence found
tape measure	measure distances	extent of fire distance from where Zach was playing to camper distance cord was moved.

5. List three possible witnesses to interview in the *Coleman v. Make Tracks, Inc.* wrongful death case (Case III) and the focus of each interview.

ANSWER:

Sam/Emma	Sean's personality/judgment
Coleman	Importance to future of farm
Jason Hackett and other friends	Events surrounding accident Recklessness, speed Effect of advertising Sean's personality/judgment
Teachers	Academic and employment potential Sean's personality/judgment
Emergency medical staff	Type, extent, and cause of injuries Cause of death

6. Write five interview questions to Jason Hackett, friend of Sean Coleman, and the specific issues in Case III that they will probe.

ANSWER: A variety of responses are possible, including the following:

- Did Sean mention any advertising for the Make Tracks vehicle? (Misleading ads.)
- How did the terrain and speed of the vehicle at the time of the accident compare to your impressions of terrain and speed in TV commercials for the vehicle? (Misleading ads.)
- Did Sean read the manual before operating the vehicle? (Comparative negligence, warranty.)
- Did you drive the vehicle before the accident? Was it difficult to control on flat terrain? Hills? (Mechanical defect.)
- Had Sean or anyone else altered the vehicle in any manner? (Defense to breach of implied or express

warranty and strict liability.)
- Were there distractions that may have caused Sean to lose control of the vehicle? (Comparative negligence.)
- What happened between the time of the accident and the time the rescue squad arrived? (Cause of death.)

7. List four methods for recording the statement of a witness and note advantages or disadvantages for each.

ANSWER:

- Witness writes own—inexpensive but not detailed, few witnesses willing.
- Court reporter—more expensive, not good for pro-client witness because inaccuracies will be recorded. Third party verification.
- Neutral third party—third party verification, may record memorandum if witness refuses to sign.
- Paralegal draft—would not be viewed as neutral party
- Audio or video recorder—must be protected from tampering. Must have full knowledge and permission of witness.

8. Make a list of leads for further investigation provided by the interview with Ms. Schnabel in the text or with Mr. Warren in Application Assignment 5.

ANSWER: A variety of responses are possible, including the following:

Ms. Schnabel:	Check road conditions and weather (how slippery) Wheels locked on van Distance from crest of hill to Ms. Forrester Speed of van Interference of coat collar
Mr. Warren:	Original placement of cord Where Mr. Ameche threw cord Flammability of grass Location where child was playing

9. Summarize either Ms. Schnabel's or Mr. Warren's statement to be included on the Witness Information Cover Sheet for the case file. Use the computer editing technique.

ANSWER: The summary for Mr. Warren depends on the statement written in Application Assignment 5. The summary could include the following:

Weather warm, dry, and windy
Warrens in site 34, Ameches in 36
Saw boy explore

Heard Ameche comment on poor electrical cord, throw "what I assume was the cord" into the grass

Was told by Ameche of electrical problems at site 36

Saw spark where boy was playing

Awoke to see fire, Mr. Ameche rescue son

Saw Ameche's face burned on left side, arms and legs burned

Much of campground and several small buildings burned

Thinks cause of fire was electricity problem stemming from faulty cord

Ms. Schnabel: At first unwilling to make statement
Conditions cold, windy, 20 percent patches of ice on both sides of road
Ann Forrester was on side of road toward house, van approached, swerved side to side, slid to middle of road, hit Ms. Forrester

Started skid 35–40 feet from Ms. Forrester

No horn, must have braked, sounded like wheels locked

Van speed 40–45 m.p.h.

Crest of hill to Ms. Forrester 100 feet

"I kind of recall her collar being up around her neck and ears—but I'm really not sure."

10. Sketch the Forrester accident scene from the viewpoint of Ms. Schnabel.

11. Work through the questions for study and review to test your understanding of the chapter.

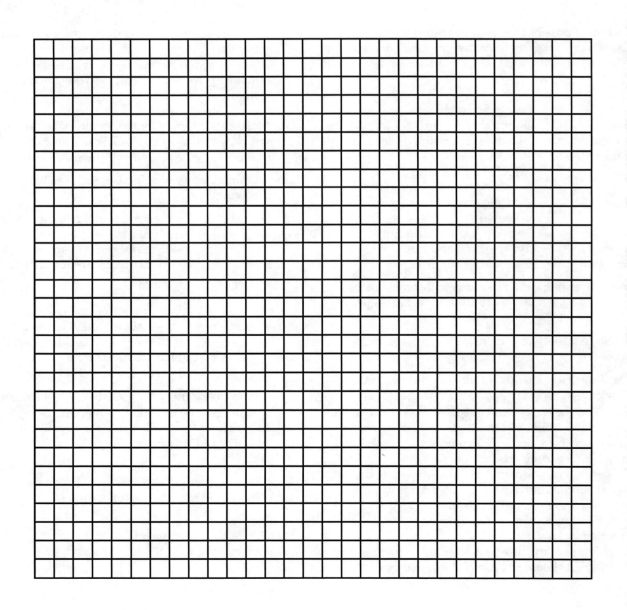

CHAPTER 3 TAKE HOME TEST

Select a factual situation such as Case II or any other case of interest or familiarity to you. Choose several aspects of the case that you would like the students to investigate (a full investigation would probably be too cumbersome, especially to critique). Have students demonstrate their ability to do the following on those aspects of the case that you have chosen:

- plan the applicable aspect of the investigation
- draft the investigative plan including a choice of methods to be used

- request documents (draft appropriate letters)
- investigate scene of accident
- locate potential expert witness (not contact—just locate)
- plan interview checklist for assigned aspects including key issue questions
- conduct interview
- draft statement
- evaluate witness
- review statement for leads and indicate needed follow-up
- indicate how evidence will be stored

CHAPTER 4

Drafting the Complaint

CHAPTER OBJECTIVE

This chapter helps the student develop the knowledge, skills, and techniques needed to draft the complaint for a civil lawsuit and gain experience in drafting complaints.

PREPARING FOR CLASS: INSTRUCTIONAL SUPPLEMENTS

1. The state rules of pleading and/or the state rules of civil procedure.
2. The federal rules of civil procedure.
3. Copies of state civil complaints that could be used as a guide and placed in the student's system folder.
4. Pertinent Web sites.

SUGGESTED CLASS ACTIVITIES

1. Invite an experienced litigation attorney to discuss drafting complaints for both state and federal court (videotape).
2. As a state and/or federal judge to explain what they look for when ruling on the adequacy of a complaint (videotape).
3. Use several anonymous examples of complaints drafted by students to demonstrate strengths and weaknesses.
4. Let groups of four or five students critique each other's complaints.

OUTLINE

I. Introduction
  A. The Task: Draft a Complaint
  B. Definition and Purpose
    Key terms: due process of law, pleadings, complaint
  C. An Example
    Exhibit 4:1, Sample Complaint (State)
II. The Complaint in Detail

A. Caption
  1. Parties
    Key terms: plaintiff, defendant
  2. Real Party in Interest
    Key term: real party in interest
  3. Standing to Sue
    Key term: standing to sue
  4. Capacity to Sue or Be Sued
    Key term: capacity, guardian ad litem
  5. Joinder of Parties
    Key term: joinder of parties
  6. Interpleader
    Key term: interpleader
  7. Class Actions
    Key term: class action
  8. Intervention
  9. "Et al."
  10. Sample Captions
    System Folder Assignment 1
B. The Body of the Complaint
  1. Jurisdictional Allegations
  2. Identification of the Parties
  3. Allegations (Cause of Action)
    a. Introduction
      Key term: cause of action
    b. What Must Be Alleged
    c. Guidelines and Techniques for Drafting the Body of the Complaint
    d. Fact (Code) Pleading
      Key term: fact pleading
    e. Notice Pleading
      Key term: notice pleading
C. Remedies and the Prayer for Relief (Demand for Judgment)
  Key terms: general damages, special damages, exemplary damages, prohibitory injunction, mandatory injunction, specific performance
  Application Assignment 1
  Internet Exercises 1 and 2

D. A Brief Guide to Causes of Action and
Remedies
Exhibit 4:2, Causes of Action and Remedies
E. Separate Counts
F. Demand for Jury Trial
G. Subscription (Rule 11)
H. Verification
III. Exhibits and Appendices
IV. System Checklist for Drafting a Complaint
System Folder Assignment 2
A. Preparation
B. Drafting
V. Sample Complaints
System Folder Assignment 3
Application Assignments 2 and 3
Internet Exercise 3
VI. Injunctions
Exhibit 4:3, Motion for Preliminary Injunction—
General Form
Exhibit 4:4, Motion for Temporary Restraining
Order
VII. Summary

SYSTEM FOLDER ASSIGNMENTS

1. Research the rules of civil procedure for your state
for the recommended caption form. If the rules of
your state do not have sample forms, go to a book
on forms for civil action in your state. Place a copy
of the state caption form with copies of the captions from the text at the beginning of the complaint section of your system folder. Also list the
applicable rules and forms.

ANSWER: Federal Rule of Civil Procedure 10 as well as
state rules.

2. Following class discussion on drafting complaints,
especially regarding state court rules, complete the
state and system folder reference blanks in the system checklist for drafting a complaint, and place it
in your system folder.

ANSWER: Note indicated state rules. Experience in
your local jurisdiction could provide helpful additions
to students' checklists.

3. Check the pleading rules of your own state. Gather
examples of local complaints by researching recent
editions of legal forms and pleading books, or obtain them from your instructor. Try to locate a full
range of examples of complaints that include
pleading in the alternative, pleading in the hypothetical joined parties, and joined claims and
counts. Place them in your system folder. Add references to the page numbers in this text where
samples of specific types of complaints can be

located. Add references to injunction and restraining
order forms.

ANSWER: Requiring the students to research local
rules and practices provides them with valuable experience.

APPLICATION ASSIGNMENTS
Assignment 1

Should an insurance company have to pay exemplary
damages on behalf of the insured? State arguments for
and against.

ANSWER: Subjective.
Yes, the policy holder pays for and relies on full liability coverage up to the amount stated in the policy.
No, exemplary damages are intended to punish the one
responsible for the injury. If the insurance company
pays, the wrongdoer is not punished.

Assignment 2

Using the checklist and examples in the text, draft a
complaint for Ann Forrester to be filed in the United
States District Court for the Eastern District of Columbia
alleging diversity jurisdiction. Place copies of the federal
(notice) complaint and the example of the state (fact)
complaint from the text into your system folder.

Assignment 3

Draft both a fact and a notice complaint for the *Ameche*
case (Case II in Chapter 1) using the facts you found
through investigation in Chapter 3.

ANSWER: You may use any of the cases in Chapter 1 for
this assignment. This assignment could be used as a test
for this chapter. These examples may be copied and used
as a guide in group critiques of the students' complaints.

INTERNET EXERCISES

1. Go to www.ojp.usdoj.gov. Using the search box, enter the search term "punitive damages, 2000." Click
Civil Trial Cases and Verdicts in Large Counties,
1996. According to that study, what was the aver-
age processing time of a case from filing to final
judgment in jury cases?

ANSWER: 22.1 months

2. The previous edition of this text stated that
Alabama had a law requiring that punitive damages over a certain amount be split with the state.
Using Westlaw, Lexis, or a lawfinder such as
www.lawresearch.com, go to state materials and
then the state statutes of Alabama. Using the index

ANSWER: Federal Notice Complaint for Ann Forrester Case

UNITED STATES DISTRICT COURT
FOR THE EASTERN DISTRICT OF COLUMBIA
Civil Action, File Number 1000

ANN FORRESTER and
WILLIAM FORRESTER,
    Plaintiffs

v.

RICHARD HART and
MERCURY PARCEL SERVICE, INC.,
    Defendants

COMPLAINT FOR NEGLIGENCE

Plaintiffs Demand Trial by Jury

Count One

1. Plaintiffs are citizens of the state of Columbia and defendants are citizens of the state of Ohio.
2. On February 26, on Highway 328 in Capitol County, Columbia, Defendant Richard Hart in the employment of Mercury Parcel Service, Inc. negligently drove a motor vehicle striking down Plaintiff Ann Forrester who was then crossing said highway.
3. As a result, Plaintiff fractured her left leg and hip bones and was otherwise seriously injured. She has been prevented from transacting her business, and has suffered and will continue to suffer great physical and emotional pain. In addition, she has incurred and will continue to incur expenses for medical attention and hospitalization in the sum of $750,000.

Wherefore plaintiff demands judgment against defendants in the sum of seven hundred and fifty thousand dollars ($750,000) together with the costs and disbursements of this action.

Count Two

1. Plaintiffs hereby incorporate by reference paragraphs 1 through 3 of Count One.
2. Because of Defendants' negligence, Plaintiff William Forrester has suffered loss of the consortium of his wife, Ann Forrester, in the amount of twenty thousand dollars ($20,000).

Wherefore, Plaintiff William Forrester demands judgment against Defendants in the sum of twenty thousand dollars ($20,000) and costs and for such other relief as this court may deem just and proper.

_____.

Arthur White
White, Wilson & McDuff
Attorneys at Law
Federal Plaza Building Suite 700
Third and Market Streets
Legalville, Columbia 00000
(111) 555-0000

(Fact Complaint)

STATE OF COLUMBIA	CAPITOL COUNTY	CIRCUIT COURT

CARL AMECHE and
ZOE AMECHE,
       Plaintiffs
     v.   Civil Action No.
MARGIE CONGDEN and
LEROY CONGDEN,
       Defendants   Plaintiffs Demand Trial by Jury

COMPLAINT FOR NEGLIGENCE

Plaintiffs allege that:

1. The jurisdiction of this court is based on the amount in controversy in this action which is more than $2500.
2. Plaintiff Carl Ameche is an accountant and resides at 222 2nd Street, Thorp, Ohio.
3. Plaintiff Zoe Ameche is the wife of Carl Ameche and resides with him.
4. Defendants Margie and Leroy Congden are the owners of the Maple Meadows Campground and reside at the campground which is located at Star Route 2, Highway 66. in the city limits of Legalville, Capitol County, Columbia.
5. On August 21, plaintiffs rented campsite 36 in the Maple Meadows Campground.
6. Defendants had negligently placed a worn extension cord running to campsite 36.
7. As a direct consequence of the defendants' negligence, a fire was started that encircled the plaintiffs' son Zachary, requiring Carl Ameche to place himself in peril in order to rescue his son.
8. Because of said negligence, Carl Ameche suffered severe burns to his face, hands, and legs that have caused him intense pain and great suffering, physical disability, considerable inconvenience, and permanent scarring.
9. As a consequence of the defendants' negligence and the aforesaid injuries, Carl Ameche has incurred and will incur the loss of considerable sums of money for hospital and medical care, loss of income and benefits, and property damage to his clothing and camper.

Wherefore plaintiff demands judgment in the amount of three hundred and fifty thousand dollars ($350,000), together with the costs and disbursements of this action and for such relief as this court may deem just and proper.

COUNT TWO

10. Plaintiffs hereby allege and incorporate by reference paragraphs 1 through 8 of COUNT ONE.
11. Because of the defendants' negligence, plaintiff Zoe Ameche has suffered loss of the consortium of her husband, Carl Ameche, in the amount of fifteen thousand dollars ($15,000).

Wherefore, plaintiff Zoe Ameche demands judgment against defendants in the sum of fifteen thousand dollars ($15,000) and costs and for such relief as this court may deem just and proper.

                                          _____
                                          Arthur White
                                          White, Wilson, and McDuff
                                          Federal Plaza Building
                                          Suite 700
                                          Third and Market Streets
                                          Legalville, Columbia 00000

(Students should include verification.)

(Notice Complaint)

UNITED STATES DISTRICT COURT FOR THE
EASTERN DISTRICT OF COLUMBIA
Civil Action, File Number _____.

CARL AMECHE
     and
ZOE AMECHE
          Plaintiffs   COMPLAINT FOR NEGLIGENCE
     v.
MARGIE CONGDEN
     and
LEROY CONGDEN,
          Defendants   Plaintiffs Demand Trial by Jury

1. Plaintiff is a citizen of the state of Ohio and defendant is a citizen of the state of Columbia. The matter in controversy exceeds the sum of $10,000, exclusive of interests and costs.
2. On August 21, _____, at the Maple Meadows Campground owned and operated by defendants, defendants negligently used a faulty extension cord, necessitating plaintiff Carl Ameche to rescue his son from a fire caused by the faulty cord.
3. As a result plaintiff was seriously burned on his face, hands, and legs, was and is prevented from transacting his business, suffered great pain of body and continues to suffer anguish and embarrassment, incurred and will continue to incur expenses for medical attention and hospitalization, and incurred property damage, all to the sum of $350,000.

Wherefore plaintiff demands judgment against defendants in the sum of 350,000 dollars and costs.

COUNT TWO

4. Plaintiffs incorporate by reference paragraphs 1 through 3 of COUNT ONE.
5. Because of defendants' negligence, plaintiff Zoe Ameche has suffered the loss of the consortium of her husband, Carl Ameche, in the amount of 15,000 dollars.

Wherefore plaintiff demands judgment against defendants in the sum of 15,000 dollars and costs.
February _____.

                                      _____.

                                      Arthur white
                                      White, Wilson and McDuff
                                      Federal Plaza Building
                                      Suite 700
                                      Third and Market Streets
                                      Legalville, Columbia 00000

to the statutes or a search box, find out if that is still the law in Alabama.

ANSWER: No, the state may not take a percentage of punitive damages, but caps are still imposed on punitive damages.

3. If you want to get actual copies of the complaint filed in a specific case, what Internet fee service might be helpful? Go to this service and see what it offers.

ANSWER: www.Juritas.com

ADDITIONAL EXERCISES

1. a. What is a syllogism and what are its components?
   b. In your own words, explain a cause of action for negligence in terms of a syllogism.

ANSWER:
a. A logical formula for an argument
   Major premise
   Minor premise
   Conclusion
b. Major Premise: Rule of law that the existence of duty plus breach of duty plus injury plus the fact that the breach caused the injury entitles the injured party to relief.
   Minor Premises:
      A duty existed.
      A breach of duty happened.
      An injury occurred.
      The injury resulted from the breach.
   Conclusion: The injured party is entitled to relief.

The minor premises are the elements that must be proven to satisfy the law (major premise) and reach the conclusion. If one element is missing, the syllogism is incomplete; there is insufficient cause of action.

2. List the five suggested references on good legal writing and add them to your system folder.

ANSWER:
Plain English for Lawyers, Wydick
Mightier than the Sword, Good
Clear Understandings, Goldfarb and Raymond
Writing to Win: The Legal Writer, Stark
Elements of Legal Style, Garner

3. What Federal Rules of Civil Procedure cover notice pleading requirements? Compare and contrast fact (code) pleading with notice pleading.

ANSWER: Rules 8, 9, 10.

Notice pleading requires only a general statement satisfying the elements of the rule of law; fact pleading requires more detailed facts to allege support for each element of the rule of law.

Notice is used in federal courts and some states; fact is used in some states.

Notice is simple and requires no technical forms; fact must be done carefully to satisfy local practice in providing enough information without revealing too much.

Rule 10 requires fact pleading in cases of fraud or mistake.

4. List and give examples of four types of remedies typically sought by plaintiffs in civil litigation.

ANSWER: Examples will vary, but may include the following:
- Damages
  a. General—money to compensate for suffering in personal injury
     Special—money to compensate for loss of profits in breach of contract
  b. Exemplary—payment required to punish company who knowingly sold dangerously defective products for immense profit
- Recovery of property—return of a painting loaned to a museum that subsequently claimed it as a gift
- Injunctions
  a. Prohibitory—stop the building of a business in a residential district
  b. Mandatory—require a resident to maintain property to the neighborhood standard
- Specific performance—force completion of a contracted construction project

5. Using the text guide to causes of actions and remedies, write the cause of action and wherefore clause (with an example of at least one type of remedy available) for a complaint in each of the following fact situations. Then state whether the syllogism is complete; that is, whether all elements are present, or what elements are lacking, to state a cause of action upon which relief may be granted.

a. Alice Jones has been transferred and must move by May 1. On her Realtor's advice and in order to help sell her home, she hires Elegance Interiors to redecorate it. Elegance contracts to complete the work by March 1 and accepts payment for materials from Jones. On February 20, Elegance returns the money and notifies Jones that another obligation prevents work on her house until April 16. Jones sues for anticipatory breach of contract.

ANSWER: May vary, but should be similar to the following:

- On February 20, _____, Defendant repudiated the contract to redecorate Plaintiff's house by March 1, _____.
- As a result, Plaintiff will incur future damages of $10,000 relating to late sale of Plaintiff's property. Wherefore Plaintiff demands judgment against Defendant in the sum of ten thousand dollars ($10,000) together with the costs and disbursements of this action.

  Syllogism is complete.

  b. Micky Speer has contracted with hall of fame trainer Eddie Fast to train Mr. Fix, a racehorse, for the Kentucky Derby. Fast resigns on April 6, _____, a month before the race, in a dispute over fringe benefits. To force Fast to train his horse through the race of a lifetime, Speer sues for specific performance.

ANSWER:

- On April 6, _____, Defendant breached a contract with Plaintiff by refusing to train Mr. Fix for the Kentucky Derby, though completion was possible.
- Without services of Defendant, Plaintiff's horse would suffer a change in training procedure that would jeopardize his chances in a once-in-a-lifetime race.

  Wherefore Plaintiff demands judgment to force Defendant to train Mr. Fix through the May 4, _____ date of the Kentucky Derby.

  Syllogism is inadequate because specific performance does not cover personal service contracts. Also, it is not clear whether Plaintiff has performed his duties under the contract (dispute over fringe benefits).

  c. Sleepy Time Motel manager Edna Bains resigns and uses an inheritance to buy the Tick Tock Inn down the street. The manager of Overroad Trucking, whose drivers always stay at Sleepy Time, shows the owners of Sleepy Time a letter from Bains offering Overroad a discount for staying at Tick Tock and referring to Sleepy Time as a dump. Sleepy Time sues for tortious interference with prospective economic advantage.

ANSWER:

- Plaintiff had a business relationship with Overroad Trucking, which was known by Defendant because of her former position at Plaintiff's business. Defendant attempted to disrupt this relationship through a derogatory letter.
- As a result, the Plaintiff's business has suffered a loss of reputation. Wherefore Plaintiff demands judgment against Defendant for exemplary damages in the amount of $10,000.

  Syllogism is inadequate; actual disruption of the relationship and actual injury must exist and be alleged.

6. Work through the questions for study and review at the end of Chapter 4 to test your understanding of the chapter.

CHAPTER 4 TAKE HOME TEST

Application Assignment 2 or writing a complaint for any of the Chapter 1 cases could be a take home test for this chapter.

CHAPTER 5

FILING THE LAWSUIT, SERVICE OF PROCESS, AND OBTAINING THE DEFAULT JUDGMENT

CHAPTER OBJECTIVE

The purpose of this chapter is to enable students to file an action properly, effect service of the summons and complaint on the defendant, and draft documents required to obtain a default judgment. They will practice working with applicable rules of civil procedure for both the state and federal systems, as well as with the documents required by each.

PREPARING FOR CLASS: INSTRUCTIONAL SUPPLEMENTS

1. A major task in this chapter is to present the specific rules of civil procedure for your state and encourage students from other states to become familiar with the rules of their states. The latter can be done through research or by having the student write to the appropriate clerks of court for current filing and service rules, procedures, and fees. You may choose to gather all the necessary state documents and have them copied for the students.

2. Since there are many documents to be drafted in this chapter, a simple process of reviewing the drafted documents for accuracy using the S (satisfactory) or U (unsatisfactory) grading system should not take too much evaluation time. Some of the documents are sufficiently simple that they could be made into transparencies for a more visually interesting class presentation. Once again, the forms and checklists in this chapter comprise valuable resources for the system folder. Complement the text with your own experiences and suggestions on techniques and pitfalls.

3. Because part of the chapter focuses on finding hard-to-locate defendants, you may choose to spend some class time on what collection practices are deemed illegal in your state and by the Federal Collection Act. An assignment in the workbook asks students to research this area.

4. Check pertinent Web sites.

SUGGESTED CLASS ACTIVITIES

1. This is a good time to visit a nearby clerk of court's office as a class, or prearrange with the clerk some small group visits at staggered times. It may be possible to get the clerk to participate in a videotaping of what goes on when a paralegal comes to file an action, taking close-ups of each type of document filed or issued, with the clerk explaining the procedure. The tape could be used in future classes. Another possibility is to have the clerks (one state and one federal) speak to the class.

2. Invite an experienced paralegal to speak on what she or he does to keep good service of process records, to locate hard-to-reach defendants, and to serve process in person.

3. If you have students from other jurisdictions, it might be interesting to have them report to the class on the specific procedures required in their state.

OUTLINE

I. Introduction
   A. The Tasks: Filing the Lawsuit, Serving the Summons, Obtaining a Default Judgment
   B. Purpose of the Tasks
      Key term: service of process
II. Preparing Documents for Filing an Action and for Service of Process
   A. Determine What Documents Are Needed
   B. Gather and Prepare the Documents Necessary for Filing and Service
      1. Introduction
      2. The Complaint
      3. Summons
         Key term: summons
         Exhibit 5:1, Summons in a Civil Action (Completed Form)
      4. Civil Cover Sheet
         Exhibit 5:2, Civil Cover Sheet (Completed Form)

5. Notice of Lawsuit and Request for Waiver of Service of Summons; Waiver of Service of Summons
Exhibit 5:3, Notice of Lawsuit and Request for Waiver of Service of Summons
Exhibit 5:4, Waiver of Service of Summons
6. Request for Service of Process
Key term: in forma pauperis
Exhibit 5:5, Process Receipt and Return
7. Motion for Special Appointment to Serve Process
Exhibit 5:6, Motion for Special Appointment to Serve Process
8. Affidavit of Service of Summons and Complaint
Exhibit 5:7, Affidavit of Service of Summons and Complaint
9. Consent to Exercise of Jurisdiction by Magistrate Judge
Exhibit 5:8, Consent to Exercise of Jurisdiction by a United States Magistrate Judge, Election of Appeal to District Judge
C. Obtain the Check for the Filing Fees
System Folder Assignment 1
Application Assignment 1
III. Filing the Lawsuit
A. Traditional Methods of Filing
B. E-Filing
Key term: e-filing
Exhibit 5:9, Colorado Rules for E-Filing
Internet Exercise 1
IV. Service of Process
V. Reference Guide and Checklist for Methods of Service
System Folder Assignment 3
A. Service on Individuals in a State or in a Judicial District of the United States
B. Service on Individuals in a Foreign Country [Rule 4(f)]
C. Service on Corporations and Associations [Rule 4(h)]
D. Service on the United States [Rule 4(i)]
E. Service on a Foreign, State, or Local Government
F. Service Outside the Geographical Boundaries of the State or Federal District Court/Long-Arm Statutes
Key term: Long-arm statute
Application Assignment 2
G. Service in In Rem and Quasi In Rem Cases
Key terms: in rem action, quasi in rem action, constructive service, substituted service
System Folder Assignment 2

H. Immunity from Service of Process
I. Locating "Invisible" Defendants
System Folder Assignment 4
Internet Exercises 2 and 3
J. Other Service of Process
K. Filing and Service of Pleadings and Papers Subsequent to the Complaint
System Folder Assignment 5
L. Keep Good Records of Service
VI. Obtaining a Default Judgment
A. Introduction
Key term: default judgment
B. The Procedure and Necessary Forms
Exhibit 5:10, Request for Entry of Default
Exhibit 5:11, Request for Entry of Default Judgment by Clerk
Exhibit 5:12, Affidavit of Nonmilitary Service of Defendant
Exhibit 5:13, Judgment of Default
Exhibit 5:14, Notice of Motion for Default Judgment by Court to Defendant Who Has Appeared in Action
C. Default and Multiple Defendants
D. Checklist for Default Judgment
System Folder Assignment 6
Application Assignment 3
E. Setting Aside a Default Judgment
System Folder Assignments 7 and 8
Application Assignment 4
VII. Summary

NOTE ON ASSIGNMENTS: Many of the tasks in this chapter require attention to state procedures and rules. You may want to take time to collect the appropriate information before the tasks are assigned.

SYSTEM FOLDER ASSIGNMENTS

Assignment 1

Obtain fee schedules for the federal, state, and local courts, including fees for service of process and the person to whom such service fees should be paid, as well as fees for the filing of subsequent pleadings and motions. If so directed by your instructor, contact the appropriate clerk of court for this information. Place the fee schedules in your system folder with a reminder to update the information periodically.

ANSWER: It may be easier for you to get fee schedules and photocopy them for the class.

Assignment 2

Look up "service of process by publication" in your state statutes. Find out when publication is required or permitted, what time limits must be observed, and what procedure must be followed. Make a short checklist of these and add them to your system folder.

ANSWER: You may want to draft your own checklist for evaluating students' work.

Assignment 3

Using an approach similar to the Reference Guide and Checklist for Methods of Service, draft a state service or process checklist for your system folder. Look up an needed information in your state's rules of civil procedure or state statutes to complete your checklist.

ANSWER: You may choose to require a copy of the service of process list in the text to be added to the system folder as a reference for federal cases.

Assignment 4

After class discussion on locating difficult-to-find defendants, add additional techniques to the Checklist for Locating Defendants. Place the checklist in your system folder.

ANSWER: Any personal experience in finding defendants that you can offer would spark interest and be a help to the students.

Assignment 5

Draft a brief Checklist for Filing and Service of Documents Subsequent to the Complaint—Federal and a similar one for your state. Note the applicable rules for future reference, including any on e-filing and service. Place the checklists in your system folder.

ANSWER: Provide state procedures and rules.

Checklist for Filing and Service of Documents Subsequent to the Complaint—Federal
1. Original and supporting documents filed with clerk of court [Rule 5(d)].
2. Copy of documents served on each of parties
   a. May be altered if there is an unusually large number of defendants [Rule 5(c)].
   b. Copy served on attorney when there is representation [Rule 5(b)].

Assignment 6

In your system folder make a reference to the checklist for default judgment. Research the rules and forms applicable to obtaining a default judgment in your state courts, and draft a state checklist for default judgment. Add needed state forms to your system folder.

ANSWER: You may choose to provide the state forms and draft a state checklist to use in evaluating student work.

Assignment 7

Refer to the motion to set aside default judgment and the notice of motion in your system folder.

Assignment 8

Your system folder should have a guide to both federal and state time limits. Two rules in this chapter give specific time limits that must be met. They are Rule 55(b)(2), which requires that notice of a hearing on an application for default judgment be served on the defendant or representative at least three days prior to the hearing, and Rule 60(b), which requires a motion to set aside a default judgment to be filed within one year from the date of the judgment in specified circumstances. Keeping tack of time requirements and calendaring them is extremely important. See the Pleadings, Motions, and Time Limits table in Chapter 6. Verify both state and federal deadlines for default judgments and all other deadlines as they arise.

APPLICATION ASSIGNMENTS
Assignment 1

Prepare the necessary documents for filing Case II, the *Ameche* case, for both federal and your state courts. Use the sample forms provided in this chapter, and the completed forms as a guide. Assume there is diversity jurisdiction. Check for accuracy. Place these samples of your work and page references to the forms in this text in your system folder.

ANSWER: Data sheets found in Chapters 2 and 3 of this manual will provide necessary information for the *Ameche* case. The purpose of this assignment is from the examples in the chapter. Check for precision. Students should have to redraft the documents until they demonstrate competency. The S/U method of grading may work best for these documents. You may choose to use this assignment as a take-home test at the end of the chapter.

Assignment 2

ANSWER: If paralegals are utilized properly, one significant responsibility will be to research memoranda on a variety of topics related to the firm's litigation. The memorandum in this assignment simulates such a situation. Students should be directed to an annotated version of the state statutes to look up any long-arm provision. Then they should research the cases listed, or research cases in the state's digest under "long-arm statutes" or "personal jurisdiction." Although the stu-

Memo to:	Terry Salyer, Paralegal
From:	Isadora Pearlman
Subject:	Research
Completion Date:	Three days from today
Issue:	What are the necessary minimum contacts required by our state statute to gain jurisdiction over a foreign corporation? Over a nonresident tort feasor? Over an Internet marketer?
Task:	Prepare a short memorandum on the state and constitutional law on this subject.
Guidelines:	Check the annotated state statutes under "long-arm statutes," "foreign corporations," and "non-resident tort feasors" for case law. Also try the state digest under similar key phrases. Since the state's long-arm statute affects both our federal and state court, decisions in both jurisdictions are helpful. See the section on researching and drafting a memorandum of law in Chapter 6.

dents will be researching state law, it is likely the cases will refer to federal precedents like *International Shoe Co. v. Washington*, 326 U.S. 310 (1945), *World Wide Volkswagen v. Woodson*, 444 U.S. 286 (1980), *Burger King Corp. v. Rudzewicz*, 471 U.S. 462 (1985), and *Zippo Manufacturing Co. v. Zippo Dot Com Inc.*, 952 F. Supp. 1119 (W.D. Pa. 1997), which will help the students gain an understanding of why minimal contacts are necessary and what those contacts must be.

Assignment 3

Assume for purposes of this assignment that Mr. Hart is an incompetent person; that he is the only defendant in the Ann Forrester case; that Mr. Hart's guardian has been served with a summons and complaint; and that the guardian did not respond within the required twenty days. Draft the necessary state documents to obtain a default judgment in the case. Use your checklist.

ANSWER: The purpose of this assignment is to have students apply what they have learned about default judgments to a specific case setting. It should also reinforce their use of checklists. Check for accuracy in names, dates (you may indicate a date for service of complaint), amount, and proper forms.

Assignment 4

Assume that you work for the firm that is representing Richard Hart and that for purposes of this problem, Mr. Hart is elderly and not well educated. He comes to your firm six months after a default judgment has been entered against him. Your attorney assigns you the task of determining if limited capacity brought on by aging and lack of education is sufficient good cause to have a default judgment set aside. Research the issue and prepare a brief outline on what facts are sufficient good cause to set aside a default judgment.

ANSWER: This research and drafting assignment should help the student better understand what factual circumstances cause a court to set aside a default judg-

ment. A brief outline of what is found is all that should be required of the student. Reference: Rule 60(b).

INTERNET EXERCISES

1. Go to www.WestFile.com and www.JusticeLink.com to compare their e-filing approaches. Who can use them and how do they work?

ANSWER: These two e-filing services will evolve over the next several years. Initially WestFile was for pro se filing, while Justice Link was solely for Colorado attorneys with subscriptions.

2. Pick a large city and use www.Deponet.com to locate two process server firms.
3. Assume you have hit a dead end trying to locate the defendant in your client's lawsuit. Your client is willing to pay only a small amount to continue the search. Go to the people locator sites listed in Helpful Web Sites and compare fees. What will the company charge if the search is not successful?

ANSWER: Because these fees will change, verify current amounts.

ADDITIONAL EXERCISES

1. Research your state counterpart to Rule 4(a) of the Federal Rules of Civil Procedure. Identify the number of the state rule and prepare a concise list of the content requirements for a valid summons in your state court. Place this in your system folder.
2. Outline the procedure for service of summons in your state. Are there special forms for request of service?

ANSWER: This assignment can be combined with the previous one.

3. Prepare the necessary state documents for filing Case IV.

ANSWER: You may choose any case to provide extra practice with state documents.

4. Outline the process of filing the lawsuit.

ANSWER:
I. Documents delivered to clerk of court
   A. personal delivery
   B. mailed (or electronic mail, if permitted)
   C. faxed
II. The clerk
   A. dates the original complaint
   B. assigns a civil case number (federal)
   C. possibly assigns judge
III. Case commences
   A. federal, upon delivery of complaint to clerk (Rule 3)
   B. state, when complaint and summons delivered to defendant
IV. Summons
   A. issued with
      1. court seal
      2. clerk signature
      3. possible clerk review of summons and cover sheet
   B. method of service checked
      1. summons returned to be served on defendant (federal)
      2. summons delivered to sheriff for service (state)

5. Who is usually immune from service of process? Speculate on why this is so.

ANSWER: Defendants and witnesses attending or traveling to and from trial; defendants brought into a state by force; and defendants served fraudulently.

Reasons will vary, but might include:

a. A witness or defendant fearing service might not show up for a trial.
b. Serving on someone who is in the state involuntarily is taking an unfair advantage, going beyond long-arm statutes.
c. Must discourage fraudulent use of the system.

6. Research Section 804 of the Federal Debt Collections Practices Act. Which of the following practices would be unlawful in trying to locate a defendant?
   a. A paralegal contacts a neighbor of the defendant to locate the defendant.
ANSWER: Lawful

   b. A paralegal informs a third party that the paralegal is a debt collector.
ANSWER: Unlawful

   c. A paralegal informs a third party that the defendant owes the plaintiff money after third party asks, "Does the defendant owe you money?"
ANSWER: Unlawful

Does your state have similar rules? Research them and describe them here. Do you believe these restrictions are wise?

ANSWER: You may choose to provide state rules. Answers to the last question are subjective, but should demonstrate an understanding of the rules and their purposes.

7. Consider grounds for setting aside a default judgment, then speculate on why an affidavit of non-military service of defendant is required in most jurisdictions.

ANSWER: Responses will vary, but may include the following:

The defendant's military service would be a good reason for not responding to the summons and complaint, may have made defendant unavailable, etc.

Without this provision, people might be discouraged from participating in military service because of possible legal penalties.

8. Research your state statutes and pertinent cases to determine the most common factual situations that are sufficient to set aside a default judgment. According to the law, what should the court consider in determining whether a default judgment should be set aside?

ANSWER: Motions to set aside a default judgment are treated liberally in most courts, so a variety of circumstances may be successfully argued. Courts are not inclined to set aside a case that is clearly without merit or where the lapse of time has been so great as to adversely affect justice (prejudice plaintiff's case). Rule 60(b) of the Federal Rules of Civil Procedure requires the court to consider time, mistake, surprise, excusable neglect, new evidence, whether the judgment was obtained by fraud, or if it was void, satisfied, or based on law recently reversed. In addition to the grounds listed in Rule 60(b) or similar state rules, the courts will consider prejudice to opponent, opponent's reliance on the default judgment previously entered, due diligence in making the motion, and concerns for fairness.

9. Work through the questions for study and review at the end of Chapter 5 to test your understanding of the chapter.

CHAPTER 5 TAKE HOME TEST

Use as a take home test Application Assignment 1, asking for preparation of all the papers necessary for filing an action and obtaining service of process for both the state and federal courts in Case II, the *Ameche* Case. Any of the cases presented in Chapter 1 could be used for this purpose.

CHAPTER 6

Defending and Testing the Lawsuit: Motions, Answers, and Other Responsive Pleadings

CHAPTER OBJECTIVE

This chapter aims to familiarize the student with the variety of pleadings and procedures that will follow service of the complaint. It covers motions in general and motions to dismiss; removal to federal court; the answer, counterclaim and cross-claim; motions on the pleadings; amendments to the pleadings; and summary judgment.

PREPARING FOR CLASS: INSTRUCTIONAL SUPPLEMENTS

1. Examples from your state of each of the forms covered in the chapter. If your state uses the demurrer and request for bill of particulars, copies of these forms are important supplements to the system folder.
2. Your state rules on motions, pleadings, summary judgments, and so on, as well as any rules setting out time limits for response pleadings and motions. Students may need regular reminders throughout the chapter to record the applicable state rules and time deadlines in the Pleadings, Motions, and Time Limits table (Exhibit 6:25) at the end of the chapter.
3. Pertinent Web sites.

SUGGESTED CLASS ACTIVITIES

1. Invite a local judge to discuss what the judge must look for in the complaint when considering a motion to dismiss the complaint, a demurrer, or other motions attacking the complaint. The judge could be encouraged to bring examples of civil cases from his/her court where complaints have been dismissed, or items stricken or made more definite and certain.
2. Invite an experienced paralegal to discuss researching, formatting, and preparing a memorandum of law in support of a motion.
3. Invite an experienced local judge, attorney, paralegal, or preferably an attorney-paralegal team to

discuss their respective roles regarding pleadings as well as what techniques they employ in good pleading practice, especially defensive pleadings.

OUTLINE

I. Introduction
II. Motions in General
   A. Introduction
      Key terms: motion, order
   B. Purpose
   C. Requirements and Components of the Motion
      Key terms: memorandum of law (memorandum of points and authorities), brief, affidavit, affiant
   D. Procedure: Filing, Service, and Time Limits
      System Folder Assignment 1
III. Motion to Dismiss
   A. Task
   B. Purpose
      Key term: demurrer
   C. Determining What to Attack
      Application Assignment 1
   D. Drafting the Documents
      Exhibit 6: 1, Motion to Dismiss Complaint
      Exhibit 6:2, General Demurrer
      Exhibit 6:3, Memorandum of Law in Support of Defendant's Motion to Dismiss Complaint
      Exhibit 6:4, Order Granting Motion to Dismiss Complaint
      Exhibit 6:5, Joint Application for Extension of Time
      System Folder Assignment 2
      Application Assignment 2
      Internet Exercises 1 and 2
   E. Other Motions to Dismiss
      Exhibit 6:6, Federal Rules of Civil Procedure Form 19: Motion to Dismiss, Presenting Defenses of Failure to State a Claim, Lack of

Service of Process, Improper Venue, and Lack of Jurisdiction Under Rule 12(b)

F. Other Motions Attacking the Complaint
   1. The Motion to Strike
   2. The Motion to Make More Definite and Certain
      Key term: bill of particulars
      Exhibit 6:7, Motion to Make More Definite and Certain
      Exhibit 6:8, Motion to Strike Redundant, Immaterial, Impertinent, or Scandalous Matter from Pleading
      System Folder Assignment 3
G. Ethics Reminder
H. Response to Motions
IV. Removal of State Action to Federal Court
A. Task
B. Purpose
C. Cases That May Be Removed
   Application Assignment 7
D. Procedure
   Exhibit 6:9, Notice of Removal
   System Folder Assignment 4
   Application Assignment 3
V. Computation of Time
   System Folder Assignment 5
   Application Assignment 4
VI. Drafting the Answer, Counterclaim, and Cross-Claim
A. Task
   Key term: answer
B. General Requirements
   1. Time
   2. Style and Content of the Answer
      System Folder Assignment 6
C. Structure of the Answer
   1. Introduction
   2. Defenses
   3. Denials
      Key term: argumentative denial
      Exhibit 6:10, Forms of Denial in Pleadings
      System Folder Assignment 7
   4. Affirmative Defenses
      System Folder Assignment 8
      Application Assignment 5
   5. Wherefore Clause
   6. Counterclaims
      Key Term: counterclaim
   7. Cross-Claims
      Key term: cross-claim
   8. Certification and Verification
D. Sample Answer, Counterclaim, and Cross-Claim
   Exhibit 6:11, Forrester Complaint: Notice Pleading
   Exhibit 6:12, Answer and Counterclaim to

Forrester Complaint: Notice Pleading
   Exhibit 6:13, Fact Complaint for Forrester Case
   Exhibit 6:14, Answer and Counterclaim to Forrester Complaint: Code (Fact) Pleading
   Exhibit 6:15, Fact Complaint Case II
   System Folder Assignment 9
   Application Assignment 6
VII. Third-Party Practice (Impleader)
A. Introduction
   Key term: third-party practice (impleader)
B. Task
C. Purpose
D. Procedure
   Exhibit 6:16, Summons Against Third-Party Defendant
   Exhibit 6:17, Third-Party Complaint
   Exhibit 6:18, Motion to Bring in Third-Party Defendant
   System Folder Assignments 10 and 11
VIII. Amending and Supplementing the Pleadings
A. Purpose
B. Procedure
   Exhibit 6:19, Amended Complaint
   Exhibit 6:20, Notice of Motion and Motion for Leave to Amend Complaint
   System Folder Assignments 12 and 13
IX. Motion for Judgment on the Pleadings
A. Task
B. Purpose
   System Folder Assignment 14
X. Motion for Summary Judgment
A. Task
B. Purpose
C. Procedure
   Exhibit 6:21, Motion for Summary Judgment by Plaintiff
   Exhibit 6:22, Notice of Motion and Hearing on Motion for Summary Judgment
   Exhibit 6:23, Affidavit in Support of Motion for Summary Judgment—General Form
   System Folder Assignments 15 and 16
XI. Keeping a Pleading Record
   Exhibit 6:24, File Pleading Log
   System Folder Assignment 17
XII. Pleadings, Motions, and Time Limits
   Exhibit 6:25, Pleadings, Motions, and Time Limits
XIII. Summary

SYSTEM FOLDER ASSIGNMENTS

Assignment 1

Locate in your state rules the requirements, procedures, and time limits that apply to motions. Write a checklist for drafting, filing, and serving motions for both state and federal court, and place it in your system folder. Verify the time limits pertaining to motions in the Pleadings, Motions, and Time Limits table at the end of the chapter. Add state deadlines.

ANSWER: You may want to draft a state checklist to use in evaluating students' work.

Federal Motions Checklist
  I. Drafting Motions, Rules 7(b) and 11
     A. Must be in writing, except at trial or hearing
     B. Grounds stated with particularity setting forth order
     C. Same caption as complaint (et al. allowed)
     D. Addresses of parties not necessary
     E. Attorney's signature and address necessary
  II. Components
     A. Motion
     B. Notice of Motion to inform opponent of motion and hearing (combined with motion)
     C. Affidavit to set forth additional facts
     D. Memorandum of law to present legal authority
     E. Order Granting Motion
  III. Filing (this is discussed in Drafting the Documents)
     A. Obtain hearing date from clerk
     B. File original documents with clerk
     C. File copies in case file
     D. Serve copies on plaintiff's attorney
  IV. Service
     A. Served on opposing attorney (Rule 5)
     B. Served not less than five days before hearing [Rule 6(d)]
     C. Affidavits served not less than one day before hearing [Rule 6(d)]

Assignment 2

Make references in your system folder to the documents in this text needed to file a motion to dismiss the complaint. Add any pertinent state practice forms.

ANSWER: Be sure that the students include state forms.

Assignment 3

Place page references to or copies of the Motion to Strike and the Motion to Make More Definite and Certain in your system folder.

Assignment 4

Enter a reference to or copy of the notice of removal to federal court in your system folder. Develop your own brief checklist for the required procedural stages and place that in your system folder.

ANSWER: Removal Procedure, 28 U.S.C. § 1446

1. File notice of removal in federal court encompassing area where state action is pending.
2. The notice should contain
   a. statement of grounds for removal
   b. copy of all papers served on defendant
   c. statute conferring federal jurisdiction
   d. facts in support of federal jurisdiction
   e. date of receipt of initial pleadings
   f. applicable removal statute [28 U.S.C § 1446(b)]
   g. statement that all defendants have joined in removal action
3. Notice must be served on all parties and filed within 30 days of commencement of state action or within 30 days after action has become removable.
4. Though bond requirement has been abolished, some language remains in statute [§ 1446(d)].
5. Upon prompt filing of the notice in state court, state court can proceed no further.
6. Plaintiff can challenge
   a. through motion to remand within 30 days after notice of removal
   b. district court's subject matter jurisdiction any time up to entry of judgment
7. If plaintiff joins additional defendants defeating subject matter jurisdiction after removal, district court may
   a. deny joinder
   b. allow joinder and remand case to state court

Assignment 5

Note the rules for calculating time for both the federal and your state jurisdiction [see Rule 6(a)] in your system folder. Include the formula and the previous example on how to calculate the due date.

ANSWER: Federal Rule 6(a) and state equivalent.

Assignment 6

Place a page reference or copy of the list of style and content suggestions for the answer in your system folder.

ANSWER:
1. Be clear and concise.
2. Use numbered paragraphs to correspond to complaint paragraphs.
3. Avoid impertinent, scandalous, or immaterial language.
4. Follow the complaint logically.
5. Reveal no more facts than necessary.
6. Avoid evidence and conclusions.
7. Be truthful.
8. State defendant's lack of information to form a belief if that is the case.
9. State separate defenses in separate paragraphs.

Assignment 7

Add Exhibit 6:10, forms of Denial in Pleadings, to your system folder, or enter a page reference to it.

Assignment 8

Place in your system folder a page reference to the steps in locating affirmative defenses.

Assignment 9

Place copies of the answers and counterclaims you drafted for Application Assignment 6 in your system folder, along with copies of or text page references to the sample answers, counterclaims, and cross-claims in this chapter.

Assignment 10

From the steps for preparing and filing a third-party complaint, create a checklist for third-party practice and place it in your system folder. See Federal Forms 22A and 22B. Note any variations in local practice.

ANSWER:
1. Obtain all necessary information on the third-party defendant.
2. Draft a motion for a third-party complaint unless the action is filed within ten days of the answer [Rule 14(a)].
3. Draft a third-party summons and third-party complaint.
4. File with the clerk of court using the summons and complaint as exhibit A.
5. On notice that the motion is approved, serve the third-party summons and a copy of the third-party complaint in the same manner that the original complaint is served (Rule 4). Attach a copy of the original complaint.
6. Calendar the due date for the third party's answer.

Assignment 11

Make copies of the third-party summons, complaint, and motion and place them in your system folder, or make page references to these forms.

Assignment 12

Enter page number references to or copies of the amended complaint and the notice of and motion to amend in your system folder.

Assignment 13

Verify in the Pleadings, Motions, and Time Limits table the deadlines for amended pleadings set out in section VIII and in Rule 15. In addition, draft a checklist of pro-cedures and time limits regarding amended pleadings and add it to the system folder.

ANSWER: Checklist for Amended Pleadings
1. Permitted any time before responsive pleading is served.
2. If no response required and not on trial calendar, within 20 days after pleading is served.
3. Otherwise only with leave of court or written consent of opponent [Rule 15(a)].
4. Response necessary within remaining response time for original pleading or 10 days of service of amendment, whichever is longer, unless otherwise ordered by court [Rule 15(a)].
5. Motion for amendment with leave of court can be brought any time, even after judgment [Rule 15(b)].
6. Amended pleading dates from time of original pleading, as long as claim or defenses in amend-ment arose from occurrence set forth in original.
7. Combine amended language with original
8. Serve amended pleading on adverse attorney.
9. File with clerk of court.
10. Consult local rules.

Assignment 14

Be sure to note the time requirements for a motion for judgment on the pleadings in the Pleadings, Motions, and Time Limits exhibit at the end of the chapter.

Assignment 15

Place text page references to or copies of the motion, notice of motion, and affidavit in support of motion for summary judgment in your system folder.

Assignment 16

Enter state time limits parallel to Rule 56 (summary judgment) in the Pleadings, Motions, and Time Limits exhibit at the end of the chapter. Fill in the state rule and deadline section up to the discovery section and add the table or page reference to your system folder.

Assignment 17

Place a page reference to or a copy of the File Pleading Log in your system folder.

APPLICATION ASSIGNMENTS
Assignment 1

You are directed to look over a complaint for negligence. The body of the complaint reads as follows:

   5. On March 22, ____, Defendant owned and oper-ated the Bay View Motel.

6. On that date Plaintiff was descending a stairway at the motel, and as a result of Defendant's conduct, tripped and fell down the stairway.

7. As a result of Defendant's conduct, Plaintiff suffered a broken wrist, a brain concussion, and numerous bruises over much of his body.

8. Because of the above injuries, Plaintiff had extensive medical bills and lost six weeks of work, to the sum of $25,000.

Using the method suggested in the Determining What to Attack section, determine if the body of this complaint is defective, and if so, why. Explain how the syllogism method of finding defects applies to this case. Be prepared to defend your conclusion.

ANSWER: This assignment gives the student a chance to apply the syllogism method of determining if defects exist in a complaint, subjecting it to a motion to dismiss for failure to state a claim on which relief can be granted. The main defect in the body of this complaint is that no breach of duty is alleged—no facts demonstrating negligence on the part of the owner of the motel are stated. Therefore, at least one of the parts of the syllogism (duty + breach of duty + harm + breach is substantial cause of harm) is missing.

Assignment 2

To reinforce your research and motion practice skills, locate a case from your state or federal jurisdiction that upheld the dismissal of a complaint for failure to state a claim. Make a copy of the complaint in the case and then draft the necessary motion. For future reference, not citations to key cases given in the opinion, and enter them in your system folder.

ANSWER: You may choose to refer your students to a particular case This same case can be used in Additional Exercise 5. If your students need research practice, you could also assign them to draft a memorandum of law and other supporting documents for this case.

Assignment 3

Draft the Notice of Removal to have the case against Allen Howard removed to federal court, as Mr. McDuff requested.

ANSWER: Encourage students to use Exhibit 6:9 in the text as their guide, with facts drawn from the case information in the Motion to Dismiss section of the chapter and from your state and federal jurisdictions. Note particularly that time limits and diversity jurisdiction are observed.

Assignment 4

Under Federal Rule 6(a), what are the following due dates?

a. Three days before a hearing on Monday, April 8.

ANSWER: Wednesday, April 3. Day of the hearing does not count. Saturday and Sunday do not count when limit is less than 11 days.

b. Three months from February 16.

ANSWER: April 16.

c. A complaint received on March 5 with an answer due in 20 days. On March 21, an enlargement of time of 30 days is granted the defendant for filing the answer.

ANSWER: April 24—original due date March 25 plus 30 days.

d. A complaint received on December 12.

ANSWER: January 2—cannot fall due on a holiday.

Assignment 5

Review the basic facts set out in Chapter 1 for Case IV, *Briar Patch Dolls, Inc. v. Teeny Tiny Manufacturing Co.*, a contract case. using the method described in the Affirmative Defenses section of the text, make an initial determination of what affirmative defenses under the topic *discharge* might be available to the defendants. Make a list of these defenses and suggest some facts that might be necessary to support the defense. Because there are numerous defenses in contract law, confine yourself in this assignment to those defenses within the concept of *discharge*.

ANSWER: The list the students prepare should identify at least some of the following possibilities:

1. Rescission—mutual agreement to rescind contract and pay for what has been done.
2. Release or contract not to sue—written release of obligation imposed by contract or contract where one party agrees not to sue the other party for breach.
3. Discharge by substitute contract—revised contract with new contract.
4. Impracticability (Impossibility) of Performance—strike in denim manufacturing industry creates acute shortage of materials from which to make doll clothing.
5. Others.

Assignment 6

Exhibit 6:15 is a copy of the code (fact) complaint in Case II, the *Maple Meadows Campground* case. Assume that your firm is defending the owner of the camp-ground. Review the complaint and draft an Answer and Counterclaim for a code-pleading state. Then draft one for a notice-pleading jurisdiction.

ANSWER: Students should draft answers similar to the ones below. The answers provided may be photocopied and given to the students for evaluation of their answer. This assignment could also be used as a test.

Answer for Case II "Code" Pleading:

STATE OF COLUMBIA   CAPITOL COUNTY   CIRCUIT COURT

CARL AMECHE and
ZOE AMECHE, Plaintiffs   Civil .Action No._____.

      v.

MARGIE CONGDEN and   JURY TRIAL IS DEMANDED
LEROY CONGDEN, Defendants

DEFENDANTS' ANSWER, NEW MATTER, AND COUNTERCLAIM

1. Admitted.
2. Admitted.
3. Admitted.
4. Admitted.
5. Admitted
6. Denied. Defendants specifically deny that the cord was worn and further deny placing said cord in location that was dangerous.
7. Denied. Defendants specifically deny that their conduct caused the fire mentioned in plaintiffs' complaint and in "new matter" allege that plaintiffs themselves caused the fire. Further, after a reasonable investigation, defendants lack sufficient information on which to form a belief as to the truth of the allegation that the fire encircled plaintiffs' son requiring plaintiff to place himself in peril in order to rescue his son, and therefore, deny same.
8. Denied. Defendants, after reasonable investigation, lack sufficient information on which to form a belief as to the truthfulness of the allegation of plaintiff's injuries in paragraph 8 of the complaint and, therefore, deny same.
9. Denied. Defendants, after reasonable investigation, lack sufficient information on which to form a belief as to the truthfulness of the allegation of loss of money in paragraph 9 of plaintiffs' complaint and, therefore, deny same.

Wherefore, defendants request that plaintiffs' complaint be dismissed and that judgment be entered for defendants for their costs and disbursements.

NEW MATTER

10. Defendants incorporate by reference paragraphs 1–9 of their answer.
11. Defendants allege that the fire was due to natural causes, an act of God.
12. Defendants allege that plaintiff is more than fifty percent responsible for the accident and resulting injuries by:
    a. negligently transferring the extension cord running on gravel to campsite 36 and placing it in brush that could catch fire.
    b. tampering with the cord and damaging said cord to point it became a fire hazard, and
    c. failing to exercise proper control and supervision of their child, causing undue delay in extracting him at the early and more harmless stages of the fire, and is, therefore, barred from recovery.

Wherefore, defendants request that plaintiffs' complaint be dismissed and that judgment be entered for defendants for their costs and disbursements.

ANSWER TO COUNT TWO

13. No response to plaintiffs' paragraph 10 is required.
14. Denied. Defendants specifically deny being negligent or responsible for plaintiff's alleged injuries. Further, defendants, after reasonable investigation, lack sufficient knowledge to form a belief as to the truth of plaintiff's allegation of loss of consortium of her husband and the amount of the loss.

Wherefore, defendants request that plaintiffs' complaint be dismissed and that judgment be entered for defendants for their costs and disbursements.

NEW MATTER COUNT TWO

15. Defendants incorporate by reference the affirmative defenses alleged in paragraphs 11 and 12 of this answer.

Wherefore, defendants request that plaintiffs' complaint be dismissed and that judgment be entered for defendants for their costs and disbursements.

DEFENDANTS' COUNTERCLAIM

16. Defendants incorporate by reference paragraphs 1 through 15 of this answer.
17. On August 21, ____, plaintiff Carl Ameche negligently
    a. transferred the extension cord running to campsite 36 that had been placed on gravel, to a brush area that could easily catch fire.
    b. tampered with said cord, damaging it and making said cord a fire hazard.
18. As a result of plaintiff's negligence, a fire did start, causing extensive damage to the trees and buildings in the campground.
19. Because of plaintiff's negligence, the defendants have sustained losses of large sums of money to remove damaged buildings and trees, to buy and plant new trees, to repair and replace buildings, and for loss of business totaling seventy-five thousand dollars ($75,000).

Wherefore, defendants demand judgment against the plaintiffs in the amount of $75,000 plus their costs and disbursement.

_____.
Attorney for Defendants
(Address)

(Students should include verification if required in your state.)

Assignment 7

Assume that a new federal agency regulation raises freedom of speech issues. Gloria, the alleged injured party, decides to sue. Assume that Gloria can sue in either state or federal court, since it is a constitutional issue. Gloria's attorney wants to sue the United States, but wants to stay out of federal court. Who should Gloria's attorney name as defendant and why?
ANSWER: The pertinent agency. File suit in state court. U.S. agencies cannot remove a case to federal court, *International Primate Protection League v. Administrators of Tulane Educational Fund*, U.S. La, 111 S. Ct. 1700 (1991).

INTERNET EXERCISES

1. Using Westlaw, go to the directory and locate the section on forms. Find examples of an answer and a motion to dismiss the complaint in *West's Legal Forms* and in *American Jurisprudence Pleadings and Practice Forms*. See whether the site has forms specific to your state.

ANSWER: The student should be able to locate several forms and identify them by title. Also, the more populous states have their forms on Westlaw.

2. Go to www.capsoft.com and explore Hotdocs to see what the service offers and what forms are available. What are some of this service's special features?

ANSWER: The service offers templates, add-ins, and directions to the next drafter on how to construct documents, avoiding goofs such as leaving information from a previous client's draft in a new draft.

ADDITIONAL EXERCISES

1. What is the purpose of motions? What are the components of motions? What federal rules establish motion requirements?

ANSWER:
- To obtain judicial relief, to narrow issues for trial, and to establish a record for appeal.
- Motion
  a. notice of motion—these two are combined in federal practice

"NOTICE PLEADING"

UNITED STATES DISTRICT COURT FOR THE EASTERN DISTRICT OF COLUMBIA
Civil Action, File Number _____.

CARL AMECHE and
ZOE AMECHE, Plaintiffs   ANSWER AND COUNTERCLAIM
v.
MARGIE CONGDEN and   DEFENDANT DEMANDS JURY TRIAL
LEROY CONGDEN, Defendants

1. Admitted
2. Admitted in part, denied in part. Admitted that Maple Meadows Campground is owned by defendants. Denied that defendants negligently used an extension cord and that defendants used a faulty cord.
3. Defendants lack sufficient knowledge to form a belief as to the truth of the allegations in paragraph 3 of plaintiffs' complaint and, therefore, deny same.

FIRST AFFIRMATIVE DEFENSE
Plaintiff was more than fifty percent negligent in causing the accident and is therefore barred from recovery.

SECOND AFFIRMATIVE DEFENSE
Plaintiff knew or should have known that there were risks in moving the electrical cord and, yet, plaintiff went ahead and moved the cord, accepting the consequences of the risks.

COUNT II
4. No answer required.
5. Denied

COUNTERCLAIM
6. Defendants incorporate by reference paragraphs 1 through 3 of this answer.
7. On August 21, ____, plaintiff Carl Ameche negligently transferred and tampered with the electrical cord running to his campsite, causing a fire that substantially damaged defendants' campground.
8. As a result of plaintiff's negligence, defendants lost numerous trees, buildings, and anticipated business, all to the sum of $75,000.

Wherefore, defendants request that plaintiffs' action be dismissed and demand judgment against plaintiff Carl Ameche for $75,000, plus interests and costs.

_____.
Attorney for Defendants
(Address)

---

b. affidavit
c. memorandum of law
d. order granting motion
• Rules 7(b) and 11

2. What weaknesses in the complaint indicate a failure to state a claim and, thus, would be grounds for a motion to dismiss?

ANSWER: Lack of a required element (minor premise), inaccurate or misconceived reading of the law (major premise), and defense to the action.

3. What grounds to dismiss a complaint are covered in Federal Rule of Civil Procedure 12(b)?

ANSWER:
• Lack of subject matter jurisdiction
• Lack of personal jurisdiction
• Improper venue
• Insufficiency of process
• Insufficiency of service of process
• Failure to state a claim
• Failure to join a party under Rule 19

4. Why should the motion to strike and the motion to make more definite and certain be kept in mind when you draft pleadings?

ANSWER: They should remind you to be concise and to the point while including all necessary information.

5. Using your case from Application Assignment 2, research legal authority and possible supporting evidence, then draft a response to the motion to dismiss.

ANSWER: Since this is a case where the motion to dismiss is successful, support for a response may be thin. You may choose a case where the motion was denied. The point of the exercise is for students to gain practice in researching and writing responses.

6. What is the purpose of removal from state to federal court, and what strategic advantages may result?

ANSWER: Purpose: to give defendant a choice of court when state and federal jurisdictions are concurrent.
- different judge
- a more competent jury
- more liberal transfer and venue rules in federal system
- more liberal discovery, evidence, and pleading rules
- less crowded docket

7. What defenses must be filed in motions previous to the answer or in the answer? Why is this important?

ANSWER: Lack of personal jurisdiction, improper venue, insufficiency of process or insufficiency of service of process is waived unless raised in the first responsive pleading or unless amendment is allowed.

8 What are the differences between denials and affirmative defenses?

ANSWER: Denials are responses to the allegations in the complaint and need no supporting facts. Affirmative defenses are new matters that are defined by substantive law and must be supported by facts in the answer.

9. Research in a legal dictionary and write brief definitions for the defenses that must be alleged affirmatively under Federal Rule 8(c).

ANSWER:
Accord and satisfaction—An agreement between parties to give and accept something (new contract) to discharge a claim (old contract).
Arbitration and award—Subject matter has been settled by prior arbitration.
Assumption of risk—Showing that plaintiff knew the dangers and risk of his action but proceeded in spite of that.
Contributory negligence—Plaintiff's lack of care which, combined with defendant's negligence, is the proximate cause of injury
Discharge in bankruptcy—Release of a debtor from obligation of debts.
Duress—Injury or threat which deprives one of exercising free will.
Estoppel—Detriment to one party who was entitle to rely on acts of another, caused by second party's failure to act (claim a right).
Failure of consideration—Consideration, originally good, has become worthless.
Fraud—False representation by one person to deceive another.
Illegality—Contrary to principles of law, not just rules of procedure.
Injury by fellow servant—Defense of employer charged with injury to employee that another employee caused the injury; abrogated by workers' compensation acts.
Laches—Unreasonable delay in asserting a right, which causes prejudice to defendant.
License—Permission to do an act that would otherwise be illegal, a trespass, or a tort.
Payment—Performance of an obligation.
Release—Giving up a claim by a person who has the right to exercise it to the person against whom the claim exists.
Res judicata—Thing already judicially decided.
Statute of frauds—No action is allowed on certain cases of contracts (involving a certain amount of money) unless the part charged or agent has signed a written contract.
Statute of limitations—Period of time in which a suit must be brought.
Waiver—Voluntarily giving up a known right.

10. Compare and contrast counterclaims and cross-claims.

ANSWER: Both are a suit within a suit, may be added to the answer, must meet pleading requirements, and remain if the original action is dismissed. Permissive counterclaims and cross-claims may be brought in separate suits.

The counterclaim is by the defendant against the plaintiff over matters arising from the original circumstances (compulsory counterclaims) or unrelated claims (permissive counterclaims), which can include other parties. Jurisdiction must be alleged independently.

The cross-claim is by the defendant against a fellow defendant over the subject matter of the original action. No further jurisdiction source is needed.

11. What may be changed or added in amendments to pleadings? What may not? Theorize about why this is so.

ANSWER: Amendments may be used to repair defects, such as elements omitted, matters improperly alleged, language too general, and so on. They may not state a claim unrelated to the original one.

Subjective speculation: Unrelated claims should be brought in a separate lawsuit; otherwise, they would result in an unfair advantage, would confuse issues, may avoid the statute of limitations, and so on.

12. What is the difference between a motion for judgment on the pleadings and a motion for summary judgment?

ANSWER: A motion for judgment on the pleadings is not supported by affidavits and other documents, and frequently results in amendments to pleadings. A motion for summary judgment is supported by additional evidence that shows that there is not genuine issue of fact and that movant is entitled to judgment.

13. Work through the questions for study and review at the end of the chapter to reinforce your understanding.

CHAPTER 6 TAKE HOME TEST

Application Assignment 6 would be a good test of the students' understanding and skill development from this chapter.

CHAPTER 7

DISCOVERY: OVERVIEW AND INTERROGATORIES

CHAPTER OBJECTIVE

This chapter gives the student background information on discovery, including Rule 26 provisions on disclosure. Interrogatories are presented in detail, helping the student develop the knowledge, skills and techniques needed to perform the tasks required of the paralegal when working in this area of discovery.

PREPARING FOR CLASS: INSTRUCTIONAL SUPPLEMENTS

1. The state rules on discovery, particularly disclosure and interrogatories.
2. The federal rules on discovery, particularly disclosure and interrogatories.
3. Copies of the most significant state forms relevant to disclosure and interrogatories.
4. A collection of your personal tips and techniques for disclosure and drafting interrogatories.
5. Pertinent Web sites.

SUGGESTED CLASS ACTIVITIES

1. Conduct a class discussion based on Additional Exercise 2.
2. Invite an experienced paralegal to discuss his or her suggestions in the areas of disclosure and interrogatories.
3. Use discovery practice to prepare for the mock trial.

OUTLINE

I. Overview of Discovery
   A. Introduction
      Key term: discovery
      System Folder Assignment 1
   B. Purpose of Discovery
   C. Mandatory Disclosure
      1. Introduction
         Key term: disclosure
      2. Initial Disclosure
      3. Disclosure of Information on Expert Testimony
      4. Pretrial Disclosures
      5. Disclosure Procedure
   D. Scope of Discovery
      1. Introduction
      2. Relevance [26(b)(1)]
         Internet Exercise 1
      3. Privilege [26(b)(1)]
      4. Trial Preparation Materials [26(b)(3)]
      5. Trial Preparation: Experts [26(b)(4)]
      6. Court Discretion and Other Limits
         Application Assignment 1
   E. Parties' Planning Meeting
      Exhibit 7:1, Form 35. Report of Parties' Planning Meeting
      System Folder Assignment 2
   F. Supplementing Disclosure and Discovery [Rule 26(e)]
   G. Ethical Considerations for Discovery and Disclosure
   H. Disclosure Time Frame Summary (Federal)
      Application Assignment 2

II. Interrogatories
   A. Task
   B. Purpose of Interrogatories
      Key term: interrogatories
      Internet Exercises 2 and 3
   C. Procedure
      System Folder Assignment 3
   D. Planning Interrogatories
      1. Introduction
      2. Determining Objectives of Interrogatories
   E. Drafting Interrogatories
      1. Review Rules and Examples
      2. Introductory Paragraphs
      3. Definitions and Abbreviations
      4. Instructions

5. Questions: The Body of the
   Interrogatories
   a. General Background
   b. Pleadings
   c. Basic Areas of the Case
   d. Opinions and Legal and Factual
      Contentions
   e. Computer Information
   f. Concluding or Summary
      Interrogatories
F. Drafting Techniques
   Exhibit 7:2, Sample Interrogatories
G. Concluding Material, Final Preparation, and
   Service of Interrogatories
   Exhibit 7:3, Checklist for Planning and
   Drafting Interrogatories
   System Folder Assignment 4
   Application Assignments 3 and 4
III. Answering Interrogatories
   A. Note Deadline, Review Case File
   B. Review Possible Objections
   C. Review Questions
   D. Gather and Record Information
      Exhibit 7:4, Letter to Client on Answering
      Interrogatories
      System Folder Assignment 5
   E. Review Techniques for Answering
      Interrogatories
   F. Draft Answers and Have Them Reviewed,
      Signed, and Served
      Application Assignment 5
   G. Update Answers
      Exhibit 7:5, Answer to Interrogatories
      System Folder Assignment 6
IV. Analyzing the Answer and Compelling a
    Response
V. Summary

SYSTEM FOLDER ASSIGNMENTS

Assignment 1

In both the ethics and discovery sections of your system folder, place your own restatement of the ethical principles covered in this chapter, and cite the pertinent ethical rules.

ANSWER: Model Rule 3.4; State Ethics Rule _____.

The attorney
- should not obstruct the other party's access to evidence, including destroying or concealing potential evidence, or advise another to do so.
- should not falsify evidence, counsel or assist in perjury, or offer illegal inducement.
- should not knowingly disobey court rules and court-approved obligations.

- should not make frivolous discovery requests; obligated to diligently comply with opponent's proper discovery requests.
- should not tell a person other than the client not to give information to the other party.

Model Rule 1.6; State Ethics Rule _____.

The attorney should not reveal the confidences of a client but may admit facts that cannot properly be denied.

Assignment 2

Place page references or copies of the form for reporting the parties' planning meeting and the Paralegal's Disclosure Checklist in your system folder. Add any suggestions from your instructor. Enter citations to the pertinent federal rules and your state rules on disclosure.

Assignment 3

Verify the deadlines for interrogatory practice by checking the Pleadings, Motions, and Time Limits tale in Chapter 6 or in your system folder. Add the time limits from your state rules. Place citations to the pertinent federal rules and state rules in your system folder, including the number of interrogatories permitted by both federal and your state rules.

Assignment 4

Place a page reference to or a copy of the Checklist for Planning and Drafting Interrogatories, Exhibit 7:3, in your system folder. Supplement the checklist with any suggestions from your instructor.

Assignment 5

Create a form letter to the client from the letter in Exhibit 7:4 and place it in your system folder. Use the copying and editing features of a computer to do this assignment.

Assignment 6

Drawing from the material covered in this section of the chapter and any information added in class, draft a checklist for answering interrogatories and place it in your system folder. The checklist should cover the basic steps and techniques for preparing, drafting, serving, and updating interrogatories.

ANSWER: Add any of your own tips to expand this checklist.

I. Techniques for Answering Interrogatories
   A. Engross the question into the answer.
   B. Write clearly and concisely.
   C. State objections with particularity.
   D. Answer ethically, accurately, and completely.

E. Disclose as little harmful information as possible without concealment.

F. Without misrepresenting, place the client in the best possible light.

G. Use Rule 33(d) to place the burden on the opposing party to search your client's records, but only if no sensitive information will be revealed.

H. Where appropriate, indicate that
1. supplements will follow
2. information is on information or belief or based on secondhand information
3. information according to person Y or records in office X
4. do not know answer but received information that _____

I. Inform attorney when an extension of time is needed.

II. Service of Interrogatories
A. Have attorney review interrogatories.
B. Have client or representative sign interrogatories (Rule 33).
C. Attach necessary exhibits.

D. Prepare certificate of service and serve according to Rule 5 or state rules.

III. Update Answers
A. Continual obligation to respond as additional information or inaccuracies are apparent.
B. Replace out-of-date page with new one restating the question accompanied by complete new answer.

APPLICATION ASSIGNMENTS

Assignment 1

Drawing from the discussion on the scope and limitation of disclosure and discovery plus the pertinent rules of evidence discussed in Chapter 3, indicate whether the following would be discoverable in the Ann Forrester case. If an item would be discoverable only on a showing of undue hardship, indicate that as well. The first item is completed for you as an example. D = discoverable, ND = not discoverable, R = reason not discoverable, E = exceptional circumstances, H = undue hardship.

ITEM	D	ND	R	E
1. Photo of accident scene taken by plaintiff's attorney		X	work product	H
2. Defendant Hart's driving schedule for day of accident and previous week	X			
3. Mercury Parcel's maintenance schedules on van	X			
4. Hart's statement to his attorney		X	atty/client privilege	
5. Forrester's medical bills	X			
6. Identification and opinion of plaintiff's trial expert on auto defects	X			Interrogatory
7. Statement Hart made to Mr. Forrester in plaintiff's possession	X			
8. Defense attorney's diagram of accident (not for trial exhibit)	X	work product	H	
9. Forrester's alleged confession to her priest that she felt responsible for accident	X	privilege		
10. Plaintiff's request for a second copy of Hart's driving schedule	X	duplicative		
11. Statement of Forrester tape recorded by her attorney's paralegal	X local			
12. Letters between attorneys for defendants discussing strategy	X	work product	H	

Assignment 2

Assume that a complaint was filed and served on the defendant in the Forrester case on Friday, March 29, or on another date supplied by your instructor. Using the Disclosure Time Frame Summary (Federal), determine the last possible date for the following:

a. The court scheduling conference
b. Parties' planning meeting
c. Report to court on parties' planning meeting
d. Disclosure from party joined on Tuesday, August 6
e. Objections to disclosure
f. Objections to any pretrial disclosure, assuming the trial date has been set for Monday, December 9

ANSWER: Normally, any due date that falls on a weekend or holiday moves to the following Monday or the next regular business day. If, however, one is counting back from a date, the reverse is true. For example, the parties' planning meeting is to be *at least* 21 days before the court scheduling conference. Therefore, if the due date falls on a weekend or holiday, the actual due date is the previous Friday or previous regular business day.

a. July 28
b. July 5
c. July 19
d. September 5
e. July 5
f. November 22 (pretrial disclosure due November 8)

Assignment 3

Drawing from the material in this chapter on planning and drafting interrogatories (including the checklist on Exhibit 7:3) and using the form interrogatories as a guide, draft a set of carefully planned interrogatories on behalf of Ms. Forrester to Mercury Parcel Service. For the purposes of this assignment, confine your drafting to the following:

1. Caption and instructions
2. Questions on:
   a. Background information, employment, and agency of Hart
   b. Inadequate maintenance of van and possible defects
   c. Time standards for operation of vehicles by drivers, and Hart's and Mercury Parcel's compliance prior to accident.
3. Concluding questions and directions
4. Signature and certificate of service

ANSWER: Since this and the next assignment require considerable time to complete, each student should do just one of them. This will work well if you have divided the class into paralegals for plaintiff and those for defendant. The interrogatories written here will be used in Application Assignment 5. Encourage students to do this work on computers if they are available. Answers will vary, but may be similar to the following example.

Note: Several paragraphs in this document are taken from *West's Federal Forms* and Haydock and Herr, *Discovery: Theory, Practice, and Procedure* as reprinted and cited in the textbook.

STATE OF COLUMBIA   CAPITOL COUNTY   CIRCUIT COURT

ANN FORRESTER and
WILLIAM FORRESTER,
    Plaintiffs

v.   Civil Action File No. <u>1000</u>

RICHARD HART and
MERCURY PARCEL SERVICE, INC.,
    Defendants

PLAINTIFF'S CONTINUING INTERROGATORIES SET ONE

To Mercury Parcel Service Inc., Defendant:
    The Plaintiff requests that the following interrogatories be answered under oath by any of your officers competent to testify in your behalf who know the facts about which inquiry is made, and that the answers be served on plaintiff within 30 days from the time these interrogatories are served on you.

I. DEFINITIONS (The definition and abbreviation section is omitted for this assignment.)

II. INSTRUCTIONS

1. To the extent that information sought by an Interrogatory can be furnished by reference to the Answer furnished to another Interrogatory, appropriate reference will be acceptable to the plaintiff. However, a separate answer should be accorded to each Interrogatory, and Interrogatories should not be joined together and accorded a common answer.

2. Each Answer should be preceded by identification and verbatim quote of the interrogatory to which the Answer regards.

3. Separate Interrogatories have been prepared for each defendant. Each Interrogatory should be answered separately by each defendant. If an Interrogatory Answer provided by one defendant contains information responsive to an Interrogatory directed to another defendant, that defendant may incorporate such Answer by reference.

4. If any Interrogatory is objected to by you as inquiring into privileged matter, set forth fully in the objection the facts which form the basis for your objection.

5. If any document, report, study, memorandum, or other written material is withheld or not identified under claim of privilege, furnish a list identifying each such document for which the privilege is claimed, together with the following information: date, author, sender, recipient, persons to whom copies were furnished, together with their job titles, subject matter of the document, the basis on which the asserted privilege is claimed, and the paragraph or paragraphs of these Interrogatories to which the document responds.

6. Divulge in your Answer all pertinent information in your possession, or in possession of the corporation, or your attorney's agents, investigators, employees, or other representatives.

(Have your students add any additional instructions that you believe are appropriate.)

III. BACKGROUND

1. Please state the:
   a. Full name of the corporation.
   b. Date and place of incorporation.
   c. Corporation's principal place of business.
   d. Type of corporation.
   e. Full name of the corporation's chief executive officer.
   f. Name of the department and its supervisor responsible for driver assignments, hours, and safety.
   g. Name of the department and its supervisor responsible for maintenance and inspection of courier vehicles.

(For purposes of this assignment skip to questions on employment and agency of Hart.)

IV. EMPLOYMENT OF MR. HART

2. Please state:
   a. Whether Mr. Richard hart, the co-defendant in this action, was an employee of your corporation on February 25 and 26, 19__.
   b. The duration of Mr. Hart's employment by your corporation.
   c. His title, job description, and the qualifications for the position.
   d. Whether Mr. Hart was assigned to and operating a courier vehicle owned by your corporation at approximately 7:30 A.M. on February 26, ____.

3. Was Mr. Hart performing his employment duties at the time of the alleged injury to Ms. Forrester at the time of the alleged incident.

V. THE VEHICLE

4. Please identify:
   a. The make, model, year, color, serial number, license number, and mileage of the vehicle operated by Mr. hart at the time of the alleged accident.
   b. All records on the maintenance and repair of said vehicle including any reports of damage, malfunctions, concerns of drivers or mechanics, and all information on known or suspected defects in the vehicle.
   c. The location and the custodian(s) of all such records, reports, and information.
   d. The names, addresses, and phone numbers of all drivers, in addition to Mr. Hart, that have operated said vehicle.
   e. The names, addresses, and phone numbers of all mechanics that have worked on and/or diagnosed problems with said vehicle.

  f. The source of the manufacturer's recommended maintenance schedule for said vehicle and state the schedule.

  g. Any documents stating the corporation's policies, guidelines, and/or directives on the maintenance and repair of courier vehicles.

  h. Any additional information you have regarding defects in said vehicle or suggesting that the said vehicle was inadequately maintained prior to and at the time of the alleged accident.

VI. TIME ON DUTY PRIOR TO ACCIDENT

 5. Please state:

  a. The exact time that Mr. Hart started the shift leading up to the alleged accident.

  b. A chronological account of Mr. Hart's pick-ups, deliveries, and rest periods providing for each the specific:

   i. time of occurrence.

   ii. duration.

   iii. location (address).

   iv. mileage between locations.

   v. name of any document(s) or record(s), including a computerized record, providing such information.

VII. LAWS, RULES, AND REGULATIONS AND RELATED SAFETY PROGRAM

 6. Please identify by appropriate number, section, and title any of the following that govern the regular maintenance of your vehicles and the frequency, duration (including overtime), and distance of driver shifts:

  a. State and federal laws

  b. State and federal administrative rules and regulations.

  c. Union or employee contract provisions.

  d. Company guidelines, policies, rules, and the like.

 7. Please describe your driver safety program and identify the document in which it is stated.

 8. State whether regular safety instruction is provided and the dates and nature of said instruction and identify any records that reflect such for the 18-month period preceding February 26, _____.

 9. Please provide the dates and identify any record of Mr. Hart's attendance at such safety instruction.

 10. State whether you have a safety library or section of a library pertaining to vehicle maintenance and driver safety and state its location.

 11. State Mr. Hart's driving record while an employee of your company.

 12. Was Mr. Hart's driving record screened prior to his becoming a driver for your company and identify any record of such.

VIII. GENERAL AND CONTINUING QUESTIONS

 13. Do you have any additional information relevant to the subject of this lawsuit not previously set out in your answers above?

 14. Have you listed and contacted all individuals that you know have, or might have, information pertaining to this lawsuit?

 15. Please identify and state the capacities of all persons who helped you obtain answers to these interrogatories, specifying the answer with which they assisted.

 16. Take notice that you have a continuing obligation to supplement your answers to these interrogatories as information is acquired by you, your agents, attorneys or representatives.

_____.
Arthur White
Attorney for Plaintiff
(address)

CERTIFICATE OF SERVICE

A copy of PLAINTIFF'S CONTINUING INTERROGATORIES SET ONE was served on Defendant mercury Parcel Service, Incorporated's attorney, Lynn Ott, located at 603 Stoker St., Cincinnati, Ohio by U.S. Mail this _____ day of _____, _____.

_____.
Arthur White
Attorney for Plaintiff
(address)

Assignment 4

To gain additional practice and confidence, reverse the situation and draft a set of interrogatories from Mercury Parcel to Ms. Forrester. confine your drafting to:

1. Caption and instructions
2. Questions on:
   a. Her background information (current employment information only)
   b. Her statements to others about the accident
   c. Her own possible negligence
3. Concluding questions and directions
4. Signature and certificate of service

ANSWER: The caption, instructions, concluding questions and directions, signature and certificate, may be done as in the answer to Assignment 3. Interrogatory questions will vary, but may be similar to the following:

III. CURRENT EMPLOYMENT
   5. In regard to your current employment, state the following:
      a. Employer(s)' name, address, phone number
      b. Your current title, position, or job level
      c. Period of time at this job level
      d. Current salary (annual)
      e. Annual fringe benefits and dollar amount for each benefit
      f. Dates you missed work, if any, due to accident allegedly caused by defendants
      g. Date, if any, you resumed work.

IV. YOUR STATEMENT TO OTHERS ABOUT ACCIDENT
   6. If you made or provided any written or oral statements to other persons, including those to insurance companies, at or following the accident, please identify:
      a. Name, address, and phone number, and title of each person
      b. Date of each statement
      c. Form of each statement; i.e., written, oral, mechanically recorded, etc., and the custodian of such statements.
   7. Please state which of the above statements you signed.

V. PLAINTIFF'S ACTIONS IMMEDIATELY PRIOR TO ACCIDENT
   8. Describe the condition of the road as affected by the weather.
   9. Did you look both directions before crossing the road?
   10. Was anything obscuring your vision or hearing?
   11. When did you first see the van?
   12. When did you first hear the van?
   13. State in detail your actions after you first saw the van up to the time of your alleged injury.
   14. Describe what, if anything, was distracting you immediately prior to the incident and the degree of distraction.
   15. State the purpose of your being where you were just prior to the accident.

Assignment 5

Exchange the interrogatories you drafted in Application Assignments 3 and 4 with a classmate, then draft answers to the classmate's interrogatories using the checklist you developed. For practice, object to at least one question and explain the basis of the objection. Also, assume you do not trust the accuracy of the information you have for the answer to one other question. You may have to create some information to answer the questions adequately.

Or, assume that you are the paralegal whose firm is representing Carl Ameche in Case II, the campground fire case. Draft answers to several of the questions in the sample set of interrogatories (Exhibit 7:2). Also practice objections and how to respond when unsure of your information in your answers.

Or, answer your own interrogatories for practice and to evaluate the quality of your interrogatories. Use the requirements set out in the preceding paragraphs.

ANSWER: If time does not permit students to respond to the entire set of interrogatories, consider having them answer only one section. many of the answers, especially those from Mercury Parcel, will have to be made up. Students should have a set of answers that includes:

1. Proper captions
2. A title: Answers to Plaintiff's/Defendant's Continuing Interrogatories Set One
3. Answers that are drafted conforming to the text list titled Review the Techniques for Answering Interrogatories
4. Engrossing
5. At least one objection in the following or similar format:
6. Did you make any statement about the accident that was mechanically recorded?
   Objection: Plaintiff objects to Interrogatory 6 because it calls for information that is protected by the attorney-client privilege and attorney work product.

INTERNET EXERCISES

1. Using Findlaw, Westlaw, or Lexis, find the Advisory Committee's Commentary on the 2000 changes to Rule 26 of the Federal Rules of Civil Procedure. What is the rationale for making disclosure mandatory? For changing the wording in

26(a)(1)(A) to "that the disclosing party may use to support its claims or defenses"?

ANSWER: The Advisory Committee Notes state that the courts and attorneys were sufficiently satisfied with mandatory disclosure to require it system-wide. It will promote justice and uniformity.

The wording was changed in 26(a)(1(A) to prevent abuses of disclosure by giving the trial court more control over some areas of discovery.

2. Find the ABA Standards on Discovery in the ABA site (or other possible site not requiring downloading). If your instructor approves, download the standards.
    a. What standard or section deals with interrogatories?
    b. According to the standard, when has a party fulfilled the obligation to respond to interrogatories?

ANSWER:
  a. III.
  b. III.7.b. says if they have:
      i.   responded timely as set by the rules, stipulation or court order;
      ii. made a reasonable inquiry of sources likely to have pertinent information, including documents;
      iii. given specific objections to specific interrogatories; and
      iv. provided responsive answers, except where there are objections.
3. Go to Findlaw and locate the Forms Exchange. List three forms either available or requested through the exchange regarding interrogatories. Then go to the Forms link and see if you can locate any forms pertinent to disclosure or interrogatories by doing a state-specific search.

ANSWER: Based on a current Web site search.

ADDITIONAL EXERCISES

1. List and define the seven major discovery devices.

ANSWER:
  a. Disclosure: giving to the opponent a broad spectrum of relevant information about the case without a specific request or use of other discovery devices
  b. Interrogatories: written questions submitted to a party
  c. Deposition: sworn oral testimony of a witness or litigant taken prior to trial
  d. Production of documents, tangible items, or entry to property for inspection
  e. Expert's report and opinion: the name, subject matter, and substance of the report of scientists and other experts to be used at trial

  f. Medical examinations: requirement upon motion that a party submit to a physical or mental examination by a doctor chosen by the opposing party
  g. Request for admission: asking the opponent to admit certain facts in writing, which then do not have to be proven at trial

2. What are two major limits to the scope of discovery?

ANSWER:
  a. Privileged information
  b. Trial preparation material (attorney work product)
  c. Matters relevant to the claim or defense of any party unless expanded by court order to matters relevant to the subject matter of the action

3. Go to the law library and find at least five federal or state court decisions that found specific kinds of discovery requests not discoverable. List these and return to class ready to report the cases and the types of requests that were denied by the court.

ANSWER: This will give students further insight into what the limits to discovery are under both federal and state rules. Because students are likely to come back with different cases, this assignment can serve as the basis for a good class discussion while providing students with good case references.

4. When does a party have a duty to update discovery information? What are the applicable federal and state rules?

ANSWER: Federal Rule 26(e); State Rule _____.
    When your own answers to opponent's interrogatories become outdated or inaccurate or new witnesses need to be added to original list.

5. Assume that you are a paralegal for a firm representing Make Tracks, Inc. In the discovery stage, your attorney asks you to draft as many questions as you can because she wants to "paper the plaintiff to death." She also says answer plaintiff's questions as narrowly as possible, and respond that requested safety rest reports have been temporarily misplaced even though you saw them in the file yesterday. What specific ethical concerns arise and what rules of professional conduct apply?

ANSWER:
Unnecessary questions: Model Rule 3.2
Frivolous requests: Model Rule 3.4(d)
Narrow answers are acceptable
Delay or concealed evidence: Model Rules 3.4(a) and (c)

6. Work through the questions for study and review at the end of the chapter to reinforce your understanding.

CHAPTER 8

DISCOVERY: DEPOSITIONS

CHAPTER OBJECTIVE

Chapter 8 continues the study of discovery with a focus on depositions. After an introduction to the topic, students learn specific tasks required of paralegals in deposition practice. The final section offers background and techniques for digesting depositions and other documents.

PREPARING FOR CLASS: INSTRUCTIONAL SUPPLEMENTS

1. The state and federal rules on discovery, particularly on depositions.
2. A collection of your personal tips and techniques for setting up depositions and for digesting.
3. Software for summarizing depositions.
4. Pertinent Web sites.

SUGGESTED CLASS ACTIVITIES

1. Conduct a live or taped deposition. Have the students plan the question outline, draft the necessary correspondence, and possibly, prepare witness files. Hold the deposition. Have the students take notes and later summarize the deposition. Choose your own facts for the deposition or conduct a fictional one for the *Forrester* case (Case I) or another case from Chapter 1.
2. It might be worthwhile spending some class time discussing and comparing the student digests of the Hart deposition.
3. Invite a paralegal to discuss deposition digesting and/or a court reporter to discuss how the reporting system works in the local courts.
4. Have students summarize a deposition, using software.

OUTLINE

I. Depositions
   A. Introduction
      Key terms: deposition, deponent
   B. Scope and Limits of the Deposition
   C. Types of Depositions
   D. Procedure
      System Folder Assignments 1 and 2
   E. Preliminary Tasks
      1. Determine Whom to Depose
         a. Organize Information to Identify Potential Deponents
         b. Designated Corporate or Agency Deponent
         c. Expert Witnesses
      2. Conduct a Preliminary Interview
   F. Coordinate the Deposition
      1. Arrange for Site and Necessary Components
         a. Time
         b. Site
         c. Method of Recording
            Internet Exercises 1, 2, and 3
         d. Oath Officer
      2. Prepare and Serve Notice of the Deposition
         Exhibit 8:1, Notice of Taking Deposition of a Witness Including Reference to Materials Designated in Attached Subpoena
      3. Subpoena the Deponent
         a. Obtain the Subpoena
            Key terms: subpoena, subpoena duces tecum
            Exhibit 8:2, Subpoena for Taking Oral Testimony and Production of Documents (Duces Tecum)

Internet Exercise 4
   b. Attach Fees
   c. Serve the Subpoena
     System Folder Assignment 3
  G. Prepare for Deposition
    1. Draft Questions or an Examination Outline
      Exhibit 8:3, Deposition Outline/Checklist (Plaintiff—Automobile)
      Exhibit 8:4, Sample Deposition Outline
      System Folder Assignment 4
      Application Assignment 1
    2. Gather and Prepare Documents and Exhibits
    3. Set Up Witness Files
      System Folder Assignment 5
    4. Assist in the Preparation of the Client or Witness for Testimony
      Exhibit 8:5, Letter to Client Regarding Deposition
      System Folder Assignment 6
  H. Attend and Review the Deposition
     System Folder Assignment 7
II. Digesting Depositions and Other Documents
  A. Introduction and Definition
  B. Purposes for Digesting Depositions
  C. Techniques for Digesting Depositions
  D. Types of Deposition Digests and Indexes
    Exhibit 8:6, Deposition Digest (Chronological)
    Exhibit 8:7, Page Extracts from Topical (Subject) Deposition Summaries
    Exhibit 8:8, Deposition Digest (Narrative)
    System Folder Assignment 8
  E. Digest Aids for Complex Cases
  F. Automated Deposition Summaries
    Exhibit 8:9, Deposition of Richard Hart
    Application Assignment 2
  G. Other Follow-Up Tasks
III. Summary

SYSTEM FOLDER ASSIGNMENTS

Assignment 1

Write a brief outline on the definition, purpose, scope, and procedure of depositions to place in your system folder.

ANSWER:

  I. Deposition: the oral questioning of a witness under oath before trial.
  II. Purposes
    A. Discover information
    B. Evaluate witness and attorney
    C. Impeach trial testimony (Rule 32)
    D. Preservation of evidence (testimony)

  III. Scope
    A. Persons other than parties can be deposed
    B. Conducted in accordance with Federal Rule of Evidence 30(c)
    C. Same scope as other discovery devices [Rule 26(b)]
  IV. Types
    A. Oral exam (Rule 30)
    B. Written questions (Rule 31)
    C. Before the action is filed (Rule 27)
  V. Procedure
    A. Time and place set
    B. Person to administer oath and record testimony
    C. Notice sent to parties
    D. Witness subpoenaed
    E. Other parties may attend and ask questions
    F. Officer swears in witness
    G. Requesting attorney asks questions
    H. Opponent may cross-examine
    I. All questions and answers are recorded
    J. Record is reviewed by witness and changes proposed in writing
    K. Record is certified [Rule 30(f)]

Assignment 2

Add or verify the deadlines for deposition practice from your state and local federal district rules in the Pleadings, Motions, and Time Limits exhibit in Chapter 6 or in your system folder. Place citations to the pertinent state or federal rules, including those covering scope and other limitations on depositions, in your system folder.

Assignment 3

Draft a checklist on preparing and serving subpoenas and place it and references to the pertinent documents in your system folder. Include citations to both state and federal rules. Note the time limits for objection to a subpoena in this section of your system folder and in your Pleadings, Motions, and Time Limits exhibit.

ANSWER: Subpoena Checklist
  I. Provide clerk of court with copy of notice to take deposition and proof of service on parties
    A. Federal: issued by clerk in district where deposition is taken or by the attorney
    B. State: sometimes where action is pending
  II. Usually clerk will sign in blank, leaving paralegal to fill in information (Rule 45).
    A. Name of issuing court and court where action is pending
    B. Title and docket number of action
    C. Name of attorney
    D. Witness's name and address with directions

for witness to attend and give testimony

  E. Date, time, place for deposition

  F. Designation of documents needed, if pertinent, including attorney's declaration that they are necessary.

  G. Text of Rule 45 (c) and (d)

III. Attach witness and mileage fees, if necessary (28 U.S.C. § 1821) [Rule 45(a)(2)].

IV. Serve subpoena personally.

  A. Warn witness, with your attorney's approval

  B. Federal: person 18 years old who is not a party

  C. States: sheriff, special bailiff, person of legal age (check local rules)

  D. Paralegals, professional servers

  E. Personally hand subpoena to deponent

  F. Explain subpoena and what is expected

  G. Acknowledge service

V. Objections served on deposing attorney within 14 days of service of subpoena or on or before deposition if scheduled less than 14 days from service. That attorney must seek court order to have subpoena complied with [Rule 45(c)(3)(A)].

Assignment 4

Draft a checklist that includes coordinating the deposition and planning and preparing an outline for taking a deposition based on the steps and recommendations made in this chapter, and place it in your system folder.

ANSWER: Checklist for Planning and Preparing for Deposition

  I. Planning for Deposition

    A. Review file information

      1. Note things witness is likely to prove or provide leads for.

      2. Note documents of physical items to be introduced through this witness.

      3. Note interrogatory answers or admissions by this witness.

    B. Review notes with attorney to find what is wanted form this witness.

    C. Review other witness deposition or outline forms from the firm or law library.

    D. Brainstorm questions.

    E. Arrange questions in outline.

    F. Review with attorney, amend, and have typed.

  II. Coordinate the Deposition: Add state process and rules

    A. Check time since service of summons and complaint: 30 days

    B. Schedule mutually available time.

    C. Select and reserve suitable site well in advance.

    D. Arrange for court reporter and/or method for taking deposition.

    E. Arrange for oath officer.

    F. Prepare and serve Notice of Deposition on each party and court reporter [Rule 30(b)(1)].

      1. time, place, name of attorney conducting exam

      2. name and address of each person to be deposed or a general description of person

      3. description of matters to be covered if business, association, or agency

      4. designate document or other tangible things to be brought

    G. Execute certificate of service.

    H. In case of cancellation or rescheduling, notify all participants by letter.

    I. Obtain subpoena and/or subpoena duces tecum by providing appropriate clerk of court with copy of notice and proof of service on parties.

    J. Fill in subpoena (Rule 45).

    K. Attach any necessary witness and mileage fees [28 U.S.C. § 1821, Rule 4 (a)(2)]

    L. Serve subpoena.

      1. Warn witness, with approval of attorney.

      2. Personal service is required in most jurisdictions.

      3. Written acknowledgment of service or an executed affidavit of service is required.

      4. Contact local court for correct procedure on out-of-town deponent.

    M. Follow up to see if served.

    N. If subpoena objected to, prepare court order for compliance [Rule 45(c)(3)(A)].

Assignment 5

Place a page reference to the Checklist for Preparing Witness Files in your system folder.

Assignment 6

Place a page reference to the Letter to the Client Regarding Deposition in your system folder

Assignment 7

Prepare a checklist for attending and reviewing the deposition and place it in your system folder

ANSWER: Attending and Reviewing the Deposition

  I. At Deposition

    A. Listen carefully.

    B. Take notes.

      1. information

      2. objections

3. effectiveness of witness and opposing counsel
C. Retrieve information and documents.
   4. Research law
   5. Make phone calls
II. After Deposition
   A. Compare notes with attorney and draft summary.
   B. Check to see that witness signs transcript.
   C. Verify certification.
      1. that witness was sworn
      2. that deposition is a true record [Rule 30(f)]
   D. File deposition with the court.
   E. Review transcript.
      1. Note questions omitted.
      2. Note inconsistencies.
      3. Note inaccuracies in the reporting.

Assignment 8

Place page references to the deposition summary examples in this chapter in your system folder. Add any other examples provided in class.

APPLICATION ASSIGNMENTS

Assignment 1

Assume you represent Mr. Hart. Prepare a deposition outline for your attorney to use in examining Ms. Forrester. For purposes of this assignment only, limit the scope of your outline to the time immediately before and during the accident. Do not get into injuries or other damages. Try using a tape recorder if one is available to dictate questions or topics. Use the sample outline, your checklist, and Exhibits 8:3 and 8:4 as guides for your work.

ANSWER: Forrester Deposition Outline
I. Events prior to Accident
   A. Duties in preparing family for the day
   B. State of mind
   C. Weather conditions
   D. Road conditions
   E. Dress
   F. Other
II. Accident itself
   A. Description (diagram) of site
   B. First awareness of van
   C. Speed of van
   D. Your location on road
   E. Your action or reaction
   F. Things that obstructed ability to see or hear

Assignment 2

Exhibit 8:9 contains excerpts from a deposition of Mr. Hart. Skim the deposition transcript first. Then read it and carefully draft the corresponding section of a chronological digest. Prepare a table of contents for the digest. Count lines from op of each page of a deposition, since no lines are provided. Then do a topical summary. Use a computer and appropriate software to do the summaries.

ANSWER: The table of contents would be similar to the page and line references on the left side of the pages.

INTERNET ASSIGNMENTS

1. Go to the *Concordance* and *Summation* Web sites. Compare the features and costs of each service. Try a demonstration of the product, if possible. Which product would you recommend and why?

ANSWER: Student should be able to report on comparative features and indicate reason for choice.

2. Using the Deponet service, locate a legal videographer and a court reporter in your area.

ANSWER: Student choice.

3. Go to one of the four on-line, real-time deposition transcript services and survey its features and costs.

ANSWER: Student choice.

4. Pick a town approximately 100 miles from your closest federal district court and located in the district. Using Mapquest™, determine if that location is within 100 miles driving distance of the district court.

ANSWER: Student choice.

ADDITIONAL EXERCISES

1. What limits are imposed on what can be asked in a deposition? What federal and state rules apply?

ANSWER: Normal discovery limitations [Rule 26(b)], plus must conform to the Federal Rules of Evidence [Rule 30(c)].

State Rules _____.

2. How do you gather a list of persons who might be deposed? How can you narrow that list?

ANSWER: By reviewing the facts, key elements, pleadings, investigation and/or evidence summaries, and opponent's answers to interrogatories.

This list is narrowed by weighing cost versus degree of need; by eliminating friendly witnesses, old or ill witnesses of the opponent, and witnesses with favorable prior statements; and by using preliminary interviews.

CHRONOLOGICAL DEPOSITION DIGEST

Page	Line	Topic	Summary
1	1–12	personal	Has lived at 1223 Penny Lane, Cincinnati, Ohio for 8 yrs.; at 4313 E. Wickland, Columbus, Ohio for 7 yrs. previous.
2	1–12	data	Married to Jessica Marie Hart 17 yrs., sons Brett, 16, and Jerome, 14. Born Aug. 13, 19__ in Columbus.
2	13–19	education	Graduated Taft High, Columbus. Army training as ambulance driver. Truck driving course 12 yrs. ago.
2	18–25	military service	Army 19__ to 19__, 2 yrs.
2	26–43	education	Ambulance training few wks./yr. at Fort Oglethorp, Ga. No special training for driving in ice and snow. Experience driving on ice: winter in Columbus. Truck training at Cincinnati Vocational Institute for 6 wks., not vans, but large trucks, didn't include winter driving. No formal training for winter driving.
2	44–49	employment	Route man, parcel delivery, often assigned Legalville, Col. route.
3	1–42		Previous deliveries on Capitol Dr. outside Legalville? "No . . . possibly . . . I'm not sure . . . maybe five or six years ago . . ." Form 30 would show addresses. Worked full-time for Mercury Parcel Service, 2 yrs. Columbus, 8 yrs. Cincinnati, always as route man. Earns 10.35/hr., usually 40-hr. weeks. Overtime when someone is sick, a lot to deliver, or volunteer. Previously worked 6 yrs for town of Jackson as ambulance driver, Rt. 3, Hwy 95, Jackson, Ohio.
3	43–49	driving record	"Yes," good driving record.
4	1–38		Accident in Cinc. while driving for Mercury, crossing lanes to exit I-75, no injuries, no citations; 5 yrs. ago in Columbus, turned to talk to wife, rear-ended car ahead. Injury, Hart's ins. paid, citation for inattentive driving. No other accidents recalled. OBJECTION: Atty. Ott objects to relevance of question, "Have you received any other traffic citations?" argued to establish pattern. As many as 6 citations, mainly for speeding in the last 5 years, Cinc. area, half on job.
4	39–48	working time	Working for Mercury at time. Started work on night shift at 11 P.M. the 25th.
5	1–11	Feb. 26,	Due back at 7 A.M. but 2 hrs. behind because of weather. Not driving constantly (out to deliver packages), but more than usual. Union rules: 2 breaks and 1/2 hr. lunch break, but took only one 3 A.M. break Nothing else unusual.
5	12–35	problem with van	Pulls to left when braked hard, allowed for that. Existed for 2 wks. 1 wk. before accident reported to Arnie Hanson and possibly Johnny Sloan, mechanics at Mercury. Form is required, but if not serious "we just mention it to one of the mechanics." Mechanics may look at if time, or wait until regular servicing. Didn't think problem of pulling left had been worked on. "Almost always" drives same van. Did not fill out a form on braking problem.
5	36–48	weather conditions	Wet at beginning, freezing spots by 3:30 A.M. Occasional slipping.
6	1–2		Ice here and there, " . . . it wasn't too bad." Slowed maybe 5 or 10 mph.
6	3–6	speed	"Well, I had just looked and I was going about 35 mph."
6	7–44	condition of driver/ driving time/ safety rules	Thinking about lateness, anxious to get home, a little tired because of the weather. Could have stopped for break but didn't because of lateness. One hour late on previous shift, snowy. 6 hrs. sleep on 25th because of son's basketball game. No company rules about amount of sleep before shift. Rules about break? "Oh, they tell us to pull over if we are real tired, but I felt OK." "Anyone who drives knows" to pull over, but safety rules posted in shop, didn't really read rules. "I think the rule is around 7 hours of actual driving time." Drove 8 maybe 9 actual hours and would have had 2 more without the accident. Doesn't know of penalty for driving over limit of hrs. Overtime pay only if unavoidable.
6	45–48	Road	"Quite narrow, hilly, and curvy." Not sure if speed limit posted.
7	1–3		Maybe a little tricky, but has driven worse.
7	4 to end	accident	"Glanced" at speedometer for "split second" then "looked up and suddenly there was this lady stepping out onto the road." Couldn't see her before because she was in dip behind hill in the road. "I thought she would stop, but she just kept looking ahead and kept walking into the road." "When I came over the hill she was barely onto the road . . . her head was tucked down into her coat and she just kept walking." Did not sound horn, did hit brakes. Truck pulled to left, fishtailed, Hart pumped brakes, lady looked up, hesitated, went "wrong way." "I couldn't avoid her" heard thump, van crossed middle of road, woman fell to right, van went into ditch and hit a tree. Van pulled to left "almost immediately. I think it might have been the same problem I described before, or it might have been the ice."

3. What are some of the ways to take depositions, other than orally, and their governing rules? What are the advantages and disadvantages of such procedures?

ANSWER:

Method	Advantage	Disadvantage	Rule
Video	Gives jury real picture, especially of inaccessible witness or test	Poor photography and sound	30(b)(4)
Phone	Cost savings	Cannot evaluate witness	30(b)(7)
Written deposition	Travel savings	Must still reserve site and get recorder	31(a-c)

4. Assume that Herbert Herbert III is the executive officer for Mercury Parcel Service, Inc. Draft a subpoena duces tecum requiring Mr. Herbert to appear at a deposition and to bring the employment and safety records of Mr. Hart. Find information in the Forrester complaint in Chapter 4 and make up remaining information, remembering the rules for deposing persons in another district

ANSWER: Check that the issuing court and location for the deposition is in the Cincinnati area. Address for Herbert/Mercury Parcel is 603 Stoker St., Cincinnati, Ohio.

5. Why is it important to prepare a client or witness for a deposition? In what ways can a paralegal assist at such a preparation conference?

ANSWER: What they say and how they appear could win favorable settlement; eliminates inconsistencies and inaccuracies which can be exploited at trial.
Paralegals can:

- Keep client informed of schedule and what to expect.
- Convey techniques for testifying.
- Answer questions.
- Draft questions likely to be used by opponent.
- Question witness in a mock exam.
- Observe demeanor.
- Make suggestions for improvement.

6. Assume that you are working o prepare Mr. Hart for his deposition by Ms. Forrester's attorney. Mr. Hart says that he is unsure about the road conditions at the time of the accident. You and the attorney know that it works against Hart to appear unsure about important facts.
   a. The attorney says to Hart, "It's best not to be unsure and, after all, the road was not very icy." Are there any ethical concerns?

ANSWER: The attorney is strongly influencing Hart's testimony, if not directly telling him what to say. This raises serious ethical concerns under Rule 3.4(b) and possibly the spirit of Rule 1.2.

   b. The attorney has left the room and you say, "Mr. Hart, do you recall that during our first interview you told me the road was not very icy?" Are there any ethical concerns?

ANSWER: If what the paralegal has said is true, there should be no ethical problem. Refreshing a witness's memory is appropriate. Also no legal advice is being given. The paralegal is simply restating a fact.

7. In what ways can a computer assist you in summarizing a deposition?

ANSWER: A computer printout of the document can be made and worked on. Information that is irrelevant to the case or unnecessary for the summary can be selected and deleted. What remains are the most critical aspects of the deposition. This remaining information can be manipulated or further summarized to form the final summary. By using the computer's editing function, the final product will be free of scratch-outs and can be printed immediately for a good clean summary.

8. Describe a narrative deposition digest and state its advantages.

ANSWER: A full-sentence paraphrasing of the deposition. It can be organized by topic, witness, or in any other way to meet the specific needs of the attorney. Particularly good for passing on to clients such as insurance companies to enhance their understanding of the evidence in the case.

9. Review the text section on digesting the deposition. Create a list of techniques for digesting a deposition.

ANSWER: Techniques for digesting a deposition:

a. Study the file for issues, legal theories, and so on.
b. Ask the attorney for an outline of questions used at the deposition, suggestions for topics, guidance on type of digest, indices, detail, format, time frame, cost, issues, and so on.
c. Skim the entire deposition for scope.
d. Draft a topical outline in the order that items are raised in the deposition.
e. Schedule blocks of time so you will not lose continuity in the deposition.
f. Use computer editing if possible.
g. Be concise.
h. Use abbreviations and short forms if they are clear.
i. Be accurate; avoid distortion or interpretation.
j. Use subheadings and write in short paragraphs.
k. Use page and line number references in margins
l. Use sheet or slip method of recording.
m. Use paraphrase or ellipsis summary.
n. Include accurate references to dates, exhibits, court reporter's notes on witness's behavior, objections, admissions, stipulations, document requests, and notes on witness effectiveness.

10. Work through the questions for study and review at the end of the chapter to reinforce your understanding.

CHAPTER 8 TAKE HOME TEST

The deposition digests assigned in Application Assignment 2 could be given as a take home test.

CHAPTER 9

Discovery: Document Production and Control, Medical Exams, Admissions, and Compelling Discovery

CHAPTER OBJECTIVE

The purpose of this chapter is to provide students with techniques and practice in further discovery procedures: document production, medical examinations, and admissions, as well as the informal use of the Freedom of Information Act. They also learn the procedure for compelling discovery. Along with each discovery device come guidelines for producing, reviewing, and organizing information, with an emphasis on using computers in the law office.

PREPARING FOR CLASS: INSTRUCTIONAL SUPPLEMENTS

1. Federal and state discovery rules.
2. After reviewing the techniques and procedures recommended in this chapter, prepare a list of any additions that might be added from your own experience.
3. Add assignments that utilize the computer software and facilities that are available to your students.
4. If the small case fill assignment (Application Assignment 4) is given, the instructor may choose to have manila folders and fasteners provided for the class.
5. Pertinent Web sites.

SUGGESTED CLASS ACTIVITIES

1. Arrange a visit to a large firm or corporate law department where a demonstration of document control, computer document retrieval, and file organization could be arranged. Alternatively, a paralegal from such an office might be willing to come to the class to discuss techniques in these areas, as well as in deposition digesting.
2. Ask a software vendor to demonstrate a document control product for the class.

OUTLINE

I. Introduction
II. Production of Documents and Things and Entry Upon Land for Inspection and Other Purposes
   A. Introduction
   B. Scope
   C. Procedure
   D. Reviewing for Production and Inspection
   E. Drafting the Request for Production and Inspection
      Exhibit 9:1, Request for Production, Inspection, and Copying of Documents, and Inspection and Photographing of Things and Property—General Form
      Exhibit 9:2, Example of a Production and Inspection Request Form
   F. Service of the Request for Production
      Exhibit 9:3, Request for Production of Documents—Business Records
      System Folder Assignments 1 and 2
III. Preparing for Production of Documents and Things
   A. Introduction
   B. Procedure
      1. Initial Steps
      2. Locate Documents/Computer Data
      3. Pull Files and Documents
         Exhibit 9:4, Document Production Original Source Log
      4. Screen Pulled Files and Documents
         Exhibit 9:5, Place Documents in an Upright Position
      5. Use a Standardized Numbering System
      6. Have the Attorney Review the Documents
      7. Extract Privileged Documents
         Key term: redaction
      8. Have Documents Copied
      9. Prepare Documents for Examination

10. Retrieve the Documents
11. Return the Documents and Retain Indexes
C. Document Production and Computers
 1. Introduction
 2. Necessary Knowledge and Skill
 3. Initial Decision
 4. Things to Look for in Systems and Software
 5. Planning the System
 6. Locating and Screening Documents
 7. Entry of Data
 8. Retrieval
 9. Quality Control
 10. Security
 11. Other Uses for Computerized Document Support
   System Folder Assignment 3
IV. Production Procedure
 A. Replying to a Request for Production and Inspection
   Exhibit 9:6, Response to Request for Production—General Form
   Application Assignment 1
 B. Assisting at the Production, Examination, or Inspection
 C. Analyzing Documents Produced by the Opponent
V. Request for Physical and Mental Examination
 A. Purpose and Scope
 B. Procedure
 C. Set Up the Exam
 D. Draft the Documents
   Exhibit 9:7, Motion for Compulsory Physical Examination
 E. Inform the Client
   Exhibit 9:8, Notice to Client of Physical Examination
 F. Request the Report
   System Folder Assignment 4
VI. Reviewing and Interpreting Medical Records and Other Technical Documents and Reports
 A. Introduction
 B. Medical Record Interpretation
  1. Resources
  2. The Mini-Guide
  3. An Example for Interpretation
    Exhibit 9:9, Example of Physician's Orders
    Exhibit 9:10, Translation of Physician's Orders
VII. Request for Admission (Rule 36)
 A. Purpose and Scope
 B. Procedure
   System Folder Assignment 5

C. Preparing the Request for Admission
   Exhibit 9:11, Federal Form 25: Request for Admission Under Rule 36
   Application Assignment 2
 D. Responding to a Request for Admission
   Exhibit 9:12, Response to Defendant's Requests for Admissions
   System Folder Assignment 6
   Application Assignment 3
 E. Review of and Reply to Response
 F. Amending Responses
VIII. Objections, Compelling Discovery, and Sanctions
 A. Objecting to Discovery: Protective Orders
 B. Compelling Discovery
 C. Motion, Order, and Sanctions
 D. Procedure for Compelling Discovery
   Exhibit 9:13, Motion to Compel Production, Inspection, and Copying of Documents in Case of Objection or Failure to Respond Plus Rule 26(c) Certification—General Form
   Exhibit 9:14, Affidavit in Support of Motion to Compel
   Exhibit 9:15, Order That Interrogatories Concerning Personal Jurisdiction Are Answered and That Personal Jurisdiction Is Established
   System Folder Assignments 7 and 8
   Internet Exercise 1
IX. The Freedom of Information Act
 A. Definition and Purpose
 B. Procedure and Limits
   System Folder Assignment 9
 C. The Role of the Paralegal
   Exhibit 9:16, Freedom of Information Act (FOIA) Sample Request Letter
X. Organizing Files
 A. Introduction
 B. Small Case File
   Exhibit 9:17, Small Case File Folder
   Application Assignment 4
 C. Large Case File
   Exhibit 9:18, Master File Index Sheet
   Exhibit 9:19, Subfile Index Sheet
   System Folder Assignment 10
   Internet Exercise 2
XI. Summary

SYSTEM FOLDER ASSIGNMENTS

Assignment 1

Draft a thorough checklist for document production and place it in your system folder.

ANSWER: Checklist for Document Production

 I. Preliminary Work

A. Review the case and opponent's production request; note the following:
   1. items requested
   2. possible objections
   3. privileged information
   4. likely location of items
   5. number of documents
B. Estimate needs.
   1. materials
   2. personnel
   3. equipment
   4. space
C. Plan document control method.

II. Locate Documents
A. Consult client.
B. Follow "chain of command."
C. Notify custodian.
D. Cooperate with custodian.

III. Pull Files and Documents
A. When the file is pulled, leave a file checkout card or replacement sheet indicating the following:
   1. who pulled file
   2. for what case
   3. next location
   4. date
B. Leave a copy labeled as such, if necessary.
C. Label each file or document as to its place in the case.
D. Prepare a file log indicating the following:
   1. source—helps with return
   2. description
   3. new working file number
   4. custodian
   5. files not found (also add to case file)
   6. unique nature of log books, journals, etc.
E. Remove documents to a separate room.
F. Inform custodian what documents have been removed.

IV. Screen Pulled Files and Documents
A. Identify documents responsive to the production request; place upright so they protrude from the file.
B. Number selected documents for identification and retrieval.
   1. set and paragraph of production request
   2. how many copies needed
   3. which cross files the copies go to
C. Note privileged or sensitive documents by colored cover sheet.
D. Classify documents.
   1. numbered
   2. privileged and other undiscoverables
   3. nonresponsive
E. Copy and return copies to original custodian.

F. Index the documents.
   1. number of document
   2. description
   3. nature (memo, letter, etc.)
   4. new file number
   5. date of document
   6. whether privileged or otherwise undiscoverable
   7. set and item of production request
   8. whether document was produced to adversary

V. Attorney Review of Documents
A. Respond to production requests.
B. Identify undiscoverable items.
C. Keep documents in original format (stapled, bound, etc.).
D. Prepare necessary copies.

VI. Extract Privileged Documents
A. Place with colored cover sheet in separate folder.
B. Keep folder in locked facility.
C. Substitute sheet with document number in original file.
D. Redaction: Extract privileged information from documents.

VII. Seek Assistance with computer Data Production

VIII. Have Documents Copied
A. Enough for the following purposes:
   1. replacement in original file
   2. duplicate of original file
   3. chronological file
   4. response request
B. During copying substitute a sheet identifying the document and the copier.
C. Copies should contain a legend stating:
   1. this is a copy
   2. where original can be found
D. Keep copies in original format (stapled, clipped, etc.).
E. Copy entire document.
F. Note uncopiable or altered documents.
G. Destroy poor copies.
H. Sort copies.
I. Keep originals in numerical order.
J. Return copies to original custodians.
   1. letter of return to custodian and case file
   2. request receipt

IX. Prepare Documents for Examination
A. Arrange by set and item of request.
B. Renumber all, or only those selected.
C. Prepare index showing the following:
   1. original number of document
   2. item to which it responds
   3. that it was produced
   4. if selected by adversary

D.   Keep a copy of all documents produced to opponent.

X.   Retrieve Documents When Necessary Using Indices
   A.   Index by date of document.
   B.   Index by name of author or recipient.
   C.   Index by number of document.
   D.   Index by issue it pertains to.
   E.   Maintain checkout system for documents.

IX.   At Close of Case Return Documents and Retain Indices
   A.   Retrieve originals from court or other parties.
   B.   Log and obtain receipt.
   C.   Shred or burn all copies.
   D.   Keep indices, return letters, and receipts.

Assignment 2

Draft a checklist for the procedure for requesting production of documents and things, the response, and the on-site examination. Add a brief checklist on what to consider when requesting computer data. Add the pertinent state and federal rules. Note deadlines in the Pleadings, Motions, and Time Limits (Exhibit 6:25) and your system folder. Insert page references to the forms and examples for document production.

ANSWER: Requesting Production, Response, Examination

I.   Request for Production: Procedure
   A.   Request for Production can be made in the following circumstances:
      1.   with summons and complaint, or any time after that in nondisclosure jurisdiction
      2.   after parties' planning meeting in disclosure jurisdictions
      3.   directly on any other party without leave of court
      4.   on third persons only through subpoena duces tecum [Rule 45(a) and 34(c)]
      5.   for specific item or category
      6.   for reasonable time, place, and manner for conducting inspection [Rule 34(b)]
   B.   Compliance
      1.   Requesting party may move for court order to comply [Rule 37(a)].
      2.   Requesting party pays for expense of production.
   C.   State Rules _____.
   D.   Draft a Request for Production and Inspection.
      1.   Begin with definitions section if necessary.
      2.   Items must be described with sufficient specificity.

      3.   Request should be organized by the type of evidence requested.
      4.   Include a paragraph on the continuing obligation of the respondent to produce pertinent documents that come into the respondent's possession after the original production date.

II.   Reply to Production Request
   A.   Reply within 30 days, or 45 days if with summons (shorter time by request to court).
   B.   Respond to each item, indicating compliance and/or objections specifically (Rule 34).
      1.   State reasons for objection [Rules 26(b) and 34(b)].
      2.   Protective order can be sought after good-faith effort to resolve [Rule 26(c)].
      3.   Only specific parts of the document may be protected [Rule 34(b)].

III.   Examination (responding to request)
   A.   Exchange may occur informally in small cases
   B.   Arrange for location.
      1.   secure
      2.   phone
      3.   copying machine
   C.   Review request and items to be produced.
      1.   indexed
      2.   responsive to but not exceeding request
   D.   Arrange documents [Rule 34(b)] in one of the following ways:
      1.   according to client's usual course of business
      2.   to correspond to categories in the request
   E.   Prepare for the examination.
      1.   Take a notepad and a numbering device.
      2.   Know where to reach the supervising attorney.
      3.   Prepare to stay for the duration of the examination.
   F.   During the examination, do the following:
      1.   Keep documents in order and in the room.
      2.   Keep a log of documents chosen.
      3.   Note special attention to particular documents.
      4.   Avoid conversation about the case or the value of documents.
      5.   Do not leave the room unless everyone else does and the door is locked.
   G.   Summarize the examination for the attorney.
   H.   Photocopy selected documents and submit them to the opponent.

IV.   Examination (for requesting party)
   A.   Review case, what to look for, budget, and methods for copying.

B. Check to see that copying equipment is available.

C. Take a notepad, a numbering device, and a tape recorder.

D. Work through documents, noting the following:
   1. type
   2. date
   3. author
   4. addressee
   5. pages
   6. attachments
   7. extraneous writing or marks

E. Cover all documents.
   1. See that all documents requested are produced.
   2. List documents not produced under claim of privilege or other objection.
   3. Note and index documents to be copied.
   4. Copy only useful documents; when in doubt, copy.

F. Summarize the examination for the attorney.

V. Requesting Computer Data

A. Consider consulting an expert.

B. Consider action to prevent destruction of information.

C. Locate data in the following places:
   1. in computer memory
   2. in backup systems
   3. in archived sources
   4. in e-mail
   5. in residual "deleted" files
   6. in buffer memories of printers and copiers

Assignment 3

Place page references to the computer terminology and procedure section in your system folder.

Assignment 4

Draft a checklist for the procedure for a request for physical and mental examination. Add references to the appropriate state and federal rules, and enter page references to the sample motion for examination and the notice to the client. Place in your system folder.

ANSWER: Request for Physical and Mental Examination: Procedure

A. Informal request is often adequate.

B. Motion for court-ordered examination includes the following:
   1. Notice of motion
   2. Affidavit
   3. Proposed order

C. Response may be objection or protective order.

D. Set up appointment with examiner and party.

E. Obtain report.
   1. Send copy to opponent, if directed.
   2. Pay and record expense.

Assignment 5

Place references to the applicable federal and state rules and time limits on requests for admission in your system folder and in the Pleadings, Motions, and Time Limits (Exhibit 6:25). Reference pages of checklists, forms, and examples in this chapter.

Assignment 6

Place a page reference to the form for a Response to Defendant's Request for Admissions in your system folder.

Assignment 7

List the key federal and state rules on compelling discovery and sanctions in your system folder.

Assignment 8

Draft a brief checklist on the procedure to follow to compel discovery; place it and page references to the motion to compel and related documents in the system folder.

ANSWER: Procedure for Compelling Discovery

A. Inform attorney of failure of opponent to comply with discovery request.

B. If decision is to compel and seek sanctions, determine in which court the motion to compel should be filed [Rule 37(a)(1)].

C. Draft the following:
   1. a motion to compel
   2. certification of attempt to resolve
   3. notice of motion
   4. memorandum of law
   5. desired court order
   6. certificate of service

D. Proof documents.

E. Have the attorney review and sign the documents.

F. Serve the documents on the opponent's attorney

G. File all documents and proof of service with the appropriate clerk of court.

Add necessary state procedures.

Assignment 9

Draft a procedural checklist for making a request pursuant to the Freedom of Information Act, both federal and state, and place it in your system folder. Include a page reference to the sample FOIA request in the chapter.

UNITED STATES DISTRICT COURT
FOR THE EASTERN DISTRICT OF COLUMBIA

ANN FORRESTER,
    Plaintiff

Civil Case, File No____.

MERCURY PARCEL SERVICE, INC.,
    Defendant

RESPONSE TO PLAINTIFF'S REQUEST FOR PRODUCTION AND INSPECTION OF DOCUMENTS, THINGS, AND REAL PROPERTY

Attorney
Address

    In response to plaintiff's request for production and inspection served on defendant _____, ____, the inspection and related activities requested will be permitted at defendant's corporate headquarters, 603 Stoker St., Cincinnati, Ohio, in room 117 as requested, except the production of item

    1.a, the specific rules and regulations of the Interstate Commerce Commission requiring regular safety checks, maintenance, and repair of vehicles used in interstate commerce

    to which production defendant objects respectfully on the grounds that such rules and regulations are as easily obtainable by plaintiff as they are by defendant.

_____.
Attorney, address
_____.
Date

ANSWER: Freedom of Information Act Procedure

A. Request FOIA material through the agency's designated information officer.
B. Demonstrate that requested information is in the records of that agency covered by the act.
C. Agency indicates compliance or denial within 10 days [5 U.S.C. § 552(a)(6)(A)(i)].
D. Appeal of denial must be made within 20 days [5 U.S.C. § 552(a)(6)(A)(ii)].
E. If appeal is denied and administrative remedies are exhausted, recourse is in federal district court.
F. Fee is charged, but waived if it contributes to public understanding [5 U.S.C. § 552 (a)(4)(A)(iii)].

Assignment 10

Add to your system folder any alternative methods for organizing a client's file suggested by your instructor.

APPLICATION ASSIGNMENTS

Assignment 1

Draft a response to Ms. Forrester's request for production of documents and things found in this chapter.

ANSWER: Response to Forrester Request for Production of Documents.

Assignment 2

Using the procedures described in this chapter, the form in Exhibit 9:11, and examples of the types and forms of questions to ask, draft a set of requests for admissions from Ms. Forrester to Mercury Parcel that covers:

- Caption
- Introductory material, if any
- Admissions on employment and agency of Hart
- Admissions on speed and exhaustion
- Admissions on forms that reflect irregular maintenance—as well as inaction on complaint about wheels locking when braking

    Assume that you have previously discovered certain facts needed to justify the requests.

ANSWER: Requests will vary, but check to see that they are drafted in accordance with the checklist in the previous assignment. Assignment 3 asks students to respond to these requests.

Assignment 3

Exchange the requests for admission you drafted in Assignment 2 with a classmate. Assume the facts are such that you can admit, deny, admit in part and deny in part, object, and state you cannot admit or deny with reasons t least once each in the response. In the alternative, draft a response to your own request.

ANSWER: Evaluate these responses according to the chapter material under Responding to a Request for Admission.

Assignment 4

Collect the documents you have gathered so far in the *Forrester* case and organize a small case file for them.

ANSWER: Although all of these assignments are optional, this file-organizing assignment may be particularly useful if students are doing a mock trial. What to include depends on what has been assigned, but could include the following:
   a. Interview and summary
   b. Pleadings and summary
   c. Motions
   d. Subpoenas
   e. Interrogatories and other discovery documents
   f. Deposition and digest of deposition
   g. Correspondence
   h. Time sheets and billing items
   i. Investigation and miscellaneous items

INTERNET EXERCISES

1. Go to the Department of Justice site on the motion to compel discovery. What databases is the plaintiff seeking?

ANSWER: The software tools that Microsoft uses to access and manipulate data contained in Microsoft's basic sales database.

2. Search Web sites listed above, www.paralegals.org, or www.nala.org for articles on discovery techniques or document management and case management (litigation) software. Briefly summarize the main points of two articles.

ANSWER: Current articles.

ADDITIONAL EXERCISES

1. What are the purposes, objectives, and concerns for the production of documents?

ANSWER: To provide the opponent a chance to see what, if any, documents support the facts to be alleged at trial; to produce documents thoroughly, accurately, and efficiently. Production should leave documents easy to retrieve and should interfere as little as possible with client's business or other operations.

2. If document production is not carefully planned, what problems are likely?

ANSWER: Delays, errors, paper shuffling, loss of valuable documents, unnecessary costs to client, court sanctions, and losing the case.

3. You are asked to draft a request for the production of documents under Rule 34(a) of the Federal Rules of Civil Procedure. The request is to get pertinent documents from Mercury Parcel Service concerning safety and vehicle maintenance. You have no idea what forms are common to this industry. How might you determine what to ask for?

ANSWER: Approach a similar business or appropriate trade association. Also, disclosure and the returned interrogatories may identify the needed documents.

4. You work for the law firm representing Teeny Tiny Manufacturing (Case IV). Your attorney wants to see Briar Patch's documents indicating the number of pieces received and, particularly, the number of unsatisfactory pieces. Further, it is necessary to inspect a generous sampling of the unsatisfactory pieces to see if they were justifiably rejected. Draft the needed request for production.

ANSWER: You may choose to have half the class draft the request and half draft the response. The example of plaintiff's request for production in this section can serve as a general guideline for this assignment.

5. What advantages does the standardized decimal document numbering system provide over other systems?

ANSWER: It is efficient, can be used in all cases, and provides considerable information about each document at a glance. It avoids confusion that results from other haphazard or inconsistent systems. It avoids telltale gaps in the identification numbers of produced documents.

6. What factors enter into a decision on whether to computerize the documents in a case?

ANSWER: The complexity of the case; the number of parties; the number of documents likely to be involved; whether the current system is adequate to handle the case; the comparative costs of using the client's, the law office's, or a private vendor's system; personnel needs; and whether it is just as easy or easier to handle the case manually.

7. Describe the difference between full-text software and indexing software in regard to document control.

ANSWER: Full-text software requires the entry of the entire text of each document and, thus, is the most expensive of the two systems. Documents can be retrieved and read on the computer monitor, and printed or faxed. An indexing system is a computerized version of the master document index, allowing for retrieval information about the document so it can be quickly located in the files. Some indexing software provides brief descriptions of documents.

8. Assume that you need to retrieve some documents from a full-text system in the *Forrester* case. You need all the letters by Herbert Herbert that mention safety violations and Mr. Hart.

   a. How would you word the query if you wanted the letters that referred to both Hart and Herbert?

ANSWER: All letters with names Herbert "and" Hart "and" mentioning "safety violations".

   b. What would the query be if you wanted all letters that mentioned Hart and all letters that mentioned Herbert, and no letters that mentioned both?

ANSWER: All letters with Herbert "or" Hart.

9. What is the danger of requesting a copy of the report of the requested medical exam? What rule applies?

ANSWER: If the medical report is requested, the opponent can discover what may have been privileged information concerning other medical examination of the client. Therefore, consideration of what could be revealed is essential before requesting the report [Rule 35(b)(2)].

10. What is the role of the paralegal at a Rule 35 medical exam?

ANSWER: The paralegal can comfort the client and, subject to the bounds of the unauthorized practice of law, protect the client from overreaching and unfair, or even irrelevant, procedures. In addition, the paralegal can take note of any important information brought out by the exam. After the exam, the paralegal can draft a request for the report and review and summarize it.

11. Interpret or define the following medical notes or terms using the Mini-Guide to Interpreting Medical Records in Appendix D of the text.
    a. DIA: FX Mid 1/3 ® tibia

ANSWER: Diagnosis: fracture of right tibia (shinbone) located at middle one third.
    b. VS q 3h; CBC, lytes; 2 u in am

ANSWER: Vital signs every three hours; complete blood count, electrolytes (lab tests); two units in morning.

c. NPO; TLC; T 98[6]; P 82; R 18

ANSWER: Nothing by mouth; tender love and care; temperature 98.6, pulse 82, respiration 18.
    d. H_2O_2 qd

ANSWER: Hydrogen peroxide every day.
    e Anorexia: without appetite
       Gastroenteritis: inflammation in middle of stomach
       Epilepsy: violent attacks over entire body
       Encephalitis: inflammation of brain

12. Assume that you have been assigned to a very complex litigation case involving a series of construction contracts for a downtown mall, office, and residential center. You have never worked in this highly technical field. Explain in general terms how you would prepare a Mini-Guide to Construction Records to assist you in interpreting such records over the next three years of litigation.

ANSWER:
   a. Research several sources on the pertinent aspects of the construction business including any dictionaries for construction vernacular.
   b. See if guides are available from national or regional contractors or construction associations.
   c. Make a list or glossary of construction terms, acronyms, abbreviations, etc.
   d. Photocopy some sample blueprints and other representative documents for purposes of adding identifying information.
   e. Add to mini-guide as new terms and procedures are encountered.

13. In Case V from Chapter 1, assume that Carlos Montez has refused Ms. Rakowski's request to produce reports of previous incidents of harassment. He has objected on the grounds that this is irrelevant. Briefly stating that this may lead to relevant evidence, draft a motion to compel the answer.

ANSWER: The student's motion should appear similar to that in Exhibit 9:12 or any state example that you may have provided.

14. What remedies are available for overreaching discovery requests? What are the applicable federal rule and state equivalent? Note these in your system folder.

ANSWER: Federal Rule 26(c); State Rule _____.
Objection, then if other party persists, motion for protective order. Remedies are:
   a. Deny the requested discovery.
   b. Grant discovery on specific terms and conditions, including time and place.
   c. Grant discovery if another method is used.

d. Grant discovery, provided certain items are not inquired into, or if the scope of the inquiry is limited.

e. Grant discovery but only in the presence of certain individuals named by the court.

f. Grant discovery, provided the deposition is sealed and opened only by court order.

g. Deny or limit discovery of trade secrets.

h. Grant discovery only if parties file specified information or documents in sealed envelopes to be opened as directed by the court.

15. Using the small case filing method described in the text, specify under which of the four general categories and, if pertinent, in what order you would place the following:

a. a letter to Ms. Forrester dated December 2 of this year

b. the complaint

c. a motion to dismiss the complaint

d. a time-slip carbon copy for 3 hours of legal research

e. the client's background sheet

f. a memorandum on the admissibility of inflammatory photographs

g. client's medical bills

h. a letter to Ms. Forrester dated May of this year

i. note on fee paid to witness for deposition

j. a memo from you to Isadora Pearlman

k. a written statement by Ms. Schnabel

ANSWER:

FACTS	PLEADINGS	CORRESPONDENCE	BILLINGS
e.	b.	a.	d.
g.	c.	h. (reverse chronological order)	i
k.	f.	j.	

16. When organizing and working with complex case files, one component is almost indispensable for organization and retrieval. What is this component?

ANSWER: A thorough index arranged by major divisions and then subdivisions.

17. Work through the questions for study and review at the end of the chapter to reinforce your understanding.

CHAPTER 10

SETTLEMENT AND OTHER ALTERNATIVE DISPUTE RESOLUTIONS

CHAPTER OBJECTIVE

The purpose of this chapter is to familiarize the student with the settlement process, applicable federal and state rules of civil procedure, formulas and processes for calculating damages, and forms common to settlement. Arbitration and mediation are presented.

CLASS PREPARATION: INSTRUCTIONAL SUPPLEMENTS

1. You may choose to provide students with copies of forms used in your office to supplement the settlement forms, précis, checklist, damage calculation and worksheet, and other items covered in the chapter.
2. Any pertinent local rules and forms unique to the student's jurisdiction would be helpful.
3. Current life expectancy charts would be useful for distribution in class.
4. Pertinent Web sites.

SUGGESTED CLASS ACTIVITIES

1. Preparation and use of a short video recreating a typical settlement conference or pretrial conference would provide a good point of reference for the paralegal student.
2. Having the students work through a specific problem, perhaps the *Forrester* case, using the damage calculations and summary worksheet would give them more confidence when asked to do this on the job.
3. Invite a guest paralegal to discuss damage calculation specifically and settlement in general from the paralegal's perspective.
4. Use application assignments in this chapter as the basis for class discussions. Application Assignments 3 and 4 could serve as take-home exam exercises.

OUTLINE

I. Introduction
II. Settlement
  A. Introduction
    Key term: settlement
    1. Definition and Purpose
      Application Assignment 1
    2. Role of the Paralegal
    3. Ethical Considerations
      System Folder Assignment 1
  B. Preparing for Settlement
    1. Introduction
    2. Early Investigation and Collection of Information
      a. Introduction
      b. Party's Social or Business Background
      c. Party's Medical Condition
        Application Assignment 2
      d. Party's Commercial Condition
      e. Special Areas of Investigation
        System Folder Assignment 2
    3. Communicate with Client and Insurance Adjuster
    4. Calculating Damages
      Exhibit 10:1, Damage Summary and Worksheet
      System Folder Assignment 3
      Internet Exercises 1 and 2
  C. Presenting the Settlement Request
    1. Introduction
      Key term: settlement précis
    2. Settlement Précis or Letter
      Exhibit 10:2, Settlement Précis—Illustration
      Application Assignment 3
    3. Settlement Brochure (Demand Package)
      Exhibit 10:3, Settlement Brochure
      Application Assignment 4

4. Video: "Day in the Life"
5. Calendaring
D. Role of the Defendant's or Insurance Company's Paralegal
E. Preparing for the Pretrial Conference
   Exhibit 10:4, Power to Settle Personal Injury Claims
   System Folder Assignment 4
F. Settlement Conference
III. Settlement Forms
A. Releases and Settlement Agreements
   Key terms: release, settlement agreement
   Exhibit 10:5, Release and Settlement of Suit for Personal Injuries
   Exhibit 10:6, Mutual Release of All Claims and Demands
   Exhibit 10:7, Covenant Not to Sue (with Reservation of Rights as to Others
   Exhibit 10:8, Settlement Agreement
B. Stipulation and Order for Dismissal
   Key terms: without prejudice, with prejudice, adjudication on the merits
   Exhibit 10:9, Stipulation and Order for Dismissal
C. Consent Decree and Order
   Exhibit 10:10, Stipulation and Consent Decree and Order
D. Settlement Distribution Statement
   Exhibit 10:11, Settlement Distribution Statement
   System Folder Assignment 5
IV. Other Alternative Dispute Resolutions: Arbitration, Mediation, and Summary Trials
A. Introduction
B. Arbitration
   Key term: arbitration
C. Mediation
   Key terms: mediation, med-arb
D. Early Case Assessment
E. Summary Jury Trial
   Key term: summary trial
F. Role of the Paralegal in Alternative Dispute Resolution
   Application Assignment 5
   Internet Exercise 3
V. Summary

SYSTEM FOLDER ASSIGNMENTS
Assignment 1

In the ethics section of your system folder, add or make page references to ethical considerations for the settlement process, the cited sections of the Model Rules of Professional Conduct, and the rules or ethical standards in your state.

ANSWER:
Model Rule 1.2: A lawyer must abide by client's decision whether to accept settlement. A paralegal may not make settlement offers, accept offers, or counsel client on settlement.
Do not reveal harmful or confidential information
Model Rule 1.4(a and b): Keep the client informed of negotiation and proposals.

Assignment 2

Draft a checklist of or enter text page references to the items that need to be researched and summarized in preparation for settlement. Indicate the sources for such information. Place the checklist in the settlement section of your system folder.

ANSWER: Preparation for Settlement

Research and Summarize	Source
I. Party's social or business background	
A. family	party
B. education	
C. character	employer/neighbors
D. occupation	party
E. income	
F. benefits	
G. advancement potential	employer
H. lifestyle	party/neighbors
I. activities and interests before and after	party
J. comparative wealth of parties	
K. effectiveness of witnesses	witnesses
L. commercial plaintiff	
1. age	party
2. income	
3. reputation	commercial community
4. status before and after	
II. Party's medical condition	
A. age, race, sex, personality	party
B. prior injuries and implications	medical reports
C. detailed injuries from accident	
D. diagnosis	
E. post-accident impediments	
F. willingness to admit disability	party
G. causal relationship between wrong and injury	party/witnesses
H. treatment required	medical reports
I. stages of healing	

J. hideous nature of injury
K. temporary disability
L. permanent disability
M. disfigurement
N. psychological and emotional injury
O. prognosis
P. need for future care
Q. pain and suffering
    1. time of accident
    2. during treatment
    3. permanent

R. change in life expectancy	actuarial tables
S. occupational implications	med. reports/ employer party
T. effect on hobbies, interests, home life	party
U. medical bills, travel, prostheses	medical reports
V. future medical expenses	

III. Party's commercial condition

A. value of land and other property before and after injury	business community
B. replacement value of property	
C. income before and after injury	party
D. loss of markets	party/expert witness
E. loss of customers	
F. loss of opportunity	
G. loss of profits	
H. past, present, future losses	
I. loss of rents	
J. loss of business reputation	
K. loss of entire business	
L. cost of delay caused by injury	
M. cost of finding alternative services or property	
N. attempts to mitigate damages	
O. relationship of wrong to injury	party/ witnesses

IV. Special areas of investigation

A. verdicts/awards	clerk of court attorneys in *ATLA Law Reporter* damages in *West's Digests* verdicts and settlements in *American Law Report*
B. expert witnesses	colleagues/ attorneys

1. reputation
2. background
3. intelligence
4. courtroom abilities

C. trial judge's attitude and decisions	attorneys/ paralegals
D. opponent's lawyer	attorneys/ clerk of court
E. track record of insurance comp.	economists/ library
F. future expenses/life expectancy statistics	
G. cost of litigation	attorneys

Assignment 3

Place a copy of or page reference to the Damage Summary and Worksheet (Exhibit 10:1) in your system folder.

Assignment 4

Place a page reference or copies of the pretrial conference preparation checklist and the attorney's authorization from the client to settle in your system folder.
Assignment 5
    Add page references or copies of each of the settlement forms and the outline of the pretrial memorandum to your system folder. If time permits, draft each form at least once and adapt it to the *Forrester* case.

ANSWER: You may choose to have students draft one or more documents for *Forrester* or another case. The Covenant Not to Sue and the Settlement Agreement are the most time consuming.

APPLICATION ASSIGNMENTS

Assignment 1

What factors either favoring or discouraging settlement do you see present in the *Forrester* case? Discuss.

ANSWER:
Factors in *Forrester* case for settlement:

- ability of defendant to pay (Mercury Parcel)
- Mercury Parcel evokes no sympathy from jury, whereas Mr. Hart may
- nature of injury
- sympathy for plaintiff
- good witness

Against settlement
- possible comparative negligence of Ms. Forrester
- ice left Mr. Hart with little he could do
- Hart is an effective witness

Assignment 2

Why would any of the matters characterized at the end of the Party's Medical Condition section as the "three strikes" work against the plaintiff? How might you overcome each of the strikes?

ANSWER: The presence of any or all three of these make it hard for a jury to believe that the injury was very serious or that it caused much pain and suffering. On the other hand, the existence on one or more of the strikes may be easily explained away. For example, the injured party may have had several bad experiences with previous doctors; may have had to go to work (even with great pain) or leave the family temporarily destitute; or may have had the belief that home remedies would complicate the serious medical condition.

Assignment 3

Using your imagination to provide missing facts, draft a settlement précis or settlement letter for the *Forrester* case. Critique these in small groups with your fellow students. Place the settlement précis or letter in your system folder. Keep in mind hat a well-drafted *Forrester* précis or settlement letter as part of a well-drafted system folder can be impressive when offered as a writing sample to a future employer.

ANSWER: Points for Evaluating the Précis
  a. The following sections should be included:
     (1) social history
     (2) medical history
     (3) facts of accident
     (4) theories of recovery
     (5) medical
     (6) employment
     (7) expenses
     (8) analysis of evaluation
  b. Medical history should clearly state that the client has been a healthy, physically active and vital person.
  c. Accurate facts; emphasis on facts that lead to an obvious conclusion that the defendant is liable. For example, in the *Forrester* case the facts should emphasize that the van veered left at braking. (This is followed under theory with reference to Mr. Hart's deposition testimony verifying this). Also, that Mr. Hart was looking at the speedometer just prior to the accident and not watching the road. (Followed in section on theory by reference to Mr. Hart's deposition testimony to this effect).
  d. Clear statement of the theory of liability and a brief summary of the strongest evidence in support of the theory. References to Hart's deposition testimony would be good to include.

  e. Medical section should show accurate but sharp and pathetic contrast to medical condition prior to accident. A few gory details with supporting evidence (photos, for example) should be mentioned in this section. Things that will get jury sympathy should be emphasized. For example, graphic description of bone sticking through flesh or the constant embarrassment caused by lack of bladder control.
  f. Total of all medical expenses should be stated with some breakdown as to type of expense.
  g. Loss of income and impairment of future earning capacity should be stressed and totals indicated.
  h. Analysis should reemphasize key points and bring together all totals plus an assessment of what the jury will do and the projected award; then provide a stated figure for immediate settlement.
  i. Wording should be evaluated for both accuracy and persuasiveness.

Assignment 4

Draft an outline of the contents of a settlement brochure for the *Forrester* case indicating what should appear and in what order. Compare your list of components and discuss the advantages of each in small groups with class members. Make a list of the typical components of a settlement brochure and place it in your system folder.

In the alternative, individual class members can accept responsibility for roughly equal parts of a *Forrester* settlement brochure. When finished, the students assigned to one part can meet, compare their individual work, and compile a model section. Eventually the various model sections can be photocopied and shared to arrive at the best complete brochure.

ANSWER: This assignment presents several different ways to approach the settlement brochure, requiring different investments of time. Choose the one approach that best suits your class situation. Doing all would be repetitive and too time consuming. The finished products should contain the following sections:
  a. The facts of the case as supported by the evidence.
  b. The personal history of the plaintiff.
  c. The prior medical history of the plaintiff.
  d. The injury and its present and long-term effects.
  e. The economic and related psychological impact of the injury.
  f. Damages.
  g. Evaluation of the claim.

Assignment 5

By researching your state statutes and local federal rules, determine whether your state has a provision for arbitration or mediation. If so, determine what types of cases and dispute amounts are considered for the program. If there your state has no such system, write a proposal to your local newspaper on why you believe there should or shouldn't be such a system. Discuss and defend your proposals in class.

ANSWER: Response depends on state practice and student opinion. If students will be writing a letter to the editor, emphasize that the letter should be sincere. Students might vote on the best letter on each side of the issue and, with permission of the authors, actually submit them to a local or campus newspaper for publication.

INTERNET EXERCISES

1. Go to MoreLaw.com. What is the current highest damage award of the month? Was it achieved through settlement or trial?

ANSWER: Current information.

2. Go to JuryVerdicts.com. What is the jury verdict publisher for your state or the nearest state where a publisher is available? What information does the publisher offer?

ANSWER: Information varies by state.

3. In the American Arbitration Association site, find the ADR guide for resolving employment disputes. What are the two acts of Congress that reaffirm the role of ADR in cases of employment discrimination?

ANSWER: The Americans with Disabilities Act of 1990 and Section 118 of the Civil Rights Act of 1991.

ADDITIONAL EXERCISES

1. Assume that the Congdens, the campground owners in Case II, are told by you that their attorney, your supervisor, advises them to agree to settle their case by paying Mr. Ameche $60,000. The Congdens say no and want to go to trial. Your attorney believes that the jury will hold the Congdens liable for $150,000.
   a. Considering that lawyers are supposed to exercise their independent judgment, may the attorney ethically accept the offer, since it is such a good one?

ANSWER: Model Rule 1.2. No, a lawyer must abide by the client's decision on whether to settle. Also see Rule 1.4 (a and b), obligation to keep client informed of negotiations.
   b. Are there any other ethical concerns raised in this scenario?

ANSWER: Yes, the paralegal may not counsel the client on whether to accept an offer. However, if the paralegal serves only as a conduit for attorney's advice, there is probably no unauthorized practice of law.

2. What is the importance of gearing timetables and preparation to the settlement process? The advantages?

ANSWER: So many cases are settled that the attorney-paralegal team needs to be prepared to make offers, counter-offers, and settle at the most opportune moment. The advantage to being prepared for settlement is not only that the settlement might be more favorable to the client than if not prepared, but also because much of settlement preparation will be applicable to trial preparation.

3. What are LOELs and why would a plaintiff want these separated from damages for pain and suffering? Do you think people ought to receive such damages? What is the problem with such damages?

ANSWER: Loss of enjoyment of life or "hedonic" damages, if separated, can be better emphasized than if included under pain and suffering. This creates the potential for larger injury awards. Student opinion is subjective. The problem with LOELs is how to place a dollar amount on such losses.

4. Which of the following are special damages and which are general?
   a. hospital bill
   b. wages lost
   c. LOELs
   d. horror of injury
   e. loss of stimulation of job
   f. lost household services
   g. pain
   h. loss of status

ANSWER:
Special damages: a, b, f
General damages: c, d, e, g, and h

5. Calculate the damage amounts in the following fact situations (show calculations on workbook page): Darlene Rakowski's damages based on $500 of embarrassment per day for 100 days; $250 of anxiety per day over losing job for 20 days; lost wages for days caused to miss work at $85 per day for 20 days; psychiatric counseling at $100 per session, 1 session per week for 8 weeks; future psychiatric sessions, 10 per year for the next five years with reduction to present cash value of 5 percent. Assume medical costs will go up 8 percent per year.

ANSWER: Special Damages: TOTAL $8,076
Past medical (psychological counseling):
$$100 \times 8 = \$800$$
Lost wages: 85×20 days $= \$1,700$
Future medical (factor in 8% increase per year)
100×10 days/year $\times 1$ year $= \$1,000$
108×10 days/year $\times 1$ year $= \$1,080$
$117^* \times 10$ days/year $\times 1$ year $= \$1,170$
126×10 days/year $\times 1$ year $= \$1,260$
136×10 days/year $\times 1$ year $= \underline{\$1,360}$
gross future medical expenses $5,870
less 5% reduction to present cash value = $5,576
total special $8,076
*figures rounded
General Damages: TOTAL $55,000
$500 FOR 100 Days = $50,000
$250 for 20 days = $5,000
total general $55,000

6. What should be included in the cover letter that goes to the opponent with the settlement brochure?

ANSWER: A date when the offer will be withdrawn and a date for the return of the brochure; a statement that the brochure is the property of plaintiff's counsel and that its use is restricted, and that an acknowledgment of receipt of the brochure and an agreement to abide by its restrictions should be returned.

7. If you work for the defendant and the plaintiff sends summarized medical reports and witness statements rather than originals, what should you do?

ANSWER: Obtain the originals; use discovery if needed. Use of summaries may indicate that there are weaknesses in the documents that have been summarized.

8. Describe the expanded purposes of Rule 16 of the Federal Rules of Civil Procedure. Does your state rule on settlement contain these broad purposes?

ANSWER: The main purposes of Rule 16 are to narrow the issues for trial, encourage settlement of the case, and in more complex cases to facilitate the overall planning and management of the case from the viewpoint of the court and the parties. State the rule.

9. What is a pretrial statement (memorandum) and what is one of its advantages?

ANSWER: An overall summary of items either agreed to at pretrial conference or to be agreed to at the conference, depending on local practice. If prepared jointly, it may facilitate settlement.

10. Research to determine if your state requires consideration to validate a release and to see if a covenant not to sue is required.

ANSWER: Response depends on local practice.

11. Using the Settlement Agreement form provided in Exhibit 10:8 of the text or your state's form and information on the *Forrester* case or other case as assigned by your instructor, draft a settlement agreement that reflects a fair settlement in the case.

ANSWER: This assignment will not only give students drafting experience regarding settlement forms, but it will raise their awareness of all the major factors that make up a final settlement. It is probably best to use a local practice form for this assignment. Check to see if the students have included amount, time, and terms of payment; nature and extent of releases that will be executed and delivered; when and how the action will be dismissed; how court costs and legal fees will be handled; whether goods or documents will be exchanged or discharged; what collateral, if any, will be used to insure the agreement; and any other pertinent items.

12. What are the primary reasons for the greater use of alternative dispute resolution?

ANSWER:
a. Keeps cases out of court, reducing loads and the time to resolve cases.
b. More informal procedure, therefore costs less.
c. Stresses reconciliation and common ground rather than adversarial confrontation.

13. After reading the Bruno arbitration case, what are your impressions bout the outcome of this case?

ANSWER: Subjective, but it would be good if the student recognized that unlike most trials, this was not an all-or-nothing decision. A sensible middle ground was reached and for far less money than if the case had gone to trial.

14. Assume that Teeny Tiny Manufacturing and Briar Patch Dolls agree to arbitrate or mediate their dispute. To whom might they turn for assistance? How can this assistance be located?

ANSWER: The American Arbitration Association, The Federal Mediation and Conciliation service, The National Academy of Arbitrators and others. Their addresses can be found on-line or in library reference rooms.

15. Work through the questions for study and review at the end of the chapter to reinforce your understanding.

CHAPTER 10 TAKE HOME TEST

Application Assignment 3 or 4.

CHAPTER 11

TRIAL PREPARATION AND TRIAL

CHAPTER OBJECTIVE

This chapter helps the student become effective in working with witnesses and investigating jurors, as well as preparing and organizing the paperwork necessary to assist the attorney at trial. Students will also learn the role of a paralegal at trial.

PREPARING FOR CLASS: INSTRUCTIONAL SUPPLEMENTS

1. Add steps and time references to the pretrial preparation checklist according to your preferences.
2. You will need your local rules and procedures on how to subpoena witnesses.
3. Your preferences for organization of a trial notebook would be helpful.
4. Your preferences on preparing witness for trial would be a valuable addition.
5. Find local rules and procedures on the voir dire process.
6. Your own experience can add to the discussion on how a paralegal can assist at trial.
7. A videotape of the voir dire process would be helpful.
8. Share with the class a list of jury instruction sources for your jurisdiction.
9. Pertinent Web sites.

SUGGESTED CLASS ACTIVITIES

1. Acquire a list of the current or upcoming jurors for the local court term, including the juror background sheets. Divide the class into plaintiff and defendant groups and have each group investigate the jurors and reach conclusions as to their pro-plaintiff or pro-defendant leanings. Use the facts in the *Forrester* case or a real case to come before the jury. If the class is preparing for a mock trial, have prospective jurors fill out juror background sheets so they can be investigated.

2. Arrange with a local court to attend a voir dire process. Prepare the class on issues and have students observe and reach conclusions about jurors. You might also ask them to record who is chosen on a jury panel chart.
3. Have an experienced trial attorney or attorney-paralegal team discuss techniques for choosing jurors and how a paralegal can assist in the process.
4. Have an experienced paralegal discuss the preparation of a trial notebook.
5. Have the students prepare a diagram of the *Forrester* accident scene to be used at trial by Ms. Forrester or other witnesses (see Application Assignment 2).
6. If your school has an instructional media department or you are located near a business that prepares audiovisual aids, visit the office and let the students see what audiovisual aids are available and how they are made.
7. Use Application Assignments 2 and 3 for class discussions.

OUTLINE

I. Trial Preparation
   A. Introduction and Trial Preparation Checklist
      Exhibit 11:1, Trial Preparation Checklist
      System Folder Assignment 1
      Internet Exercise 1
   B. Preliminary Trial Preparation Tasks
      Exhibit 11:2, Case Status Sheet
   C. Subpoena Witnesses
      System Folder Assignment 2
   D. Jury Investigation
      1. Introduction
         Exhibit 11:3, Juror Data Sheet
         System Folder Assignment 3
         Application Assignment 1
      2. Sources for Juror Information
         System Folder Assignment 4

3. Ancillary Investigation
E. Preparing Demonstrative Evidence
  1. Introduction
    Exhibit 11:4, Demonstrative Evidence
  2. Evidentiary Concerns
  3. Technology
  4. ABA Standards
    System Folder Assignments 5 and 6
    Application Assignment 2
F. Trial Notebook
  1. Introduction
    Exhibit 11:5, Outline of Trial Notebook
    System Folder Assignment 7
  2. Legal Research
  3. Motions
    Key term: in limine
    Exhibit 11:6, Motion for Mistrial
    Exhibit 11:7, Motion for Directed Verdict
    Exhibit 11:8, Motion in Limine
    System Folder Assignment 8
  4. Voir Dire Questions
  5. Jury Instructions
    Exhibit 11:9, Jury Instructions
    Application Assignment 3
  6. Witness Questions
  7. Juror Notebooks
  8. Noting Special Details
G. Preparing the Client and Witness for Testifying at Trial
  1. Task
    Exhibit 11:10, Guidelines for a Witness's Trial Testimony
    System Folder Assignments 9 and 10
  2. An Ethics Reminder
H. Additional Preparation
II. Assistance at Trial
A. Introduction
  Key term: prima facie case
  Exhibit 11:11, Stages in Trial Procedure
B. Jury Selection
  Key terms: voir dire, challenge for cause, peremptory challenge
  Internet Exercise 2
C. Shadow Jury
D. Witness Control
E. Documents and Exhibits
F. Exhibit and Witness Logs
G. Trial Notes
H. Trial Day Review Meetings
I. When the Paralegal Must Testify
J. Polling the Jury
K. Findings of Fact and Conclusions of Law
  Key term: findings of fact and conclusions of law

    Exhibit 11:12, Findings of Fact and Conclusions of Law
    System Folder Assignment 11
III. Summary

SYSTEM FOLDER ASSIGNMENTS

Assignment 1

Expand the trial preparation checklist in the text in any way recommended by your instructor and file it at the beginning of the pretrial preparation section of your system folder.

Assignment 2

Place a list of or page reference to the steps in obtaining and serving subpoenas in your system folder. Having the list in both the deposition and trial preparations sections will prove useful.

Assignment 3

Place the juror data sheet or page reference to it in your system folder.

Assignment 4

Reference the various sources and methods for conducting jury investigations in your system folder.

Assignment 5

Locate the applicable local, state, and federal rules of evidence on demonstrative evidence. Place these in your system folder.

ANSWER: The general practice in federal and most state courts is that maps, charts, diagrams and most other demonstrative evidence, if helpful to the fact-finder, may be used. They are subject to the limits of Rule 403 regarding prejudice and other reasons.

Rules that apply are: 401 relevancy, 403 and 901(a) authentication, 1002 best evidence (original document) rule, and 1006 summaries of large amounts of data. please add your state rules to this list.

Assignment 6

Use the Internet or page through legal periodicals such as bar journals, *Legal Assistant Today, The National Law Journal*, and others and develop a brief bibliography or source list of companies that prepare, sell, or rent audio-visual aids. Seek information on vendors that provide such services in your area. Add this information to your system folder.

ANSWER: It would be good to require material from at least three different sources.

Assignment 7

Place a copy of or page reference to the Outline of Trial Notebook in your system folder.

ANSWER: If time permits, you may want to have students organize at least a simulated trial notebook for *Forrester* or another case. Individual sections represented by a single sample sheet could be set up.

Assignment 8

Add copies of or references to the trial and in limine motions to both the trial and motions sections of your system folder.

Assignment 9

Draft a checklist for preparing clients and other witnesses for testifying at trial. Include a special section on preparing expert witnesses. Place the checklist in your system folder.

ANSWER: Checklist for Preparing the Client and Witness for Testifying at Trial

I. Communicate frequently.
   A. Inform on trial and office appointment dates.
   B. Inform about items to bring to trial.
   C. Review deposition.
II. Familiarize witness with courtroom surroundings and procedures.
   A. witness box
   B. communication with jury
   C. jury box
III. Observe witness during preparation with attorney.
   A. Note idiosyncrasies, inconsistencies, impressions.
   B. Carefully critique and encourage witness.
IV. Videotape mock testimony.
V. Locate and enlist expert witness.
   A. Gather data on qualifications.
   B. Provide facts, theories, etc. of the case to inform expert.
   C. Note suggestions from expert on helpful materials needed.
   D. Prepare expert for courtroom.
      1. Familiarize expert with courtroom.
      2. Guide against defensiveness.
      3. Guide against condescension.
      4. Guide against jargon.
VI. Inform all witnesses.
   A. time changes
   B. locations
   C. testimony of other witnesses
   D. theory of the case

Assignment 10

Place a copy of or page reference to the Guidelines for a Witness's Trial Testimony in your system folder.

Assignment 11

Place a copy of or page reference to the form for drafting findings of fact and conclusions of law in your system folder.

APPLICATION ASSIGNMENTS

Assignment 1

What special information might you want to know about jurors for the *Forrester* case? Case II?

ANSWER: This assignment should encourage students to think bout what information might specifically allow them to make an educated guess about whether a juror will be pro-client or pro-defendant. In addition to the general information sought in the juror Data Sheet, some specific ideas that the students might list include the following:

Juror Information
Case I, *Forrester* Case

Pro Forrester
   Mothers working outside the home
   Teachers
   Persons with family, close friends, or relatives having similar disabling injuries and who might be aware of tremendous costs of care and outside help.
   Married men whose wives are teachers, professionals.
   Professional persons in general
   Democrats—less likely to favor big business
   Persons with excellent driving records

Pro Mercury Parcel and Hart
   Business managers, supervisors, especially of delivery businesses
   Republicans—tend to favor big business
   Taxi, bus, and other drivers likely to be empathetic with Hart
   Blue collar family members
   Persons with not-so-good driving records
   Mechanics and factory workers
   Macho, chauvinist male types who may generalize that Forrester was a careless female
   Insurance people who believe damage awards are too high and litigation too frequent

Case II, *Ameche* Case

Pro Ameche
   Young parents
   Campers
   Firefighters, especially if they have had to rescue others

Burn victims or those having friends or relatives who are burn victims

Very orderly business owners or managers with excellent safety records

Business persons who have a history of correcting problems immediately

Macho, risk-taking types

Pro Congdens

Middle aged to older operators of business

Electricians, power company workers, etc., if experts advise that extension cord was not likely cause of fire

Older persons without children, likely to believe that child was not adequately supervised and was the cause of the accident

Insurance company employees

Persons working in fire extinguisher sales or business who might conclude that Ameches should have carried a fire extinguisher

Cautious, not-so-macho types

Assignment 2

What audiovisual aids would be useful in the *Forrester* case for the plaintiff? For the defendant? Using the information that you have gathered on the scene of the accident in the *Forrester* case, prepare a courtroom diagram of the accident scene.

ANSWER: You may choose to assign other kinds of demonstrative evidence, especially if the diagram has been done earlier. The class could be divided to make different kinds of demonstrative evidence for both sides of the mock trial.

Audiovisual aids for Forrester

Video: "day in the life"

Diagram of accident

Chart of potential income lost

Audiovisual aids for defendant

Photograph or video showing low visibility at scene

Photograph showing damage to van

Assignment 3

Research form books for jury instructions in your jurisdiction. Place a list of the major sources in your system folder. Then make a list of instructions that you believe will be needed in the *Forrester* case. Compare your list to those made by others in your class.

ANSWER: You may want to research standard jury instructions from your jurisdiction. Instructions likely to be used in the *Forrester* case, or any negligence case, may include the following:

Negligence

Ordinary care

Proximate cause

Comparative fault and apportionment of responsibility

Pedestrians/crossing highway

Brake failure

Defective inspection or repair

Excessive speed

Sleepy driver

Employer liable for tort of employee/scope of employment

Personal injury

Pain and suffering

Medical expenses

Loss of time

Future lost earnings

Loss of consortium

Injury to personal property/reduction in value of goods/loss of use

Loss of employment

Last clear chance

Burden of proof

INTERNET EXERCISES

1. Go to the site for the ABA Civil Trial Practice Standards. With permission from your instructor, download copies of the standards. Note those that apply to pretrial preparation and use of technology and place these in your system folder.

ANSWER: Copy of standards.

2. Go to the ABA Civil Trial Practice Standards. Are there any standards that encourage the use of note-taking by jurors or questioning of witnesses by jurors?

ANSWER: The standards encourage juror notetaking and questions with restrictions.

3. Go to the sites for the National Jury Project and the Jury Research Institute. Compare services offered and note the nature of any articles available.

ANSWER: Current Web site information.

ADDITIONAL EXERCISES

1. What is a case status sheet and how is it helpful in trial preparation?

ANSWER: It is a checklist of tasks, documents, due dates, and other matters that form the steps leading up to trial. it should be started very early in the case so that everyone working on it will understand what has been done and what remains to be done. It is valuable in preventing important steps from being overlooked or delayed.

2. How can you help prepare for objections or arguments that might arise at trial?

ANSWER: Draft motions, then research and draft memoranda of law to support them, because there will be little time for this during trial.

3. What are the pros and cons of subpoenaing witnesses from each side?

ANSWER: Unfriendly witnesses should be subpoenaed to ensure their presence at trial. Friendly witnesses may be insulted, but a subpoena may be advisable if explained. neutral witnesses may appreciate a subpoena to maintain the appearance of neutrality.

4. What is the purpose of jury investigation?

ANSWER: To find information on the juror's likely response to the issues in the case so that those likely to be unsympathetic with your client will be eliminated from the panel and those likely to favor your client will be included.

5. Which three of the jury investigation methods would you like to participate in and why? Show your understanding of the method and its advantages in your answer.

ANSWER: Responses will vary, but should display an understanding of the process and effect of the method on jury selection.

6. Make a list of types of demonstrative evidence and their advantages.

ANSWER: Demonstrative Evidence
   Diagrams: Inexpensive, versatile, simple to make or find.
   Charts and graphs: Inexpensive, easily made, make complex data understandable.
   Animation: Expensive if done professionally, good for sequence of events and from variety of viewpoints, shows obstructed views.
   Models: Expensive, require professional skill to make, good for depicting parts of the body, buildings, equipment, and so on. Computerized models are expensive but effective, can be manipulated.
   Photographs: Inexpensive, dramatic, can be digitized and easily projected.
   Slides: Inexpensive, vivid, good for detail and sequence.
   Film: Expensive, outmoded, requires expertise, good quality.
   Videotape: Inexpensive, easy to make, can be magnified, good for "day in the life;" can be digitized for precise editing and for showing brief clips.

Overhead transparencies: Easily made, effective.

7. Describe research and writing tasks that a paralegal can do in preparing the trial notebook.

ANSWER:
   Research for the trial brief section: Research evidence and draft elements, jury instructions, memoranda.
   Motions: Draft standard motions and orders in general to be filled in as needed.
   Voir dire: Research questions and supporting legal authority.
   Jury instructions: Research instructions favorable to the client's position that have been upheld, draft standard instructions, draft special instructions supported by legal authority.
   Noting special details: Use your familiarity with the case to find details to help sway a jury.

8. In a role-playing situation, familiarize a classmate/witness with a mock courtroom and offer guidance for trial testimony. Discuss clothing, demeanor, techniques, and ethics for answering questions.

ANSWER: Students from an Introduction to Law class could serve as unprepared witnesses. This assignment could be part of the preparation for the mock trial. Otherwise, you could assign specific cases and viewpoints to the witnesses to help make the guidance more pointed. Directions should conform to the Guidelines for a Witness's Trial Testimony in the text.

9. What miscellaneous tasks can a paralegal do to help things go smoothly for the legal team outside the courtroom during trial?

ANSWER: Outside Preparation for Trial
   Make hotel reservations for the trial team.
   Arrange transportation to the trial site.
   Arrange and pay for parking.
   Arrange and pay for meals.
   Collect receipts for expenses.
   Arrange and have cash ready for emergency copying, phone calls, and so on.
   Deliver trial materials, diagrams, files, and so on, to court.

10. Briefly, what are the stages in trial procedure (Exhibit 11:11)

ANSWER:
- Jury selection
- Opening statements
- Plaintiff's case in chief
- Defendant's motion for dismissal or directed verdict
- Defendant's case in chief
- Plaintiff's rebuttal

- Defendant's rejoinder
- Motions for directed verdict or judgment as a matter of law
- Conference on jury instructions
- Closing arguments
- Charge to jury
- Jury decides case
- Motion for judgment notwithstanding the verdict
- Motion for new trial
- Entry of judgment

11. Compare and contrast a trial and an arbitration hearing.

ANSWER: Both have a fact finder, opening arguments, witness testimony, cross examination, and the presentation of evidence.

The primary differences are that arbitration is far briefer in each of these stages, uses more relaxed rules of procedure and evidence, and there is no jury. The burden of proof in arbitration is generally not as stringent.

12. Prepare a list of paralegal tasks to assist the attorney at trial.

ANSWER: Assisting at Trial

I. Jury Selection
   A. Chart voir dire responses.
   B. Note observations and previously researched facts.
   C. Keep track of voir dire questions.
   D. Chart final jury.

II. Witness Control
   A. Locate and subpoena if necessary.
   B. Notify of when to appear.
   C. Meet with and reassure witnesses.
   D. Arrange witness payment, lodging, transportation.

III. Custodian of Documents and Exhibits
   A. Prepare all items needed each day.
   B. Store all items securely.
   C. Maintain list of who has what, and where.

IV. Exhibit and Witness Logs
   A. Keep track of all exhibits of both sides.
      1. as presented
      2. objected to
      3. accepted
   B. Keep track of all witnesses and testimony.
      1. those called
      2. whether testimony deviates from expectations
      3. follow question outlines to make sure attorney hasn't forgotten anything

V. Trial Notes
   A. Use pre-numbered notebook.
      1. summary/outline on left
      2. details on right
   B. Attorney specifies areas to note.
      1. staff
      2. parties and attorneys
      3. witnesses
      4. exhibits
      5. objections and rulings
      6. times
         a. recesses
         b. conferences at bench
         c. conferences in chambers
         d. resumption of trial

VI. Trial Day Review Meetings
   A. Compare notes.
   B. Offer suggestions.
   C. Put motions into final form.

VII. Paralegal Testimony
   A. Be prepared by attorney.
   B. Put aside advocacy, maintain professionalism and truth.

VIII. Notes During Polling of the Jury

13. What two paralegal tasks during trial seem most important to you? Why?

ANSWER: Responses are subjective, but should show an understanding of the tasks.

14. Work through the questions for study and review at the end of the chapter to reinforce your understanding.

CHAPTER 12

POST-TRIAL PRACTICE FROM MOTIONS TO APPEAL

CHAPTER OBJECTIVE

This chapter provides the necessary background and skills for the paralegal to effectively assist in preparing post trial motions, enforcing judgments, and appealing cases.

PREPARING FOR CLASS: INSTRUCTIONAL SUPPLEMENTS

1. You will need examples of post-trial motions for your state.
2. A description of how to enforce a judgment in your state with examples of the necessary state forms would be helpful.
3. Your state rules on appellate procedure are important for the students to have.
4. You may want to provide an example of an appellate brief prepared for your state's appellate court.
5. Pertinent Web sites.

SUGGEST CLASS ACTIVITIES

1. Have a paralegal experienced in collections lecture on enforcing judgments.
2. Have a clerk of the appellate court discuss appellate procedures and requirements and address the most common errors to avoid.
3. Have each student turn in their litigation system folder for review and grading.

OUTLINE

I. Introduction
II. Post-Trial Motions
   Key terms: remittitur, additur
   Exhibit 12:1, Renewal of Motion for Judgment as a Matter of Law (State: Motion for Judgment Notwithstanding the Verdict
   Exhibit 12:2(a), Motion for New Trial in Nonjury Case
   Exhibit 12:2(b), Motion for New Trial in Jury Case
   System Folder Assignment 1
III. Judgment and Bill of Costs
   Exhibit 12:3, Bill of Costs
   System Folder Assignment 2
IV. Enforcement of the Judgment
   A. Introduction
      Key terms: judgment creditor, judgment debtor, lis pendens
      Exhibit 12:4, Notice of Lis Pendens
   B. Locating the Assets of the Judgment Debtor
      Key terms: judgment proof, postjudgment interrogatory, post-trial request for production of documents, post-trial deposition, supplementary proceedings
      Exhibit 12:5, Informal Investigative Techniques to Discover the Assets of the Judgment Debtor
      Exhibit 12:6, Written Interrogatories to Judgment Debtor
   C. Obtaining the Assets of the Judgment Debtor
      1. Introduction
         Key term: supersedeas bond
         Exhibit 12:7, First Letter to Judgment Debtor
         Exhibit 12:8, Follow-Up Letter to Judgment Debtor
      2. Execution
         Key terms: execution, levy, receivership
         Exhibit 12:9, Writ of Execution for Specific Property (or its Value)
         System Folder Assignment 4
         Application Assignment 1
      3. Garnishment
         Key terms: garnishment, garnishee
         Exhibit 12:10, Application and Affidavit for Writ of Garnishment after Judgment
         Exhibit 12:11, Writ of Garnishment
         System Folder Assignment 5
      4. Domesticating a Judgment
         Key term: exemplified
         System Folder Assignment 6

5. Keeping Track of Collections of Judgment
System Folder Assignment 7
Application Assignment 2

V. Appeal
A. Introduction
Key terms: question of law, question of fact, harmless error
B. Appellate Procedure Checklist
Exhibit 12:12, Notice of Appeal
Exhibit 12:13, Designation of Record on Appeal
Exhibit 12:14, Motion for Enlargement of Time—Court of Appeals
Exhibit 12:15, Appellate Brief—Notice of Filing
System Folder Assignment 8
Application Assignment 3
Internet Exercises 1 and 2
C. Assisting in the Appeal
1. Introduction
2. Deadline Control and Appeal Management
3. Research
4. Verifying the Record
5. Assisting with the Appellate Brief
Exhibit 12:16, Sample Appellate Brief
System Folder Assignment 9
6. Oral Argument
VI. Summary
System Folder Assignment 10

SYSTEM FOLDER ASSIGNMENTS

Assignment 1

Enter the ten-day time limit for filing post-trial motions in the Motions, Pleadings, and Time Limits exhibit in Chapter 6. Place copies of or page references to the motions in your system folder, both in a post-trial motion section and in your motion practice section. Indicate what federal and state rules govern the motions.

ANSWER: Motion for judgment as a matter of law: Rule 50, Federal Rules of Civil Procedure.

Motion for new trial: Rule 59, Federal Rules of Civil Procedure. Add your state rules.

Assignment 2

Place a page reference to or a copy of the bill of costs in your system folder. If your state has a similar form, include it. Note the applicable state and federal rules.

Assignment 3

Research the rules of procedure and law in your jurisdiction on the availability of formal supplementary proceedings for locating a judgment debtor's assets. Check the U.S. Code as well as for any such procedures. Then list the procedures and applicable rules and statutes in your system folder. Place a copy of or a page reference to the notice of lis pendens and the post-judgment interrogatories in your system folder.

ANSWER: rules 64 and 69 of the Federal Rules of Civil Procedure require the U.S. District Courts to employ the supplementary proceedings permitted by the state in which the district court is located. Where there are applicable federal rules or statutes, however, the district courts must apply these rules or statutes. Some of the relevant federal laws and commentary follow:

Federal Rules: 62, 64, 69, 70
28 U.S.C. § 1962: judgment on lien
§ 1963: if registered, good in any district court
§ 2001–2007: execution and judicial sales
§ 2710–2717: attachment
§ 2405: garnishment
§ 1292: appeal of order affecting provisional remedies.
Commentaries: C.J.S. §§ 1254–1272
Moore's Federal Practice, Part VIII, Chapter 64

Assignment 4

Research your state law to determine what assets of a judgment debtor are exempt from execution on the judgment. List these in your system folder.

ANSWER: This assignment and most of those following require research into requirements for your state.

Assignment 5

Research the forms and procedures for garnishment in your state. Make a checklist and place it and copies of or references to the appropriate forms in your system folder.

Assignment 6

Make an outline of the procedure for domesticating a judgment in another state and in federal court. Place the outline in your system folder.

ANSWER: Domesticating a Judgment

I. Investigate assets.
II. Locate court that has jurisdiction over assets.
III. File application in foreign court.
A. State that enforcement of judgment is not barred by statue to limitations in either state.
B. State that no stay of execution on the judgment is in effect.
C. State that judgment remains unsatisfied.
D. State that no other action based on the judgment is pending.
E. State that no judgment based on the original judgment has previously been entered in the foreign state.

F.   Include names and addresses of debtor and judgment creditor.

G.   Attach authenticated, exemplified, or otherwise certified copy of original judgment.

IV.   Article 4, § 1 of U.S. Constitution elicits "full" faith and credit to judgments from state to state.

A.   Once domesticated, judgment entered with foreign state the same as original state.

B.   Procedure may vary for foreign countries.

V.   Judgment debtor has burden of proof in challenging original court jurisdiction or showing that judgment has been paid.

VI.   Federal judgments are registered from court to court under Title 28 U.S.C. § 1963.

VII.   Describe state procedure.

Assignment 7

Check the law library for form and procedure books on enforcement of judgments or collections for your state. Draft a step-by-step checklist for enforcing a judgment in your state. Place the checklist and any pertinent forms in your system folder.

Assignment 8

Place a page reference or copy of the checklist for federal appellate procedure (appellant) in your system folder. Research appellate procedure for your state and make a separate state appellate checklist for your system folder. Verify appellate time requirements in the Motions, Pleadings, and Time Limits exhibit and add state time limits.

Assignment 9

Place page references or a copy of the skeletal appellate brief in your system folder. Enter applicable rule references. Research the format of an appellate brief for your state. Include a copy in your system folder plus references to rules on the required format.

ANSWER: If students have a copy of at least the key components of an appellate brief for both the federal and state jurisdiction, they will be more confident when faced with these tasks in the law office.

Assignment 10

Complete your litigation system folder, update its table of contents, and prepare it for grading.

ANSWER: If you have emphasized the system folder, this assignment will be the culmination of much of the students' effort and will reemphasize the importance of a good system folder.

APPLICATION ASSIGNMENTS

Assignment 1

Assume that your client has a judgment for $250,000 against X, who lives in your state. You know that X has $100,000 in liability insurance, a $100,000 home and land, a small cottage worth $60,000 (but only $15,000 paid for), two vehicles each worth $10,000 (both paid for), a boat worth $7,000, and an online coffee business that generates $30,000 in gross annual income. Under your state statutes, what of X's assets are not exempt from execution on the judgment?

ANSWER: Describe your state law provisions.

Assignment 2

Assume that you represent a judgment debtor who has recently paid off a judgment. Under your state law, what procedure must one follow to record a release of judgment?

ANSWER: Describe your state law.

Assignment 3

When must a notice of appeal be filed under your state's rule of appellate procedure? Can this time be extended by the court?

ANSWER: Describe your state rules.

INTERNET EXERCISES

1.   Go to www.ca6.uscourts.gov/. What types of information does this site have or link to that would help you if you had an appellate case in the 6th Circuit?

ANSWER: Court contact information, court opinions, docket and calendars, forms, and rules.

2.   Substituting your circuit number for the 6 in the Web site in Internet Assignment 1, what helpful information is available for appellate practice in your circuit?

ANSWER: Depends on extent of the applicable circuit court Web site.

ADDITIONAL EXERCISES

1.   If a defendant has moved for a judgment as a matter of law (directed verdict) based on the weight of the evidence and the motion was denied, what motion may the defendant file after the trial if the defendant believes the jury's verdict is against the weight of the evidence? What motion should be

filed if the defendant believes a serious procedural error was committed by the judge? What state rules govern these motions?

ANSWER: Renewal of Motion for Judgment as a Matter of Law, federal, JNOV, state.

Motion for new trial. Add your state rules

2. Assume for purposes of this assignment that, contrary to the weight of the evidence the jury returned a verdict against Ms. Forrester. The areas that you believe the jury ignored are (a) that Hart was looking at the van radio just prior to the accident; (b) that several of Mercury Parcel's documents showed the van had faulty brakes; and (c) that defendants offered no evidence whatsoever that Ms. Forrester was careless or contributed in any way to the accident. Using your state form, draft a motion (no supporting affidavit or memo-randum) for judgment notwithstanding the verdict.

ANSWER: this assignment requires the state form, but the student's motion should appear similar to that in Exhibit 12:1 stating the reasons mentioned in the problem.

3. Work through the questions for study and review at the end of the chapter to reinforce your understanding.

CHAPTER 12 TAKE HOME TEST

1. Draft a motion for a new trial.
2. Draft a checklist for the appellate procedure in your state.
3. Draft a checklist for enforcing a judgment for money in your state.

TEST BANK

TEST BANK

CHAPTER ONE: WELCOME TO THE LAW OFFICE

Multiple Choice

1. An active founding owner of a law firm is often called
   a. senior associate
   b. associate
   c. senior partner
   d. of counsel

   ANS: c

2. A lawyer who works for a firm, but is not yet a partner in the firm is
   a. an associate
   b. a paralegal
   c. a law clerk
   d. a legal aide

   ANS: a

3. An example of an intellectual property case is a
   a. negligence case
   b. civil rights case
   c. products liability case
   d. copyright case

   ANS: d

4. An incidence of food poisoning might lead to a
   a. contract case
   b. civil rights case
   c. corporation case
   d. products liability case

   ANS: d

5. A paralegal is valuable to a law firm because a
   a. paralegal will make a good partner
   b. paralegal's time is billed at the same rate as an attorney's
   c. paralegal is not bound by ethical standards
   d. paralegal can help the law firm efficiently deliver legal services to more people

   ANS: d

6. Keeping track of how you spend your time in the law office
   a. is called docket control
   b. is called disbursement entry
   c. may be done on-line
   d. is the responsibility of your supervising attorney

   ANS: c

7. Under task-based billing, clients are charged
   a. for the number of hours required by a task
   b. a set fee for a particular task
   c. only if the case is won
   d. for the attorney's work, but not the paralegal's work

   ANS: b

8. Professional telephone use includes
   a. a chatty conversation
   b. repetition of facts
   c. lengthy discussions of sensitive matters
   d. anonymous calls

   ANS: b

9. The litigation system is least helpful to the paralegal in
   a. saving time
   b. assisting with unique and irregular tasks
   c. preparing for the job
   d. saving effort

   ANS: b

10. Paralegals may
    a. give legal advice to a friend
    b. accept cases for the firm
    c. represent clients at federal administrative hearings
    d. split fees with an attorney

    ANS: c

11. Ethical responsibility in a law firm rests with
    a. attorneys only
    b. the senior partner only
    c. paralegals only
    d. all employees

    ANS: d

12. To avoid the unauthorized practice of law, the paralegal's work
    a. must be delegated by an attorney
    b. must not include drafting documents
    c. must not involve the client
    d. must be kept separate from the attorney's work

    ANS: a

13. A conflict of interest occurs when a paralegal assists
    a. on a case for a bank where the paralegal has an account
    b. an attorney representing his or her family
    c. on a case against a store in which the paralegal occasionally shops
    d. on a case against a good friend

    ANS: d

14. Confidentiality would be at risk in the
    a. office reception area with the paralegal, client, and the client's mother-in-law present
    b. paralegal's office with the paralegal and the client alone
    c. paralegal's office with the paralegal, client and supervising attorney present
    d. client's home with the client and paralegal alone

    ANS: a

15. Disclosure of confidential information is always unethical when the
    a. client consents in writing
    b. disclosure is necessary to prevent death
    c. disclosure is to an attorney not involved in the case
    d. disclosure is necessary to prevent financial injury by fraud

    ANS: c

16. An intermediate appellate court
    a. exists in all state systems
    b. has original jurisdiction
    c. considers only questions of law
    d. considers only questions of fact

    ANS: c

17. Most court cases are disposed of by the
    a. trial court
    b. intermediate appellate court
    c. highest appellate court
    d. U.S. Supreme Court

    ANS: a

18. A court of general jurisdiction
    a. hears military cases only
    b. usually has appellate jurisdiction only
    c. is common to the federal court system
    d. is common to the state court system

    ANS: d

19. When a judge or jury attempts to answer the question "what happened?" it is trying to answer a question of
    a. law
    b. fact
    c. venue
    d. jurisdiction

    ANS: b

20. A United States District Court can have
    a. general jurisdiction
    b. diversity jurisdiction
    c. appellate jurisdiction
    d. unlimited subject matter jurisdiction

    ANS: b

21. A court has personal jurisdiction
    a. when a summons and complaint are served
    b. when a warrant is served
    c. over everyone in its district
    d. over everyone named in an action brought in its district

    ANS: a

22. The jurisdictional amount
    a. an determine in which court a case can be tried
    b. is the attorney's fee
    c. is the same in all courts
    d. can be waived for indigents

    ANS: a

23. Legislative courts do not include United States
    a. Claims Court
    b. District Court
    c. Tax Court
    d. Court of Veterans Appeals

    ANS: b

24. The jurisdictional amount in federal diversity cases
    a. is the combined claim for multiple plaintiffs
    b. is the value of all claims made by one plaintiff against one defendant
    c. can never include attorney's fees
    d. does not apply to class action suits

    ANS: b

25. The U.S. Supreme Court
    a. is the highest authority on the federal law
    b. is an intermediate appellate court
    c. has seven associate justices
    d. has no original jurisdiction

    ANS: a

26. Venue includes
    a. each county where multiple plaintiffs reside
    b. the same as jurisdiction
    c. the county most convenient for all parties
    d. the county where the incident occurred

    ANS: d

True/False

27. Sexual harassment is likely to lead to a contract suit.

    ANS: False

28. Pro bono cases deal with corporation law.

    ANS: False

29. Paralegals are responsible for clerical and word processing services for the law firm.

    ANS: False

30. Timekeeping is important for analyzing productivity.

    ANS: True

31. A tickler system is a calendaring process.

    ANS: True

32. Disbursements are expenses incurred on behalf of the client.

    ANS: True

33. When speaking to a witness on the phone, it is best not to identify your firm.

    ANS: False

34. One of the most common problems in using the telephone is failing to record phone numbers and addresses accurately.

    ANS: True

35. Use your clients' first names to help them feel comfortable.

    ANS: False

36. Paralegals may represent clients in court if the amount in controversy is less than five thousand dollars.

    ANS: False

37. Generally, paralegals may have business cards with the name of the firm on them.

    ANS: True

38. Poor research is the most frequent reason for malpractice suits.

   ANS: False

39. Professional development requires that you join the ABA.

   ANS: False

40. Ethical standards are set in each jurisdiction by the local judge.

   ANS: False

41. There would be a conflict of interest if you assisted in representing a client in a suit against your cousin.

   ANS: True

42. Only attorneys need concern themselves with professional ethics.

   ANS: False

43. Paralegals must be licensed in 13 states.

   ANS: False

44. Venue is determined in the same way as jurisdiction.

   ANS: False

45. The Supreme Court has original jurisdiction over controversies between two states.

   ANS: True

46. A court can have personal jurisdiction based on Internet contacts.

   ANS: True

47. The jurisdictional amount for federal diversity cases is $25,000.

   ANS: False

48. Federal question cases go directly to the Supreme Court.

   ANS: False

49. Domicile is established for the purposes of appeal.

   ANS: False

50. Trial courts decide questions of law and questions of fact.

   ANS: True

51. The U.S. Court of Appeals for the Federal Circuit hears appeals from the U.S. Commissioner of Patents.

   ANS: True

Short Answer

52. What is the role of the paralegal in the law firm?

    ANS: Complete tasks assigned by attorneys: Gather and organize information; draft documents; research and investigate; assist at hearings and trials; file matters; inform clients on case status; generate income for the firm through billable hours; and benefit clients through lower rates and efficient work.

53. Define double billing and describe the ABA Formal Opinion on it.

    ANS: It is charging each of several clients for the full amount of time spent on behalf of all of them. The ABA prohibits double billing as unfair.

54. Define professional ethics as applied to attorneys and discuss its significance to the paralegal.

    ANS: Professional ethics are the rules of conduct and guidelines to behavior that govern the practice of law. The actions of the attorney as well as of those persons supervised by the attorney must conform to the standards of professional ethics. Failure to comply with the standards can result in damage to the reputation of the firm, the disbarment of the attorney, loss of employment for the paralegal, and possible prosecution of the paralegal under the state statute for the unauthorized practice of law.

    It is essential for the paralegal to be familiar with the ethical standards imposed on attorneys, and at what points in the litigation process one or more of those standards become particularly important in order for the paralegal to work within those standards. The significance of professional ethics pervades everything paralegals do, for honesty, integrity, and fairness are at the core of their work.

55. How can a paralegal continue professional development?

    ANS: Keep informed of what is going on in your field, attend continuing education seminars, participate in paralegal associations, and subscribe to paralegal literature.

56. List the courts in your state system and their primary jurisdictions.

    ANS: Your state information.

57. What is the domicile of a corporation? An insurance company?

    ANS: The state in which it is incorporated and its principal place of business; the state in which it is incorporated and its principal place of business, plus the state of the insured person.

58. Explain the differences between venue and subject matter jurisdiction.

    ANS: Subject matter jurisdiction defines what subject, including amount in dispute, a court is authorized to hear; venue permits a court to hear a case because that is the geographical location in which the defendant lives or in which the cause of action arose. What versus where.

59. How is forum non conveniens used?

    ANS: It is used to transfer a case to another court having requisite jurisdiction and venue if the original court is inconvenient to the defendant.

60. One of the following steps in the flow of a case is out of chronological order. Which is it?
    a. accident or event
    b. informal investigation
    c. motion for summary judgment
    d. file complaint

    e. file answer
    f. discovery
    g. trial
    h. appeal

ANS: c

CHAPTER TWO: THE INITIAL INTERVIEW

Multiple Choice

1. A good interview form
    a. gives you all the questions you will need
    b. requires specific information on damages
    c. meets ABA standards
    d. is available from the clerk of court

    ANS: b

2. A paralegal should not rely entirely on model interview forms because they
    a. are usually too long
    b. are usually too short
    c. do not always allow for the uniqueness of the individual case
    d. often waste time

    ANS: c

3. A good source for researching the elements of a cause of action or defense thereto is a
    a. legal practice manual
    b. state or federal jury instruction book
    c. law office procedures manual
    d. court clerk

    ANS: b

4. That aspect of law that defines the rights of individuals and the duties owed one person by another is the definition of
    a. substantive law
    b. procedural law
    c. ethics
    d. negligence

    ANS: a

5. If A has a miscarriage and sues her doctor for malpractice for giving her x-rays before realizing she was pregnant, and A reveals on the witness stand that she fell down the stairs at home just before the miscarriage, the element of the plaintiff's proof that is in jeopardy is
    a. duty
    b. breach of duty
    c. proximate cause
    d. injury

    ANS: c

6. A orders a large pitcher of beer, as does B. A proceeds to drink his pitcher and half of B's. A dies of asphyxiation (drowning). In an action by A's estate against the bar that sold the beer, the defense most applicable to the action is
   a. contributory negligence
   b. comparative negligence
   c. assumption of risk
   d. last clear chance

   ANS: c

7. A boat strays into the swimming area of a lake. A swimmer sees the boat, but swims directly in front of it to retrieve a beachball and is injured when the boat hits him. The boat operator has the defense of
   a. breach of duty
   b. comparative negligence
   c. assumption of risk
   d. procedural law

   ANS: b

8. In regard to scheduling the initial interview, it is best to
   a. schedule about an hour and to end at a specified time so the interview will not be unduly prolonged
   b. leave it open ended to provide flexibility and an unhurried environment
   c. leave time to allow clients to chat as long as they want
   d. schedule twenty minutes and let the client know at the end of that time that you have more important things to do

   ANS: b

9. The best way to record a client interview is to
   a. take notes
   b. tape record it
   c. have the client sign a written statement
   d. videotape it

   ANS: a

10. Body language of a person may best be assessed to determine
    a. whether the person is lying
    b. whether the firm should take the person's case
    c. how a jury will perceive the person
    d. a person's intelligence

    ANS: c

11. Fee agreements
    a. are never discussed by paralegals
    b. are set by paralegals
    c. are always based on billable hours
    d. require the client's signature

    ANS: d

12. Doctors or others holding confidential information are authorized to give that information to a lawyer or paralegal through
    a. docket control forms
    b. release forms

    c.   summons

    d.   writ of certiorari

ANS: b

13. An example of a good interview question is:
    a.   You stopped to look before you crossed the road, didn't you?
    b.   Why didn't you pay more attention to traffic?
    c.   Do you know what Statute CS § 127 requires?
    d.   How long did it take you to cross the road?

ANS: d

14. Professional ethics require the paralegal
    a.   to give reliable legal advice to the client
    b.   to question the truth of what the client says
    c.   to keep client information confidential
    d.   not to ask questions that would embarrass the client

ANS: c

15. The client should be told not to make statements to others about his or her case or injuries, because such statements
    a.   might cause gossip
    b.   can be used against the client in court
    c.   might damage the attorney's reputation
    d.   are against the law

ANS: b

16. In concluding the interview, be sure to
    a.   have the client sign necessary documents
    b.   have the client sign a statement
    c.   avoid any conversation that is not pertinent to the case
    d.   encourage the client to promote his or her side of the case among friends.

ANS: a

17. Typically, at the initial interview the client should sign a
    a.   motion to dismiss
    b.   medical information release
    c.   sworn statement about the accident
    d.   malpractice release for the attorney

ANS: b

18. One of the most frequent client complaints is addressed by paralegals providing
    a.   more relaxed interviews
    b.   better legal forms
    c.   better billing procedures for clients
    d.   increased communication with the client

ANS: d

19. In preparing the interview site the paralegal should
    a. keep other client files on the desk to show how much business the firm has
    b. have all paper, pencils, diagrams, and forms ready
    c. arrange the office seating to keep distance between client and interviewer
    d. arrange for all calls to be put through to the interview site

    ANS: b

20. Thinking of questions to ask in an interview is a matter of
    a. applying common sense to the substantive law (legal elements)
    b. studying the steps of procedural law
    c. good psychology
    d. being a good conversationalist

    ANS: a

21. In some states where comparative negligence is the rule of law, the plaintiff will not be able to recover if the jury determines the plaintiff was
    a. 30 percent negligent
    b. 51 percent negligent
    c. 10 percent negligent
    d. even slightly negligent

    ANS: b

22. When an angry client is ranting in your office, first
    a. call the police
    b. call your supervising attorney
    c. allow the client to vent
    d. leave the room as fast as you can

    ANS: c

23. The interview summary is helpful for
    a. publicizing the case
    b. quick review of facts
    c. evidence at trial
    d. keeping the client informed

    ANS: b

True/False

24. The initial client interview can provide valuable information essential to forming the basis of a lawsuit or a defense thereto.

    ANS: True

25. The initial interview sets the tone for the entire relationship between the plaintiff and the defendant.

    ANS: False

26. Elements of a cause of action can be found in jury instructions.

    ANS: True

27. The most frequent complaint of clients is that they have to communicate with paralegals.

    ANS: False

28. Defendants usually pay attorneys on the basis of a contingent fee agreement.

    ANS: False

29. For the most efficient interviews, use only form questions.

    ANS: False

30. Since each case is unique, interview form questions are not helpful.

    ANS: False

31. An event can be a contributing cause of an injury without being the proximate cause.

    ANS: True

32. One element of negligence is that a breach of duty has to be the proximate cause of the injury.

    ANS: True

33. Duty of care is an element of negligence.

    ANS: True

34. Contributory negligence is not a defense in most states.

    ANS: True

35. Comparative negligence is not a defense in most states.

    ANS: False

36. Assumption of risk and last clear chance are elements of negligence.

    ANS: False

37. It is best to let the client know that it is the client's responsibility to provide for any special needs, such as interpreters, for the initial interview.

    ANS: False

38. Because toys are a distraction, do not keep them in the room when interviewing children.

    ANS: False

39. In the interview, encourage the client to give all information about the accident, even if it is not in the client's favor.

    ANS: True

40. Euphemisms are a good way to deal with sensitive issues in interviews.

    ANS: False

41. Pace and lead is a technique used to elicit information during the client interview.

    ANS: False

42. A plaintiff may have to undergo an examination by a doctor hired by the opposition.

    ANS: True

43. Signed docket control forms allow confidential information to be given to a lawyer.

    ANS: False

44. You know your client is telling the truth if he or she looks you straight in the eye.

    ANS: False

45. Procedural law includes the rules for filing a lawsuit.

    ANS: True

46. Substantive law includes defenses to actions.

    ANS: True

47. The statute of limitations defines the range of damages that can be requested.

    ANS: False

48. A paralegal may explain the terms of a fee agreement to a client.

    ANS: True

49. An interview summary must be filed with the court within 20 days of the interview.

    ANS: False

50. "What do you mean by the phrase 'high as a grasshopper's knee'?" is a good interview question.

    ANS: True

51. Time that a defendant spends outside the state may extend the time limit for filing a case.

    ANS: True

Short Answer

52. The initial client interview is significant for what three reasons?

    ANS: Establishes client-firm relationship, establishes client-paralegal relationship, begins investigation.

53. Define substantive law and procedural law.

    ANS: Substantive law defines the duties owed by one person to another. Procedural law defines the steps that must be followed in a lawsuit.

54. What is an interview plan? State its purposes.

    ANS: An interview plan is a step-by-step procedure for planning all details of an upcoming interview. Its purpose is to see that the maximum benefit is derived from the time spent with the client and that important areas of questioning are not missed.

55. How do you generate interview questions for specific cases?

    ANS: Consider what is needed to prove elements of substantive law.

56. List and define the elements of negligence and related defenses.

    ANS:
    - Duty: The existence of a duty of due care owed by one person to another.
    - Breach of duty: Failure to conform to the required standard of care; that is, what is reasonable under the circumstances.
    - Cause of the injury: the conduct in question (the breach) was the natural and probable (proximate) cause of the resulting harm.
    - Injury in fact: An actual injury or loss must have resulted.
    - Contributory negligence: Any negligence on the part of the plaintiff which contributes to the plaintiff's injury is a bar to plaintiff's recovery.
    - Last clear chance: Defeats defense of contributory negligence by showing defendant had the last clear chance to avoid the accident or injury and defendant did not avoid the injury to plaintiff.
    - Comparative negligence: A process whereby plaintiff's own negligence is assessed at a certain percentage of the entire responsibility for the injury and plaintiff's award is reduced accordingly. In some states if a plaintiff is assessed at more than 51 percent of the responsibility, the plaintiff may not recover.
    - Assumption of risk: A doctrine which denies any recovery of the plaintiff if the plaintiff knows the risks and still enters into the conduct in question.

57. (Special direction to instructor: Give each student a copy of the facts in Case I, Chapter 1.) Referring to the facts on the attached sheet (Case I) and the elements and defenses to negligence, discuss whether there may be a cause of action for negligence and defenses thereto.

    ANS:
    - Duty: It is clear that Mr. Hart had a duty to avoid unreasonable risk to Ms. Forrester, a pedestrian
    - Breach of duty: Investigation would have to reveal whether Mr. Hart was inattentive, reckless, speeding, or had obscured vision. There is a good possibility of such a breach.
    - Cause of injury: It would seem highly likely that Ms. Forrester's injuries were the actual and probable consequences of Mr. Hart's conduct. There is room however for the fact that the most natural cause of the injury was Ms. Forrester's own carelessness in crossing the highway.
    - Injury: Because Ms. Forrester was hit by the van it is likely that there would be some injuries.

Defenses:
- Contributory negligence: If Ms. Forrester failed to check for traffic and/or kept her head tucked into her coat such that she could not see, there is a good possibility of contributory negligence.
- Last clear chance: If it can be demonstrated that Mr. Hart had a chance to avoid the accident despite any carelessness of Ms. Forrester, Ms. Forrester should be able to recover.
- Comparative negligence: Possibility for this as indicated in contributory negligence response. It may also be possible that Ms. Forrester's own negligence could be so great as to bear 51 percent of the fault.
- Assumption of risk: It seems unlikely there will be evidence of this.

58. In planning any initial interview, what special needs should be anticipated? List three.

   ANS: The need for an interpreter; the need for playthings for a child; preparation in special vernacular or medical terminology; and the need to deal with special sensory impairments.

59. What are some considerations in choosing an interview site?

   ANS: Convenience, privacy, access to evidence.

60. Is the client going to be the one who is suing or being sued in a contingent fee agreement? Explain.

   ANS: The one suing. Must be likely to win damages to pay the attorney a percentage.

61. What is an Authorization for Release of Information form? Why is it important?

   ANS: A document which, when signed by the client, authorizes holders of confidential records regarding the client to release those records to the paralegal. The information released by the document can be essential to investigation and may not be available by other means.

62. What kinds of materials should the personal injury client bring to the interview?

   ANS: Information on employment, insurance, medical treatment, bills, etc.

63. List three things clients should not do in order not to jeopardize their case.

   ANS: Sign documents releasing others from liability, accept payment for damages, make statements to others about the case, file an accident report without attorney approval.

64. Assume that you are a paralegal in a firm working for the defendant, Mr. Hart, in Case I. For an interview with Mr. Hart:
   a. Draft a set of five questions pertinent to the element of breach of duty, specifically Mr. Hart's attentiveness.
   b. Draft five questions for Mr. Hart regarding plaintiff's comparative negligence.

   ANS: Questions on attentiveness could cover:
- Distraction on either side of road
- Reaching for anything in car
- Adjusting radio, tape player, clock, etc.
- Lighting cigarette, pushing in lighter
- Reading directions to house
- When first saw plaintiff
- How long did it take to brake
- Others

Questions on comparative negligence could cover:
- When did plaintiff see you?
- Where was plaintiff looking when you first saw her?

- Did she move further into the path of the van after you saw her?
- Was anything obscuring her vision?
- What was she wearing?
- Was she walking fast or slow?
- Once you saw her, was there anything she could have done to avoid the accident?

65. On what two calculations are attorneys' fees based?

    ANS: Fees are calculated as a percentage of the award or by an hourly rate.

66. Define and explain the significance of the statute of limitations.

    ANS: The statute of limitations defines the period of time in which a particular type of action must be brought. Should the statute's deadline be missed, the plaintiff may not sue.

67. Describe the technique of pace and lead in dealing with difficult clients.

    ANS: The interviewer first identifies with the emotion of the client, agreeing with opinions expressed by the client, then sympathetically leads the client toward a more compliant attitude.

68. What are three ways you can help keep your client informed?

    ANS: Schedule regular client report letters, promptly respond to all client inquiries, acknowledge receipt of information and material sent to you from the client.

CHAPTER THREE: EVIDENCE AND INVESTIGATION

Multiple Choice

1. To be admissible, evidence must be
   a. direct
   b. cumulative
   c. material
   d. privileged

   ANS: c

2. The probative value of evidence must outweigh
   a. the opponent's evidence
   b. its admissibility
   c. prejudice it causes
   d. its materiality

   ANS: c

3. To be authenticated, physical evidence must be
   a. identified as genuine
   b. stipulated by the opponent
   c. direct
   d. circumstantial

   ANS: a

4. The formal exchange of information in litigation is called
   a. investigation
   b. discovery
   c. evidence
   d. relevance

   ANS: b

5. Care in drafting an investigation plan is important because it
   a. must be authenticated by a judge
   b. must conform to Rule 6(a)
   c. is a record for billing
   d. saves time and resources

   ANS: d

6. Attorney's work product is
   a. all the evidence gathered
   b. motions and briefs
   c. privileged
   d. authenticated

   ANS: c

7. Judicial notice permits the introduction of
   a. irrelevant evidence
   b. immaterial evidence
   c. physical evidence
   d. evidence without authentication

   ANS: d

8. Expert witnesses are best for presenting
   a. the chronology of the event
   b. technical evidence
   c. background on the client's character
   d. demonstrative evidence

   ANS: b

9. Tire tracks at the scene of an accident are most likely to be
   a. physical evidence
   b. direct evidence
   c. inadmissible evidence
   d. demonstrative evidence

   ANS: a

10. To be relevant, evidence must
    a. be given by an eyewitness
    b. be direct
    c. tend to prove or refute a fact of consequence
    d. show a chain of custody

    ANS: c

11. A chain of custody establishes
    a. that a piece of evidence is authentic
    b. who owned an item at the time of the accident
    c. which side gets to present a piece of evidence at trial
    d. who takes custody of the item after trial

    ANS: a

12. Evidence that opposes your client's case
    a. is irrelevant
    b. is circumstantial
    c. is helpful in preparing for trial
    d. should be destroyed

    ANS: c

13. Professional ethics require paralegals to
    a. make well-prepared statements to the press
    b. give loyalty to the client top priority
    c. refrain from obstructing opposition access to evidence
    d. ignore fraudulent behavior of clients if it is privileged

    ANS: c

14. When speaking to witnesses a paralegal should reveal
    a. the amount of damages at stake
    b. that the defendant is insured
    c. nothing
    d. that he or she is a paralegal

    ANS: d

15. Evidence is best gathered from key witnesses through a
    a. modem
    b. personal interview
    c. professional research service
    d. letter

    ANS: b

16. When interviewing witnesses
    a. ask questions that focus on elements of substantive law
    b. bring several together to save time
    c. don't worry about planning; go with your instincts
    d. never pay them a fee

    ANS: a

17. If you need to interview an evasive witness it is best to
    a. visit without calling first
    b. call for an appointment
    c. pretend you represent the other side
    d. wait until close to time for trial

    ANS: a

18. Rules of evidence are explained in
    a. federal statutes
    b. Advisory Committee Notes
    c. Federal Rules of Civil Procedure
    d. ABA Guidelines

    ANS: b

19. Res gestae statements are
    a. inadmissible because they are hearsay
    b. statements of reputation
    c. excited utterance
    d. always relevant

    ANS: c

20. Hearsay is inadmissible if it is a
    a. res gestae statement
    b. quote of what someone said to a witness
    c. statement made to receive medical diagnosis
    d. statement of reputation

    ANS: b

21. Self-authenticating evidence includes
    a. federal documents
    b. blood test results
    c. videotapes
    d. tire tread marks

    ANS: a

22. A witness may be impeached
    a. by a two-thirds vote of the Senate
    b. if the witness is shown to be telling the truth
    c. if trial testimony deviates from the signed statement
    d. by the judge

    ANS: c

23. Hearsay is the firsthand observation of
    a. a witness
    b. a client
    c. a person other than one testifying
    d. an expert witness

    ANS: c

24. Computer data is hearsay evidence unless it
    a. is relevant
    b. was entered by someone not connected to the case
    c. is authenticated by an expert witness
    d. was entered automatically by the computer

    ANS: d

25. A statement of reputation is admissible
    a. if it bears on a witness's truthfulness
    b. if it is based on religious belief
    c. to prove the actions of the defendant
    d. only if it is based on a criminal record

    ANS: a

26. The best evidence rule means that
    a. the side with the strongest evidence wins
    b. only the original document or item is admissible
    c. only the most important evidence may be presented
    d. no circumstantial evidence is allowed.

    ANS: b

27. A presumption is
    a. not admissible in court
    b. a form of hearsay
    c. assumed true unless disproved by the opponent
    d. a statement of the elements of the case

    ANS: c

28. An important focus for all steps of investigation is
    a. The Federal Rules of Civil Procedure
    b. state procedural law
    c. elements of substantive law
    d. jurisdiction and venue

    ANS: c

29. If a test is likely to damage or destroy evidence
    a. it should not be performed
    b. it should be performed in court
    c. the opponent should not be told
    d. it should be recorded in photographs or on videotape

    ANS: d

30. As evidence, photographs may be
    a. testimonial evidence
    b. found to be prejudicial
    c. thrown away if they support the opponent's case
    d. digitally altered to favor the client's case

    ANS: b

31. Information gathered in informal investigation can be kept organized and under control with the help of
    a. witness information cover sheets
    b. docket control software
    c. a chain of custody
    d. expert witnesses

    ANS: a

32. A review of information from the informal investigation will help the attorney decide
    a. how much to charge the client
    b. what expert witnesses to have testify at trial
    c. whether to file a complaint
    d. whether to split the fee with the paralegal

    ANS: c

True/False

33. Civil cases must be proved beyond a reasonable doubt.

    ANS: False

34. A stipulation is permission from the judge to introduce evidence.

    ANS: False

35. It is helpful to investigate an accident scene at the same time of day and the same day of the week that the accident occurred.

    ANS: True

36. The more evidence collected to prove a single point, the better.

    ANS: False

37. Circumstantial evidence can be valuable to a case.

    ANS: True

38. A chain of custody is a locking device used to prevent removal of valuable evidence.

    ANS: False

39. You have no need to collect evidence that does not support your client's case.

    ANS: False

40. You should always answer the questions of a witness about a case.

    ANS: False

41. The opposing attorney's work product is evidence that can be obtained only through formal investigation.

    ANS: False

42. Sherlock Holmes' tools, such as a magnifying glass and a stopwatch, are silly and no help to a serious investigator.

    ANS: False

43. A signature on a contract is direct evidence of agreement to the contract.

    ANS: True

44. Illegally obtained evidence, though inadmissible in criminal trials, is admissible in a civil trial.

    ANS: False

45. Evidence is material if it is of consequence to the determination of the action.

    ANS: True

46. Privileged evidence is most useful at trial.

    ANS: False

47. When requesting records, remember that follow-up letters are irritating to busy doctors and should be avoided.

    ANS: False

148 Since it may make witnesses more cooperative, you should tell them the details of your client's case.

    ANS: False

49. Under some circumstances, witnesses may be paid.

    ANS: True

50. A third party at a witness interview can verify that the witness statement is true.

    ANS: False

51. Hearsay is admissible if it is a present sense impression.

    ANS: True

52. A witness's capacity to observe may not be questioned.

    ANS: False

53. When drafting the statement of an uneducated witness, it is best to change the language to sound more sophisticated.

    ANS: False

54. Once drafted, the witness statement cannot be changed.

    ANS: False

55. Newspapers are self-authenticating as evidence.

    ANS: True

56. Authentication of computerized data relies in part on how the data was processed.

    ANS: True

57. Judicial notice and stipulation save time.

    ANS: True

58. Investigation raises few ethical concerns since it does not usually bring paralegals into contact with the public.

    ANS: False

59. There is no point in taking the statement of a witness who says she didn't see anything.

    ANS: False

60. Photographs may be difficult to authenticate.

    ANS: True

61. Sketches used as evidence should always be drawn to scale.

    ANS: True

62. It is best to be the first investigator at the scene because you can take evidence so your opponent does not find it.

    ANS: False

63. A witness statement should be signed in the presence of a third party, if possible.

    ANS: True

Matching

64. *Match each item with the following correct statement.*

    a. testimonial evidence
    b. documentary evidence
    c. real evidence
    d. demonstrative evidence

    1. A witness statement that the defendant was intoxicated
    2. A model of the product in a liability case
    3. The charred remnant of a shoe worn by the plaintiff during the accident in question
    4. Canceled checks showing payment from plaintiff to defendant

    1. **ANS:** a
    2. **ANS:** d
    3. **ANS:** c
    4. **ANS:** b

Short Answer

65. List the three levels of the burden of proof, from weakest to strongest, and the type of case to which they apply.

    ANS: Preponderance of evidence, civil; clear and convincing evidence, special civil cases (fraud);proof beyond reasonable doubt, criminal.

66. List four types of evidence and an example of each.

    ANS:
    - Testimonial—witness statement
    - Documentary—business records
    - Real—defective product
    - Demonstrative—photo of scene of accident

67. Why is evidence of habit or routine generally admissible?

    ANS: Their invariable regularity and frequency make them valid and reliable.

68. What is the difference between judicial notice and stipulation?

    ANS: Judicial notice permits the judge to allow evidence without authentication.
    Stipulation permits an agreement between parties to allow evidence without authentication.

69. List in order at least four of the steps in planning an investigation. Why is that plan important?

    ANS:
    1. Review file and information.
    2. Identify elements of proof.
    3. Identify facts to prove elements.
    4. Determine sources for facts.
    5. Record investigative plan.
    6. Consult with attorney.
       The plan helps make efficient use of time and resources for effective results.

70. Briefly outline the procedure for requesting reports, records, and other documents.

    ANS:
    - Be sure client has signed current authorization.
    - Call records custodian for fees, procedures, etc.
    - Send letter properly identifying persons, dates, and specific information needed.
    - Attach signed release and fee

71. Write a list of things to remember when requesting employment and financial information.

    ANS:
    1. Have the client sign a release of employment information at the initial interview to include with the request.
    2. Request a brief history of annual earnings, current salary or hourly wage, days of work missed since accident, overtime and bonuses missed, and disability insurance coverage.

72. What should you look for when you receive a reply to your request for records?

    ANS: Check that information is correct and clear.
    Check that vernacular can be deciphered.
    Request corrections or explanations immediately.

73. Why is it helpful to investigate an accident scene at the same time of day and day of the week that the accident occurred?

    ANS: To observe traffic patterns, light, possible witnesses.

74. Give two reasons for contacting witnesses early.

    ANS:
    1. They forget details with time.
    2. They tend to form attachments to the first side who contacts them.

75. What are three ways to find an unknown jogger who may have witnessed your client's accident?

    ANS: Newspaper ad, canvass neighborhood, review photos, visit accident scene at same time, ask local running groups.

76. List three ways a witness statement can be useful to a case.

    ANS:
    1. Tells the attorney what facts can be corroborated or refuted. (Reveals strengths and weaknesses of case.)
    2. Serves as a record of witness's recollection of facts:
       a. Used later to refresh memory of witness.
       b. Used later to impeach witness.
    3. May help settle case.

77. Why should great care be taken with the wording of a witness statement? The initialing and signing of a witness statement?

    ANS: Wording could indicate uncertainty or inaccuracies.
    Initialing and signing are verification of statement.

78. Identify and give the importance of *Daubert v. Merrell Dow Pharmaceuticals, Inc.* (1993) and *Kumho Tire Co. Inc. v. Carmichael* (1999). List the resulting standards.

    ANS: Daubert v. Merrell Dow is the Supreme Court case that confirmed the test for admissibility of scientific opinion. Kumho extended the test to all types of expert testimony.
    1. The testimony must be relevant and helpful.
    2. The expert must be specially qualified.
    3. The methodology used must be reliable.
    4. The evidence must be capable of being and actually be applied reliably to the facts of the case.

79. How do you decide which view of a scene is best for sketches or photos?

    ANS: Look for clarity in depicting the event and the points of view of parties and witnesses. Show significant features and relationships.

80. Why is it necessary to preserve evidence in its discovered state?

    ANS: Any changes may obscure the facts of the event, resulting in unprofessional conduct charges against you or the attorney.

81. Why are non-professional photos subject to question as evidence?

    ANS: Perspective, light, and color may be distorted.

CHAPTER FOUR: DRAFTING THE COMPLAINT

Multiple Choice

1. A person shall not be deprived of life, liberty, or property without
   a. capacity
   b. verification
   c. due process of law
   d. litigation

   ANS: c

2. Pleadings are
   a. formal documents that set out claims and defenses
   b. statements of guilt or innocence
   c. informal exchanges between parties
   d. discovery devices

   ANS: a

3. Pleadings include
   a. cross claims
   b. memoranda
   c. motions
   d. evidence

   ANS: a

4. A complaint does not
   a. introduce the cause of action
   b. present defenses
   c. invoke the court's jurisdiction
   d. inform the defendant of the action

   ANS: b

5. In drafting a caption, be sure to include
   a. main points of substantive law
   b. main points of procedural law
   c. addresses of the parties
   d. the name of the court

   ANS: d

6. Federal Rules of Civil Procedure cover pleadings contents in
   a. Rule 10
   b. Rule 14
   c. Rule 8
   d. Rule 25

   ANS: a

7. A real party in interest is
   a. the employer of the injured person
   b. a key witness
   c. the person who caused the injury
   d. the attorney for the plaintiff

   ANS: c

8. An example of a person who has standing to sue is
   a. a retailer who will lose business next year because of an unfulfilled advertising contract
   b. the adult daughter of a man who suffered food poisoning at a restaurant
   c. a woman who was upset when a friend's dog was killed by a reckless driver
   d. a homeowner who thinks a neighbor intends to let his property become an eyesore

   ANS: a

9. To sue, a party must have
   a. capacity
   b. domicile
   c. interest
   d. caption

   ANS: a

10. A guardian ad litem permits suit when
    a. a corporation is a party
    b. there is no interpleader
    c. there is a lack of capacity
    d. multiple parties are joined

    ANS: c

11. Class action suits require that
    a. the action of the adverse party is inconsistent toward members of the class
    b. members of the class claim the same amount of damages
    c. the representative is chosen by a majority vote of the class
    d. there are common questions of law and fact

    ANS: d

12. A lawsuit may be prevented if the defendant
    a. is a child
    b. is unknown
    c. has sovereign immunity
    d. is an unincorporated association

    ANS: c

13. Language in the complaint needs to
    a. prove the plaintiff's case
    b. be assertive
    c. address possible defenses
    d. state the law

    ANS: b

14. Joinder of parties is
    a. bringing parties together for settlement
    b. inclusion of all persons involved in one side of a lawsuit
    c. always a class action
    d. necessary when corporations are parties

    ANS: b

15. The interpleader rule allows
    a. persons without capacity to sue
    b. joinder of parties in counterclaims
    c. one person to sue as representative of a class
    d. deceased persons to sue

    ANS: b

16. When a person's interest in a suit is not represented by existing parties, that person can become a party through
    a. a guardian ad litem
    b. a petition to include
    c. a motion to intervene
    d. a cross-claim

    ANS: c

17. Jurisdictional allegations
    a. are not necessary in federal court
    b. are always necessary in state court
    c. should be left for the defendant to allege
    d. should be stated in the first paragraphs of the complaint

    ANS: d

18. Statement of parties' domiciles is necessary in alleging
    a. jurisdiction
    b. capacity
    c. procedural law
    d. in rem rules

    ANS: a

19. A syllogism is
    a. a logical formula helpful in determining whether there is a cause of action
    b. an allegation
    c. required below the caption of the complaint
    d. corporate representation in a lawsuit

    ANS: a

20. The basis for a cause of action is
    a. the amount of damages
    b. the rule of law
    c. the complaint
    d. The Federal Rules of Civil Procedure

    ANS: b

21. A complaint should
    a. state all the available facts
    b. anticipate defenses
    c. state the law if the action is pursuant to specific provisions of a particular statute
    d. avoid naming all the defendants

    ANS: c

22. Notice pleading is
    a. used in all states
    b. used in federal cases
    c. more detailed than fact pleading
    d. no longer used

    ANS: b

23. Exemplary damages
    a. compensate for emotional trauma
    b. seek recovery of property
    c. punish particularly reckless conduct
    d. force performance of a contract

    ANS: c

24. A remedy requiring the defendant to fulfill the terms of a contract is
    a. special damages
    b. specific performance
    c. exemplary damages
    d. prohibitory injunctions

    ANS: b

25. Types of contracts recognized by law include
    a. injunction contract
    b. consideration contract
    c. oral contract
    d. exemplary contract

    ANS: c

26. Rescission includes an action seeking
    a. to cancel a contract made under duress
    b. performance of a contract as it was written
    c. a change in terms of a contract
    d. special damages

    ANS: a

27. A wherefore clause states the
    a. demand for relief
    b. cause of action
    c. elements of law
    d. counterclaim

    ANS: a

28. Demand for jury trial should
    a. be postponed until beginning of trial
    b. be made within thirty days of service of the last pleading
    c. always be included in the complaint
    d. be conspicuous

    ANS: d

29. The complaint must always include
    a. appendix
    b. verification
    c. exhibit
    d. subscription

    ANS: d

30. Exhibits attached to complaints can include
    a. temporary restraining order
    b. explanatory material
    c. contracts
    d. demand for relief

    ANS: c

True/False

31. A complaint is the formal introduction of a lawsuit.

    ANS: True

32. A poorly drafted complaint can cause dismissal of the suit.

    ANS: True

33. Due process of law is guaranteed in the Fifth and Fourteenth Amendments.

    ANS: True

34. The caption of a complaint states the cause of action.

    ANS: False

35. Ms. Schnabel is a real party in interest in the Forrester case.

    ANS: False

36. Jurisdictional amount must be alleged in federal question complaints.

    ANS: False

37. An injured child has capacity to sue.

    ANS: False

38. Briar Patch Dolls (Case IV) does most of its business in Columbia, where Teeny Tiny Manufacturing is located, but federal diversity exists because Briar Patch is incorporated in Ohio.

    ANS: False

39. Corporations are considered persons under the law.

    ANS: True

40. The abbreviation *et al.* may not be used in the complaint caption.

    ANS: True

41. A claim can be made against an unknown defendant.

    ANS: True

42. Venue must be alleged in federal complaints.

    ANS: False

43. It's best to avoid the archaic language found in some legal forms when you draft documents.

    ANS: True

44. The cause of action is stated in the body of the complaint.

    ANS: True

45. Requirements for drafting the cause of action vary from jurisdiction to jurisdiction.

    ANS: True

46. It is not proper to use persuasive language in a formal pleading.

    ANS: False

47. Fact pleading is the simplest form of pleading.

    ANS: False

48. Notice pleading does not require attention to the elements of law.

    ANS: False

49. Special damages are not a direct consequence of a defendant's wrong.

    ANS: True

50. The wherefore clause contains the rule of law.

    ANS: False

51. If one party repudiates a contract before the time of performance, the injured party may sue for anticipatory breach of contract.

    ANS: True

52. Relief in a wrongful death action may include parental damages.

    ANS: True

53. If you sued your neighbor to keep his irrigation water from washing across your fields, you probably would seek a mandatory injunction.

    ANS: False

54. Injunctions are remedies to prevent future harm.

    ANS: True

55. Demand for a jury trial is assumed unless otherwise stated in the complaint.

    ANS: False

56. Legal writing usually requires language that is difficult for an ordinary person to understand.

    ANS: False

57. Some states limit the liability of "deep pocket" defendants according to their percentage of the degree of fault.

    ANS: True

Short Answer

58. What do pleadings have to do with our right to due process?

    ANS: Pleadings clarify issues and inform parties of the basis for claims or defenses, keeping the litigation procedure open and fair; we cannot be deprived of property without the opportunity to defend our property.

59. a. Why can the caption of Case IV read *Briar Patch Dolls, Inc. v. Teeny Tiny Manufacturing Co.* rather than *Heinz v. Smith and McGinnis*?
    b. If Teeny Tiny were owned solely by Ethel Meyers, now deceased, could Briar Patch still sue? Why?

    ANS:
    a. Corporations are considered persons. The contract was between corporations, not individuals.
    b. Yes. Her estate would be responsible for her legal obligations.

60. Explain the difference between "real party in interest" and "standing to sue."

    ANS: A real party in interest has the legal capacity to sue even if the injury is to another; for example, the guardian of an injured minor. To have standing to sue, a person must be directly and actually injured.

61. List four ways that related claims are handled to save costs and time, and their pertinent Federal Rules of Civil Procedure.

    ANS:
    a. Joinder of parties—Rules 19(a) and 20(a)
    b. Interpleader rule—Rule 22
    c. Class actions—Rule 23
    d. Motion to intervene—Rule 24(c)

62. What information must be presented to allege jurisdiction in a state court?

    ANS: Names and domiciles of parties; cause of action and its location; reference to controlling state statute on jurisdiction; any jurisdictional amount.

63. Why must jurisdiction always be alleged in federal courts but not in all state courts?

    ANS: Federal courts are courts of limited subject matter jurisdiction, so jurisdiction must be demonstrated. State trial courts are courts of general jurisdiction, meaning they will hear almost everything.

64. Why does venue not have to be alleged in complaints in federal court?

    ANS: Venue is considered a matter for the defendant to raise; may be waived.

65. How are separate claims stated in a complaint?

    ANS: In separate counts, each having its own body of allegations, damages, and demand for judgment; and incorporating common information from introductory paragraphs.

66. Why is it necessary to research local practice in drafting complaints in a particular state jurisdiction?

    ANS: Pleading rules and procedures vary from one jurisdiction to another. If the complaint is inadequate, it may be dismissed or have to be amended.

67. Discuss the importance of "subscription" to the paralegal in the context of drafting and filing a complaint.

    ANS: Federal Rule of Civil Procedure 11 requires subscription, that the complaint is signed by the attorney, or party if unrepresented, including the attorney's address and phone number. The paralegal must be confident that there is substance to the cause of action alleged in the complaint to avoid frivolous lawsuits and the consequences of sanctions.

68. The elements of an action for quantum meruit (unjust enrichment) include:
    a. defendant requested plaintiff's performance
    b. plaintiff performed the services requested
    c. services performed by plaintiff had a fair and reasonable value
    d. the defendant failed to pay for the goods or services rendered

    The remedies available are damages equal to the value of the goods and services and other remedies.

    Draft the complaint language for the cause of action paragraph, the remedy paragraph, and the wherefore clause for the facts given, then state whether the syllogism is complete and, if not, what is lacking.

    Merit Landscaping has agreed to care for Harry Berry's yard during a three-month absence for the sum of $300. Berry returns to find the yard mowed, but hears from neighbors that it was overgrown most of the summer, and refuses to pay. Merit sues for quantum meruit.

ANS:
1. Plaintiff performed landscaping service at (address) from June 2 to Aug. 29, __, at request of Defendant and for anticipated payment of $300.
2. Defendant failed to pay for services rendered in the amount of $300.
Wherefore Plaintiff demands judgment against Defendant in the amount of three hundred dollars ($300) together with the costs and disbursements of this action.
Syllogism lacks one element—service rendered had a fair and reasonable value—needs to allege worth of $300.

69. Discuss the reasons for joining parties and the limits to joinder. What federal rules govern joinder of parties?

    ANS: Federal Rules 19, 20, and 21 govern joinder.
    Limits: May join if person is subject to service and if it will not deprive court of jurisdiction.
    Purposes:
    • To grant complete relief to the parties (avoid subsequent individual suits)
    • To get at more parties and deeper pockets
    Defendants can join other parties as well.

70. Name two documents filed to require a party to do or refrain from doing some act.

    ANS: Preliminary injunction, temporary restraining order

CHAPTER FIVE: FILING THE LAWSUIT, SERVICE OF PROCESS, AND OBTAINING A DEFAULT JUDGMENT

Multiple Choice

1. Filing the complaint
   a. is the process described as the beginning of an investigation of a lawsuit
   b. marks the official beginning of the case in the federal system
   c. is always the official beginning of a case
   d. is never the beginning of a case

   ANS: b

2. The summons
   a. gives the court personal jurisdiction over the defendant
   b. officially starts the action in federal court
   c. provides the defendant with notice of the lawsuit so a defense can be prepared
   d. is not required in some states

   ANS: a

3. The best person to contact to find out what documents are necessary to file a lawsuit is the
   a. bailiff
   b. clerk of the specified court
   c. county clerk
   d. court administrator

   ANS: b

4. Except when the federal waiver of service is used, at the start of a civil lawsuit the defendant must be served with the
   a. summons and warrant for arrest
   b. affidavit of service and acknowledgement
   c. summons and complaint
   d. complaint and proof of service

   ANS: c

5. In preparing for the filing of an action, it is a good idea for a paralegal to see that the attorney signs the
   a. complaint
   b. process receipt and return
   c. the summons
   d. consent to exercise jurisdiction

   ANS: a

6. The filing fee for a civil action in federal court is
   a. $120.00
   b. $25.00
   c. $150.00
   d. $80.00

   ANS: a

7. The issuing of a summons requires the signature of the
   a. attorney
   b. judge
   c. clerk of court
   d. defendant

   ANS: c

8. The preferred method of service in federal procedure is the
   a. process prescribed by Rule 3
   b. use of the notice of lawsuit and request for waiver of service of summons
   c. personal delivery of the summons and complaint on defendant
   d. postal delivery of the summons and complaint to the defendant

   ANS: b

9. At the time of filing an action, paralegals should know
   a. the type of service to be used and who needs to be served
   b. all addresses for the defendant
   c. all the newspapers needed for publication
   d. what evidence will be presented at trial

   ANS: a

10. The Federal Rules of Civil Procedure do not allow service of process by
    a. personal delivery
    b. delivery to any person at defendant's house
    c. delivery by first class mail
    d. publication under prescribed circumstances

    ANS: b

11. Under the Federal Rules of Civil Procedure, when serving a corporation, proper service is made on
    a. any employee
    b. the CEO only
    c. an agent
    d. corporate headquarters

    ANS: c

12. Generally speaking, in order for a long-arm statute to extend to an individual or a corporation, the individual or corporation must have
    a. state long-arm certification
    b. its primary place of business in the state
    c. the necessary minimum contacts with the federal court
    d. the necessary minimum contacts with the state

    ANS: d

13. Service of process can be effected on a
    a. resident of the county in which the court has jurisdiction
    b. defendant brought into the state by force
    c. witness attending a trial
    d. defendant fraudulently served process

    ANS: a

14. In state court, the person most likely to serve process is the
    a. attorney
    b. marshal
    c. sheriff
    d. paralegal

    ANS: c

15. Service of papers subsequent to the complaint
    a. is covered in Rule 5 of the Federal Rules of Civil Procedure
    b. is directly on the party, not the party's attorney
    c. must be preceded by filing them with the clerk of court
    d. must be in person

    ANS: a

16. The Federal Rules of Civil Procedure give the court the power to dismiss a lawsuit if, after the complaint has been filed, service has not been achieved within
    a. 120 days
    b. 60 days
    c. 20 days
    d. 90 days

    ANS: a

17. Default may be entered if the
    a. defendant fails to enter an appearance or otherwise file a responsive pleading in the prescribed time period
    b. plaintiff fails to enter an appearance or otherwise file a responsive pleading in the prescribed time period
    c. defendant files a responsive pleading but fails to enter an appearance in the prescribed time period
    d. defendant is a minor and has no legal representation

ANS: a

18. If a default judgment is not set aside, the
    a. defendant wins
    b. defendant may then file an answer
    c. plaintiff loses
    d. plaintiff is limited to the amount of damages
       requested

    ANS: d

19. A request for entry of default judgment is often accompanied by an affidavit to show
    a. jurisdiction
    b. incapacity of defendant
    c. nonmilitary service
    d. service of process

    ANS: c

20. If the award requested in an action is a sum certain and the defendant is neither a minor nor incompetent, judgment shall be entered by the
    a. clerk
    b. judge
    c. plaintiff
    d. defendant

    ANS: a

21. If a hearing is to be held on an application for entry of a default judgment, notice of the hearing must be given to the adverse party
    a. 5 days before the hearing
    b. 3 days before the hearing
    c. 10 days before the hearing
    d. 1 day before the hearing

    ANS: b

22. Good cause to set aside a default judgment does not include
    a. illness of defendant's attorney
    b. that the judgment has been satisfied
    c. that the amount of damages requested is unfair
    d. misconduct of adverse party

    ANS: c

True/False

23. The summons is the document that states the time in which the plaintiff must appear and defend.

    ANS: False

24. Case deadlines stem from the initial client interview.

    ANS: False

25. Documents to file a lawsuit must be delivered to the clerk of court in person.

    ANS: False

26. Typical long-arm statutes require service of process through the secretary of state.

    ANS: True

27. The summons may not be served electronically.

    ANS: True

28. A civil cover sheet is required in filing lawsuits in some states but not in federal cases.

    ANS: False

29. In serving an officer of the United States, service is complete simply by serving a copy of the summons and complaint on the U.S. Attorney General.

    ANS: False

30. Service of process establishes personal venue.

    ANS: False

31. Internet contacts are insufficient for the use of long-arm statutes.

    ANS: False

32. Ask the clerk of court what documents are needed for filing a lawsuit in a state court.

    ANS: True

33. U. S. Senators are immune from service of process.

    ANS: False

34. A judge for the lawsuit may be assigned by the clerk of court.

    ANS: True

35. In rem actions attach property to pay a judgment in an unrelated case.

    ANS: False

36. Constructive service is most often used in in rem actions.

    ANS: False

37. The Federal Collections Act is important in quasi in rem cases.

    ANS: False

38. Entry of a default judgment ends the case in favor of the plaintiff.

    ANS: True

39. The judge enters a default judgment for a sum certain.

    ANS: False

40. A sum certain is a flat fee paid to an attorney.

    ANS: False

41. Papers subsequent to the complaint should be served on the party's attorney.

    ANS: True

42. A defendant who returns waiver of service waives defenses and objections to the complaint.

    ANS: False

43. Out-of-state defendants can be served through long-arm laws if they have sufficient contacts with the plaintiff.

    ANS: False

44. Service of process should be accomplished by mail only if personal service fails.

    ANS: False

45. The Freedom of Information Act can help you obtain a defendant's forwarding address from the Post Office.

    ANS: True

46. A default judgment hearing requires evidence to prove a cause of action.

    ANS: False

47. A default judgment against one defendant may preclude proceeding against other defendants.

    ANS: True

48. In default judgments a monetary amount not readily challengeable or subject to reasonable dispute is called special damages.

    ANS: False

49. Default judgments may award amounts greater than those requested in the complaint.

    ANS: False

Short Answer

50. Why is it important to confirm the method of service of process with the attorney before filing?

    ANS: Documents delivered to the clerk of court for filing may be different for different types of service.

51. Generally, when does an action officially begin in state court and in federal court?

    ANS:
    State court—when complaint and summons are served on defendant
    Federal court—when complaint is delivered to the clerk of court

52. What does the clerk of court do in filing a case?

    ANS: Dates original complaint; assigns a civil case number; possibly assigns judge; issues summons; checks summons and civil cover sheet.

53. How is federal service of an in-state corporation accomplished?

    ANS:
    a. If no waiver is obtained, according to law of state in which the pertinent district court is located, *or*
    b. serve an officer, general agent, or any other agent authorized by law or appointment to receive service (often secretary of state) and,
    c. if statute requires, mail copy to defendant [Rule 4(C)(1 or 2)]

54. Compare in rem and quasi in rem actions.

    ANS: Both involve the attachment of property: in rem, to resolve claims to the property itself; quasi in rem, to pay a judgment in an unrelated case where personal jurisdiction has not been established over the defendant.

55. What cautions should be observed in locating defendants?

    ANS: Federal Collections Act and local laws to avoid harassment or illegal collection practices.

56. What is the difference between the entry of default and the entry of default judgment?

    ANS: Entry of default establishes the time of the default after which defendant generally cannot contest liability. Entry of default judgment determines plaintiff's victory and remedy.

57. To whom is the request for entry of default judgment submitted?

    ANS: To the clerk if award is sum certain, to the court if the award is yet to be determined.

58. What cautions apply when seeking default judgments against multiple defendants?

    ANS: Some jurisdictions allow only one judgment, precluding action against other defendants. Other jurisdictions allow designating the judgment as joint and several.

59. What time limits are involved in setting aside a default judgment?

    ANS: Motion must be made in reasonable time (up to a year from judgment for Rule 60(b)(1–3)). Notice of a hearing on an application for default judgment must be served on the defendant or representative at least three days prior to the hearing (Rule 55(b)(2). If successful, answer can be filed as if time limit had not expired.

60. What documents are needed to properly prepare a civil case for filing in your state?

    ANS: Your state information.

CHAPTER SIX: DEFENDING AND TESTING THE LAWSUIT

Multiple Choice

1. The purposes of a motion include to
   a. state the claim against the defendant
   b. begin the lawsuit
   c. narrow the issues for trial
   d. calculate damages

   ANS: c

2. The basic requirements for a motion are set out in Federal Rule of Civil Procedure
   a. 4
   b. 12(e)
   c. 7(b)
   d. 59

   ANS: c

3. In responding to the complaint, the defendant may not
   a. default
   b. file a motion to dismiss the action
   c. file a motion to strike
   d. file a motion for a new trial

   ANS: d

4. The federal rule of civil procedure that governs when an answer to a complaint shall be served is
   a. 7(c)
   b. 12(a)
   c. 15
   d. 54(c)

   ANS: b

5. An answer may contain
   a. denials
   b. injunctions
   c. third-party complaints
   d. motions

   ANS: a

6. Once the possible defenses to a claim have been located along with the kinds of facts needed to allege the existence of the defense, the next step is to
   a. draft the answer
   b. draft the defense
   c. compare the kinds of facts that have been located to the known facts in the case at hand to see if the defenses are applicable
   d. determine whether the defenses are affirmative or negative

   ANS: c

7. Judgment on the pleadings and summary judgment vary in that
   a. only judgment on the pleadings is raised by motion
   b. only summary judgment is designed to reach behind the pleading to other evidence
   c. any summary judgment is appropriate for third party practice
   d. only judgment on the pleadings can end the lawsuit

   ANS: b

8. A motion for summary judgment may be filed
   a. 10 days after the commencement of the action
   b. 5 days after the commencement of the action
   c. 20 days after the pleadings are closed
   d. 20 days after the commencement of the action

   ANS: d

9. Documents filed with a motion include the
   a. complaint
   b. notice of motion
   c. summons
   d. answer

   ANS: b

10. Federal Rule 6(d) requires that the motion be served on the adverse party
    a. 10 days prior to the hearing on the motion
    b. 3 days prior to the hearing on the motion
    c. 1 day prior to the hearing on the motion
    d. 5 days prior to the hearing on the motion

    ANS: d

11. If a complaint is dismissed
    a. the lawsuit is over
    b. a demurrer must be filed
    c. the plaintiff will probably amend the complaint
    d. the defendant will probably amend the motion

    ANS: c

12. A motion to strike seeks to rid a pleading of
    a. prejudicial language
    b. indemnification
    c. interpleaders
    d. defensive language

    ANS: a

13. In analyzing a complaint for a motion to dismiss for failure to state a claim on which relief can be granted, a good target for attack is the
    a. caption
    b. wherefore clause
    c. verification
    d. matching of facts to elements for a cause of action

    ANS: d

14. It is always best to check with your supervising attorney before drafting a motion to dismiss the complaint because
    a. some jurisdictions do not allow paralegals to write rough draft motions
    b. the motion may alert the plaintiff to a weakness better exploited at a later stage
    c. drafting such a motion is exclusively attorney work
    d. a demurrer is usually the preferable approach, especially in federal court

    ANS: b

15. A response to a motion
    a. may be sufficient for a judge to deny the motion without a hearing
    b. can become the basis for a possible oral argument before the judge
    c. is unnecessary if there is a hearing
    d. may not include legal authority

    ANS: b

16. Lack of jurisdiction, improper venue, and insufficient service of process are all cause for
    a. motions for default
    b. motions to dismiss
    c. motions for failure to state a claim
    d. petition for removal

    ANS: b

17. Removal of action to federal court is
    a. required when federal and state courts have concurrent jurisdiction
    b. available to the plaintiff only
    c. accomplished by filing notice of removal in federal court
    d. accomplished by filing a motion for change of venue

    ANS: c

18. Notice of removal should
    a. be served with the answer
    b. state facts in support of state jurisdiction
    c. state that all defendants have joined in the removal action
    d. remand the action to state court

    ANS: c

19. A special demurrer is similar to
    a. a motion to make more definite and certain
    b. a motion to strike
    c. a motion for summary judgment
    d. default

    ANS: a

20. A fact that defeats a plaintiff's claim, even though all allegations are true, is
    a. an argumentative defense
    b. a persuasive defense
    c. an affirmative defense
    d. a quasi-defense

    ANS: c

21. Affirmative defenses are
    a. the same as denials
    b. available for only a few types of cases
    c. defined by substantive law
    d. defined by procedural law

    ANS: c

22. Defenses to be alleged affirmatively include
    a. res gestae
    b. failure of payment
    c. latches and hinges
    d. estoppel

    ANS: d

23. Permissive counterclaims
    a. may include unrelated claims
    b. do not require an assertion of jurisdiction
    c. must be brought in the answer
    d. are claims against codefendants

    ANS: a

24. A complaint brought by a defendant against a previously unnamed party is a
    a. counteraction
    b. cross-claim
    c. third-party answer
    d. third-party complaint

    ANS: d

25. A third-party defendant's responsibility for paying a judgment against the third-party complainant is
    a. an impleader
    b. indemnification
    c. joint liability
    d. the result of a cross-claim

    ANS: b

26. A motion for summary judgment must
    a. allege that there is no question of fact
    b. allege that there is no question of law
    c. not include evidence
    d. be filed before the answer

    ANS: a

True/False

27. Parties generally cooperate in filing a joint application for an order for extension of time.

    ANS: True

28. A motion must be accompanied by a notice of motion.

    ANS: True

29. An acceptable way to gain time to prepare the answer is to file a motion to dismiss.

    ANS: False

30. If a complaint is dismissed, the defendant may collect damages.

    ANS: False

31. Cases that establish precedent should be cited in pleadings.

    ANS: False

32. An order is a request by the plaintiff for relief.

    ANS: False

33. A notice of motion notifies the opponent of the hearing time.

    ANS: True

34. Legal authority is presented in a memorandum of motion.

    ANS: False

35. Prejudicial language is subject to a motion to strike.

    ANS: True

36. Pleadings, once filed, cannot be changed.

    ANS: False

37. A motion can be made orally at trial.

    ANS: True

38. A complaint can be dismissed for defective service.

    ANS: True

39. Filing a motion to dismiss is an acceptable way to gain time, even if that is the only purpose for filing the motion.

    ANS: False

40. Unless they are denied, allegations in the complaint are deemed admitted.

    ANS: True

41. United States government agencies may not remove a case to federal court.

    ANS: False

42. A bill of particulars is part of the list of damages.

    ANS: False

43. Removal of a case to federal court may allow for more complete discovery.

    ANS: True

44. Affirmative defenses are due 21 days after the answer.

    ANS: False

45. The answer may contain counterclaims or cross-claims, but not both.

    ANS: False

46. An answer must be served within 30 days of receipt of summons.

    ANS: False

47. Argumentative denials are the most persuasive.

    ANS: False

48. It is best not to plead inconsistent facts where verification is required.

    ANS: True

49. Compulsory counterclaims may not be the basis for a separate lawsuit.

    ANS: True

50. All amendments to pleadings must be completed before trial.

    ANS: False

51. A motion for summary judgment must be filed at least 10 days before the hearing on the motion.

    ANS: True

52. A pleading log must be filed with the court clerk within 10 days of receipt of the answer.

    ANS: False

Short Answer

53. What are the basic requirements of a motion in Rule 7(b)?

    ANS:
    - It must be in writing, except at trial or hearing.
    - Grounds must be stated with particularity, setting forth order.
    - It must have the same caption as the complaint (et al. allowed).
    - Addresses of parties are not necessary.
    - Attorney's signature and address is necessary.

54. What does it mean to use a motion to preserve the record for appeal?

    ANS: The motion is the record of a question of law that can be the basis for appeal.

55. List four grounds for dismissing a complaint.

    ANS:
    - lack of jurisdiction
    - improper venue
    - insufficiency of process
    - insufficiency of service of process
    - failure to state a claim

56. What is the purpose of a notice of motion?

    ANS: The notice gives the adverse party a fair chance to be prepared to refute the motion. The fundamental fairness that due process aims for requires this balance. See Rule 7(b).

57. In what way is a memorandum of law and an affidavit in support of a motion similar in purpose? In what ways are their purposes different?

    ANS: Both the memorandum of law and the affidavit in support of a motion are intended to assist the judge by providing information beyond that in the complaint or other pleadings. They are different in purpose, however, in that the memo provides arguments of law and authority on which to base a decision, while the affidavit provides factual evidence on which to base a decision.

58. What is a syllogism? Describe how it can be used in determining how to attack a complaint; give examples.

    ANS: A syllogism is a form of reasoning that employs a major premise, a minor premise, and a conclusion. An example of a major premise is, "if A + B + C exist, then Y (conclusion)." The minor premise uses specific facts to prove that the major premise exists, resulting in the same conclusion. For example, "A, B, and C exist, therefore Y (conclusion)." The conclusion, Y, cannot be reached if A, or B, or C or any consideration of those parts, is missing. Because a complaint states a minor premise it must show that each of the required elements exist in order for relief (Y) to be granted. Therefore, if it can be shown that one or more of the elements is missing in the complaint, the plaintiff has no claim. Further, the minor premise is based on the belief that the major premise is true. Thus, if it can be shown that the major premise is in fact not true, then even if the elements of the minor premise exist, the complaint does not state a cause of action. In either case, the defendant has grounds to have the complaint dismissed.

59. What does an attorney's signature on a document mean?

    ANS:
    - that the attorney has read it
    - that it has or is likely to have evidentiary support
    - that it is warranted by law or good faith argument to alter law
    - that it is not offered for improper purposes
    - that any denials of federal contentions are warranted or reasonably based on lack of information or belief

60. Give three strategic advantages for removing an action from state to federal court.

    ANS: A different judge, a more competent jury, a potentially less crowded docket, more liberal transfer rules, or more complete discovery rules.

61. According to Federal Rule 6(a), if a complaint is received on Friday, June 14, what is the last date for filing the answer within a 20-day time limit?

    ANS: Friday, July 5th, because it cannot be filed on July 4, a holiday.

62. List four possible components of the body of the answer.

    ANS: Legal defenses, admissions, denials, affirmative defenses, counterclaims, and cross-claims.

63. What is the penalty for claiming insufficient information to form a belief in the answer simply to avoid the work of investigation?

    ANS: A finding that the allegation is admitted or other Rule 11 sanctions.

64. How may a plaintiff respond to affirmative defenses?

    ANS: Response is not required, but motion to strike or dismiss is allowed, or demurrer in some jurisdictions.

65. What is the difference between compulsory and permissive counterclaims?

    ANS: Compulsory counterclaims arise from original circumstances of the action and may not be the basis for a separate lawsuit. Permissive counterclaims may include unrelated claims, may join other parties, and may be the basis for a separate lawsuit.

66. What is the purpose of impleader and what federal rule governs it?

    ANS: To litigate at one time all claims that arise from a single set of circumstances; Rule 14.

67. How can a pleading log be important?

    ANS: It can help you keep track of the many time limits involved in filing pleadings.

CHAPTER SEVEN: DISCOVERY: OVERVIEW AND INTERROGATORIES

Multiple Choice

1. Mandatory disclosure is governed by
   a. Federal Rule 33
   b. Federal Rule 26(a)
   c. Federal Rule 18(c)
   d. most state rules

   ANS: b

2. Mandatory disclosure includes
   a. only documents
   b. attorney work product
   c. information to support a defense
   d. all information connected to the case

   ANS: c

3. Unless directed otherwise by the court, initial disclosure takes place
   a. within 14 days of the planning meeting
   b. before the scheduling conference

    c. when each party completes its investigation
    d. after a motion to disclose has been filed

    ANS: a

4. Information exchanged in disclosure could include
    a. the names of attorneys for the defense
    b. a letter from the defendant to her attorney
    c. a written statement of expert witness opinion
    d. a copy of all the defendant's business records

    ANS: c

5. Disclosure of information on expert testimony
    a. includes a statement of general viewpoints
    b. can be directed by the court or by stipulation between parties
    c. cannot reveal the amount of compensation for the testimony
    d. is a simple matter

    ANS: b

6. Initial disclosure eliminates the need for
    a. depositions
    b. summons and complaint
    c. early interrogatories
    d. requests for admissions

    ANS: c

7. Pretrial disclosure must be made
    a. in response to a motion for disclosure
    b. at least 30 days before trial
    c. in the presence of a judge
    d. before depositions are taken

    ANS: b

8. In order for an item to be discoverable it must be relevant and
    a. answer questions of law
    b. appear that it will lead to admissible evidence
    c. privileged
    d. authenticated

    ANS: b

9. The federal rule of civil procedure that defines the general scope and limits of discovery is Rule
    a. 26
    b. 30
    c. 33
    d. 25

    ANS: a

10. Federal rules require a party withholding privileged information to
    a. provide identification of that information to the opposing party
    b. be penalized
    c. file an affidavit with the court
    d. reveal the information 30 days before trial

    ANS: a

11. The federal court may limit the volume of discovery devices if the
    a. discovery requested is annoying to the opponent
    b. discovery requested is too expensive for the opponent's resources
    c. information requested is privileged
    d. parties are late in responding

    ANS: b

12. A party must amend their list of witnesses and any prior response to a discovery request, if it is no longer accurate, by
    a. 30 days before trial
    b. 120 days before trial
    c. 30 days after the parties' planning meeting
    d. filing a motion to amend

    ANS: a

13. According to ABA Formal Opinion 92-368, the attorney or paralegal receiving protected information inadvertently sent by the opposing party should
    a. use the information to his or her client's advantage
    b. inspect the information carefully
    c. notify the client
    d. notify the opposing attorney

    ANS: d

14. A report of the parties' planning meeting
    a. must be filed within 14 days
    b. is unnecessary
    c. is an optional reminder for the attorneys
    d. is submitted to the client for approval

    ANS: a

15. Federal Rule 33 covers
    a. disclosure
    b. privileged communication
    c. paralegal ethics in discovery
    d. interrogatories

    ANS: d

16. With mandatory disclosure, interrogatories
    a. are not allowed in federal court
    b. take the place of document production
    c. serve as a follow-up
    d. make depositions unnecessary

    ANS: c

17. An example of an item unsuitable for interrogatories is the
    a. identity of a witness to an accident
    b. existence and location of specific records
    c. physician's detailed account of an operation on plaintiff
    d. insurance coverage of defendant

    ANS: c

18. Valid objections to interrogatories include that
    a. information sought is a factual conclusion
    b. information sought is already known by opponent
    c. question seeks admission
    d. question is too broad

    ANS: d

19. In answering interrogatories always
    a. save time by allowing the other party to search your client's records
    b. object in general to general questions
    c. avoid distortion or misrepresentation
    d. leave blank any questions you are unsure of

    ANS: c

20. A set of interrogatories must be signed by the
    a. paralegal
    b. client
    c. clerk of court
    d. judge

    ANS: b

21. Interrogatories should be answered
    a. orally, if stipulated by all parties
    b. under oath
    c. without objection
    d. without revealing the true answer

    ANS: b

22. Answers to interrogatories should
    a. put the client in the best possible light
    b. include an objection to each question
    c. never include complete documents
    d. not require the involvement of the client

    ANS: a

23. If answers are incomplete, the requesting party can
    a. do nothing
    b. file a motion to compel
    c. refuse to respond to discovery requests by the opponent
    d. have the case dismissed

    ANS: b

True/False

24. The best tactic for winning a lawsuit is surprise.

    ANS: False

25. The cost of discovery is about fifty percent of the cost of litigation.

    ANS: True

26. A motion for mandatory disclosure must be filed within 60 days of the service of summons.

    ANS: False

27. Redundant discovery requests are discouraged.

    ANS: True

28. Discovery helps preserve evidence.

    ANS: True

29. Disclosure is required in all federal courts.

    ANS: True

30. Mandatory disclosure replaces document production in discovery.

    ANS: False

31. Under federal rules, attorneys must meet to plan disclosure and discovery.

    ANS: True

32. Insurance agreements likely to cover damages are revealed through discovery.

    ANS: True

33. Under federal disclosure, information unfavorable to your client's case need not be disclosed.

    ANS: True

34. An exhibit that may be used at trial must be identified in pretrial disclosure.

    ANS: True

35. The amount of compensation to an expert witness is privileged information .

    ANS: False

36. Trial preparation materials must be identified to the opposing party.

    ANS: True

37. Confidential information from the client must be revealed if it is requested through discovery.

    ANS: False

38. Discovery of computerized information requires no more than basic word-processing skills.

    ANS: False

39. Paralegals can help their clients by concealing discoverable evidence.

    ANS: False

40. The parties' planning meeting is held after the scheduling conference or order.

    ANS: False

41. Interrogatories are a good way to find information before a lawsuit begins.

    ANS: False

42. Interrogatories are authorized in Federal Rule 33 and parallel state rules.

    ANS: True

43. Federal rules limit the number of interrogatories to 50.

    ANS: False

44. Information stored in computers is secure, so its discovery can be left until later in the case.

    ANS: False

45. Interrogatories require the attorney's signature and certificate of service.

    ANS: True

46. Abbreviations are never allowed in interrogatories.

    ANS: False

47. Interrogatories may not seek inadmissible evidence.

    ANS: False

48. Client participation is important in answering interrogatories.

    ANS: True

49. Interrogatory questions should be engrossed with the answer.

    ANS: True

50. You cannot object to part and answer part of the same interrogatory.

    ANS: False

51. Updating discovery information is not necessary unless it is requested by the other side.

    ANS: False

52. Not all courts require that interrogatories be filed.

    ANS: True

53. If the answer to an interrogatory is unavailable or uncertain, you should state on information or belief.

    ANS: True

Short Answer

54. List three purposes of discovery.

    ANS:
    a. to eliminate surprise as a basis for winning a lawsuit
    b. to narrow the issues in the case
    c. to provide a basis for early settlement or summary judgment

55. List seven discovery devices.

    ANS: disclosure, interrogatories, depositions, production and inspection, expert opinion, medical exams, request for admissions

56. What are the advantages of interrogatories?

    ANS: They are relatively inexpensive; the answering party has a duty to find the answer; they can "pierce the corporate veil."

57. How can your understanding of the elements of the case help you in drafting interrogatories?

    ANS: Questions need to elicit evidence to support those elements.

58. You need to find out if the defendant's automobile had defects in the steering column, brakes, exhaust, or electrical circuits during the year of the accident and also during the preceding year. Write one simple interrogatory question to elicit these multiple answers.

    ANS: Please identify all defects in the automobile from (date) to (date).

59. Why is it important to word interrogatories carefully?

    ANS: You save time by eliciting the wanted information the first time and without causing objections.

60. When interrogatory answers are returned needing clarification, what are the options?

    ANS:
    * The attorney takes over.
    * You request more information from opposing representation.
    * You draft, file, and serve a motion to compel and affidavit.

61. Why is it a good idea to photocopy interrogatories submitted to you?

    ANS: You can write notes on the working copy; it facilitates analysis of interrogatories and preparation of answers.

CHAPTER EIGHT: DISCOVERY: DEPOSITIONS

Multiple Choice

1. The person to be examined at a deposition is referred to as
    a. the notary
    b. the depositor
    c. the deposer
    d. the deponent

    ANS: d

2. Depositions vary from the scope of most other discovery devices because they
    a. are not limited to the other party
    b. are not limited by relevancy
    c. may provide access to documents
    d. are not limited by privilege

    ANS: a

3. A deposition may be taken without leave of court under Rule 26(a) only if the
    a. deponent is not a party
    b. deponent does not have an attorney
    c. deposition takes place outside the jurisdiction of the court
    d. parties' planning meeting has taken place.

    ANS: d

4. A videotape of the deposition is advantageous because
    a. a good quality tape is easy to produce
    b. a laboratory demonstration can be shown
    c. editing can make the testimony more effective
    d. it makes summarizing the deposition easier

    ANS: b

5. Depositions are specifically covered in the Federal Rules of Civil Procedure in rules
    a. 22–25
    b. 37–40
    c. 27–32
    d. 33–36

    ANS: c

6. Depositions
    a. are by oral exam only
    b. require an oath

    c. are by written questions only

    d. may not take place before the action is filed

ANS: b

7. The notice of deposition does not include
   a. a list of documents to be brought to the deposition
   b. business topics the deposition will cover
   c. the method of recording the testimony
   d. a list of damages to be calculated

ANS: d

8. A party to be deposed must receive a
   a. motion to depose
   b. court order
   c. notice of deposition
   d. summons

ANS: c

9. Rule 45 governs the use of
   a. depositions
   b. interrogatories
   c. requests for admission
   d. subpoenas

ANS: d

10. Upon proper notice, a corporate agent to be deposed is
    a. named by the corporation
    b. the party requesting the deposition
    c. the opposing party
    d. the judge

ANS: a

11. When the opposing party is to bring documents to a deposition she or he should be served with a
    a. Rule 34 request
    b. summons
    c. subpoena duces tecum
    d. court sanction

ANS: c

12. Objections to a subpoena must be served on the other party
    a. within 10 days of service
    b. within 14 days of service
    c. within 20 days of service
    d. any time before trial

ANS: b

13. A subpoena is issued by a clerk in the federal system in
    a. the district where the deposition is to be taken
    b. any district that has jurisdiction

   c. the location most convenient for the deponent
   d. the district where the action is pending

ANS: a

14. Subpoenas are usually issued in
   a. medias res
   b. toto
   c. forma pauperis
   d. blank

ANS: d

15. A subpoena must be served by a
   a. federal marshal
   b. sheriff
   c. person of legal age
   d. paralegal

ANS: c

16. If a deposition is taken in a different district from where the action is pending, the subpoena caption must state the name of the court
   a. that issues the subpoena
   b. where the action is pending
   c. in both districts
   d. in neither district

ANS: a

17. The best procedure for generating possible questions for a deposition is
   a. writing out the potential questions
   b. dictating the potential questions on tape
   c. using videotape
   d. dictating to a legal secretary

ANS: b

18. In preparing for a deposition a client should be told
   a. to be truthful
   b. how to answer
   c. to constantly look at his or her own attorney for signals
   d. to memorize answers

ANS: a

19. Documents or photos may be introduced at depositions so that
   a. the deponent can be convinced of your client's position
   b. they can be authenticated
   c. they can be verified
   d. document production is unnecessary

ANS: b

20. When preparing witnesses for testimony
    a. have them review all recorded statements
    b. tell them the answers they should give
    c. tell them to be impartial
    d. tell them to answer questions quickly

    ANS: c

21. An important paralegal task at the deposition is to
    a. instruct the witness
    b. record the testimony
    c. summarize the deposition
    d. listen and observe

    ANS: d

22. If the deponent refuses to sign the deposition transcript, it is signed by
    a. the court reporter
    b. the judge
    c. the attorneys
    d. no one

    ANS: a

23. Inconsistencies in deposition testimony
    a. are sufficient reason for a second deposition
    b. make the deposition useless
    c. are irrelevant
    d. can be used to impeach a witness

    ANS: d

24. Changes to the deposition transcript can be made by
    a. the attorney
    b. the deponent
    c. the court reporter
    d. no one

    ANS: b

25. Under federal rules, a deponent may review the deposition transcript
    a. after a motion is submitted
    b. with a court order
    c. if a request is entered into the deposition record
    d. without restriction

    ANS: c

26. Immediately following the deposition, the paralegal who attended the deposition should
    a. wait for the typed record of the deposition
    b. prepare interrogatories
    c. prepare requests for production of documents
    d. summarize the deposition

    ANS: d

27. Digesting documents makes it easier to
    a. impeach them
    b. compare evidence
    c. retrieve details
    d. have them admitted as evidence

    ANS: b

28. Types of deposition digests include
    a. narrative
    b. witness
    c. cursory
    d. intermittent

    ANS: a

True/False

29. Depositions are used to evaluate the opposing attorney.

    ANS: True

30. Because depositions are expensive, they are rarely used.

    ANS: False

31. Federal rule limits depositions to a seven hour day.

    ANS: True

32. If your state has a long-arm statute, any deponent may be brought from a distant state for a local deposition.

    ANS: False

33. Only parties and eyewitnesses may be deposed.

    ANS: False

34. If a witness dies before trial, that witness's deposition may not be used.

    ANS: False

35. Normally, no more than 10 depositions are allowed.

    ANS: True

36. A deposition by written questions is best because the other party cannot ask cross questions.

    ANS: False

37. Depositions can be taken before an action is filed.

    ANS: True

38. The defendant may not be represented at a deposition conducted by the plaintiff.

    ANS: False

39. The party requesting the deposition must pay recording costs.

    ANS: True

40. A deposition may not be taken before the parties' planning meeting without leave of the court, under Rule 26(a).

    ANS: True

41. A plaintiff can be required to attend a deposition in the jurisdiction where the action was brought.

    ANS: True

42. A certified court reporter usually records depositions.

    ANS: True

43. A subpoena duces tecum allows a witness to submit answers in writing without appearing in person.

    ANS: False

44. In the federal system, an attorney can issue a subpoena for a deposition.

    ANS: True

45. Subpoenas in the federal system are served by a sheriff.

    ANS: False

46. An objection to a subpoena can be served any time before the deposition.

    ANS: False

47. Witnesses should not be paid a fee.

    ANS: False

48. Paralegals can serve subpoenas.

    ANS: True

49. Paralegals may question deponents if the supervising attorney is not present.

    ANS: False

50. A preliminary interview can help determine whom to depose.

    ANS: True

51. If a party is unable to obtain counsel, a deposition without leave of court may not be used at trial against that party.

    ANS: True

52. A witness may be deposed up to three times.

    ANS: False

53. If a deposition is conducted by written questions, the requesting party must serve the questions on every other party.

    ANS: True

54. If a party is to be deposed, a subpoena must be prepared.

    ANS: False

55. Witnesses are more accurate if they refer to a diagram.

    ANS: True

56. Good objections suggest answers to the deponent.

    ANS: False

57. Copies of documents reviewed by witnesses before the deposition must be made available to the opposing party.

    ANS: True

58. The official deposition transcript cannot be changed.

    ANS: False

59. Deposition digests should include pertinent notes on the deponent's demeanor.

    ANS: True

60. Cross-indexing deposition testimony is likely to lose information.

    ANS: False

Short Answer

61. Depositions can be useful for what reasons?

    ANS: They are useful to explore points raised in interrogatories, evaluate witnesses and the opposing attorney, impeach witnesses, serve as evidence if the witness is unavailable for trial, sharpen the focus of the case, question persons other than parties, and authenticate documents.

62. How can computers be used in deposition practice?

    ANS: Internet searches for transcription services and oath officers, real-time transcript services during deposition, accessing transcripts, and summarizing transcripts.

63. Compare the scope of questioning at a deposition to that at trial.

    ANS: Deposition allows more latitude, such as questions that might reasonably lead to evidence: hearsay, identification of witnesses and evidence.

64. Why is preparation of your client for a deposition important?

    ANS: Effective testimony may bring the case to an early and favorable settlement. Inconsistencies in the deposition will damage your client's case.

65. What is the paralegal's role in preparing for deposition, at deposition, and after deposition?

    ANS: Preparing for the deposition:
    - Arrange for the date, site, method of recording, and oath officer.
    - Prepare and serve notice of deposition.
    - Subpoena the deponent.
    - Draft questions.
    - Gather documents.
    - Set up witness files.
    - Prepare the witness.

    At the deposition:
    - Listen.
    - Take notes on information, objections, and the effectiveness of witness and opposing counsel.
    - Catch missed questions.
    - Retrieve information and documents.

    After the deposition:
    - Compare notes with the attorney.
    - Draft the summary.
    - Submit any changes.
    - See that the deponent signs the transcript, if necessary.
    - Verify certification.
    - Mark documents as exhibits.
    - Review the transcript.
    - Digest the deposition and transcript.
    - Update the case file.

CHAPTER NINE: DISCOVERY: DOCUMENT PRODUCTION AND CONTROL, MEDICAL EXAMS, ADMISSIONS, AND COMPELLING DISCOVERY

Multiple Choice

1. The purpose of document production is to
   a. confuse the opponent with a mass of paper
   b. provide the opponent an opportunity to review documents
   c. prevent the opponent's access to documents
   d. complete all case paperwork before trial

   ANS: b

2. The production of documents and things is not the proper discovery device to gain access to
   a. writings and drawings of the other party
   b. computer data compilations of the other party
   c. entry to land of a non-party
   d. samples of tangible things held by the other party

   ANS: c

3. Often the best source for determining the location of documents is the
   a. paralegal
   b. client
   c. attorney
   d. corporate president

   ANS: b

4. Production of electronic data may require the assistance of
   a. an electrician
   b. a forensic software analyst
   c. a motion for electronic inventory
   d. anyone who can do computerized word processing

   ANS: b

5. The most significant index to be prepared is the
   a. master index
   b. privileged information index
   c. product index
   d. chronological index

   ANS: a

6. When photocopying documents, remember that poor copies should be
   a. kept in an "extras" copy file
   b. placed behind the original document
   c. thrown away
   d. destroyed

   ANS: d

7. At the examination of the documents, you do not need to
   a. copy each document chosen by the opponent
   b. copy each privileged document chosen by the opponent
   c. make an index of chosen documents
   d. arrange the documents to be examined according to the opponent's request

   ANS: b

8. When copying documents for production,
   a. staple copies if originals were stapled
   b. copy only the pertinent pages of large documents
   c. keep any poor copies for use as scratch paper
   d. take copies for the case file and return originals to the custodian

   ANS: a

9. If documents are properly identified and indexed, locating them requires
   a. a thorough search of all file boxes
   b. a search of computer files
   c. the number of the document
   d. the assistance of a forensic software analyst

   ANS: c

10. When returning original documents to their custodian, it is improper to
    a. keep ample copies of all returned documents
    b. log all returns
    c. keep all indexes and return letters
    d. obtain a receipt for each returned document or file

    ANS: a

11. Because searches in a full-text computer system are done by key words,
    a. it is important to standardize key terms
    b. standardization is unimportant
    c. standardization is often suggested but it is too cumbersome
    d. use KEYNOTE software

    ANS: a

12. A coded entry system
    a. is a full-text system
    b. requires uniformity
    c. eliminates the need for searches
    d. requires scanners for document entry

    ANS: b

13. The final decision on document production methods is made by the
    a. attorney
    b. paralegal
    c. client
    d. custodian of the documents

    ANS: a

14. At the close of the case, copies of documents should be
    a. returned with original documents
    b. kept in the case file
    c. destroyed
    d. kept in a computer file

    ANS: c

15. In planning document production, you need to consider
    a. access to the courthouse
    b. preparation of witnesses
    c. clarity of answers
    d. work space

    ANS: d

16. During production, privileged documents should be
    a. hidden
    b. carefully identified
    c. kept accessible to all parties
    d. destroyed

    ANS: b

17. One party may request the other party to undergo a physical or mental exam under Federal Rule
    a. 30
    b. 35
    c. 37
    d. 26

    ANS: b

18. When reviewing technical documents, it is best to
    a. disregard them because the jury will not understand them
    b. create a glossary of technical terms raised in a particular case
    c. assume all abbreviations are standardized in any particular field
    d. rely on your common sense to translate them

    ANS: b

19. A request for admission is a request for
    a. factual information, leads to evidence, and the location of documents
    b. the opponent's description of facts, documents, or physical evidence
    c. the opponent's confirmation of the truthfulness and accuracy of facts, opinions, or the application of law to facts
    d. a statement of the opponent's responsibility for injuries

    ANS: c

20. A request for admission seeks to
    a. discover new evidence
    b. narrow the issues for trial
    c. confirm that previously discovered information is admissible
    d. have the case dismissed

    ANS: b

21. A response to a request for admission must be made in
    a. 10 days
    b. 20 days
    c. 60 days
    d. 30 days

    ANS: d

22. Compelling discovery is covered in detail in Federal Rule
    a. 23
    b. 26
    c. 34
    d. 37

    ANS: d

23. An order obtained by the court that prevents a party from obtaining specified information in discovery is called a
    a. screen order
    b. protective order
    c. dismissal order
    d. compliance order

    ANS: b

24. The Freedom of Information Act allows access to
    a. classified national defense documents
    b. information not relevant to the case for which the request is made
    c. trade secrets
    d. geological information on oil wells

    ANS: b

25. The first step of a Freedom of Information Act search is to
    a. find forms at the Internet site of the applicable agency
    b. submit an FOIA notice to the court
    c. request permission from your congressional representative
    d. have both sides stipulate to the search

    ANS: a

26. The fact section of a small case file should include
    a. the complaint
    b. medical bills
    c. records of witness fees
    d. letters from the client

    ANS: b

27. Large case files usually
    a. have to be organized by different methods for each case
    b. are no more complex than small case files
    c. do not need indices if they are organized properly
    d. are divided and subdivided numerically

    ANS: d

True/False

28. Discovery of documents is available only through the device of document production.

    ANS: False

29. Failure to organize documents can mean the loss of the case.

    ANS: True

30. A very important aspect of document control is maintaining indexes.

    ANS: True

31. Document production may be accomplished by exchange of a CD-ROM.

    ANS: True

32. Full-text computer entry of documents is best for cases involving thousands of documents.

    ANS: False

33. When you take original files for production, it is wise to leave a tip for the custodian.

    ANS: False

34. An original source log is most helpful when returning documents to their custodians at the end of a case.

    ANS: True

35. Classifications of documents should be set out before production begins.

    ANS: True

36. Document production should be coordinated with the custodian of the documents.

    ANS: True

37. Produced documents belonging to the same category should be stapled together.

    ANS: False

38. Original documents should be returned to their custodian as soon as they are copied.

    ANS: False

39. Computerization of document production is prohibitively expensive.

    ANS: False

40. A uniform decimal system is best for numbering documents in small cases.

    ANS: False

41. The ABA's Legal Technology Advisory Council is set up to help firms handle large volumes of documents.

    ANS: False

42. A party may request an admission that a certain piece of evidence is genuine.

    ANS: True

43. A medical records librarian is a good source for interpreting doctors' orders.

    ANS: True

44. Federal Rule 37 covers requests for medical examinations.

    ANS: False

45. Paralegals should not accompany clients to medical exams.

    ANS: False

46. A request for a medical examination does not require the party to undergo the exam.

    ANS: True

47. For a medical exam to be ordered, the alleged condition must be in controversy.

    ANS: True

48. If the opponent refuses to undergo a medical exam, the requesting party has no recourse.

    ANS: False

49. Protective orders may allow a party not to answer interrogatories.

    ANS: True

50. Failure to cooperate with discovery may result in criminal charges.

    ANS: True

51. The billing section of a small case file should include the client's medical bills related to the case.

    ANS: False

Matching

52. Match each item with the following correct statement.

    a. Admission of fact
    b. Admission of opinion
    c. Admission regarding the application of law to fact

    1. Mr. Hart was intoxicated at the time of the accident.
    2. There was ice on the road at the time of the accident.
    3. Mr. Hart was acting in an agency capacity for Mercury Parcel Service at the time of the accident.
    4. Mr. Hart was driving too fast for conditions as defined in Columbia Statute 390.25.
    5. The temperature was 15°F the morning of the accident.

    1. **ANS:** b
    2. **ANS:** a
    3. **ANS:** c
    4. **ANS:** c
    5. **ANS:** a

Short Answer

53. What basic needs should you plan for in document production?

    ANS: Materials, personnel, equipment, and space.

54. How can you make production less difficult for your business client?

    ANS: Notify supervisors of reason for search and what is needed. Keep disruption of routine to a minimum, safeguard documents, and leave copies and notification where originals can be found; inform custodian what documents have been removed.

55. How does a uniform decimal system of numbering documents work?

    ANS: Digits in each position of the number refer to a specific category to which the document belongs, allowing it to be organized and retrieved for a specific purpose.

56. When you screen files and documents for production, what three tasks must you do?

    ANS: Identify items responsive to the request; identify privileged documents; number and classify documents.

57. How should you handle privileged documents during production?

    ANS: They should first be identified with a colored sheet, then both should be pulled and placed in a locked facility.

58. What entity of the ABA tests software for law offices and can provide assistance in choosing a program?

    ANS: The Legal Technology Advisory Council.

59. What security precautions need to be taken in computer document control?

    ANS: Backup disks should be made, all disks should be kept in a locked facility, passwords should be used, privileged and work product materials should be kept in a separate data base.

60. List three places to look for computerized data to comply with discovery requests.

    ANS: Files in computer and network memory; backed up data; retired or archived sources; e-mail; residual "deleted" data; and data in buffer memories.

61. How can computers help with document production?

    ANS: They can search, sort, and store a variety of data and make it accessible at any time. They reduce mistakes and save time and space.

62. At the close of the case, what should be done with original documents? Indexes? Copies of documents?

    ANS: Returned to custodians; kept in case file; destroyed.

63. Name three helpful resources for interpreting documents.

    ANS: A medical records librarian, specialized dictionaries, textbooks, professional organizations.

64. How can a master topical digest help organize depositions?

    ANS: It brings together information from all depositions in a case on one topic.

65. What are the advantages in using the Freedom of Information Act for discovery?

    ANS: Can be used without filing an action; relevance does not apply; access is available to anyone with a bona fide request; not restricted to information from a party.

66. What are four general categories to be included in a small case file?

    ANS: Facts, pleadings, correspondence, billing.

67. What indexes are necessary for a large case file?

    ANS: Master index, subfile indexes.

CHAPTER TEN: SETTLEMENT AND OTHER ALTERNATIVE DISPUTE RESOLUTIONS

Multiple Choice

1. The percentage of civil cases that are settled is
   a. 70–75 percent
   b. 50 percent
   c. 80 percent
   d. 90–95 percent

   ANS: d

2. The primary role of the paralegal in the settlement process is to
   a. negotiate with the adverse party
   b. organize information
   c. put information in a persuasive, presentable format
   d. arbitrate the case

   ANS: c

3. The decision to accept settlement is made by the
   a. judge
   b. attorney
   c. client
   d. mediator

   ANS: c

4. In preparing a settlement précis or in discussions with the adverse party's attorney, the paralegal
   a. needs to be cautious about revealing too much information
   b. has no need to seek the guidance of the attorney
   c. has no need to be concerned about revealing confidential information
   d. has no need to be concerned about any embarrassment to the client

   ANS: a

5. A well-prepared settlement proposal usually
   a. prolongs a case
   b. is unproductive
   c. assists in the preparation for trial
   d. is of little value in preparing for trial

   ANS: c

6. It is best to prepare a settlement proposal
   a. even before investigation
   b. as early in the case as investigation and discovery will permit

   c. just before the final pretrial conference

   d. just before trial

ANS: b

7. Producing a settlement brochure
   a. is too expensive for most cases
   b. must be done by professional printers
   c. is not a good use of resources if liability is unclear
   d. requires avoidance of emotional issues

ANS: c

8. An example of an incorrect damage calculation formula is
   a. Future medical costs: current daily cost times the number of days needed per year times the number of years times adjustments for growth in medical cost and reduced for present cash value.
   b. Future wages cost if victim deceased: most recent normal year's wages times years of work expectancy times percent reduction to present cash value.
   c. Personal property damage if item destroyed: market value less salvage.
   d. Real property, temporary damage: reduction in rental or other profit value plus injury to crops, buildings, and improvements plus restoration costs plus any applicable interest.

ANS: b

9. Calculating damages does not include
   a. losses that occurred before the cause of action
   b. losses that occurred since the cause of action
   c. losses that are anticipated but have not yet occurred
   d. hedonic damages

ANS: a

10. The settlement brochure
   a. should be informal, like a family scrapbook
   b. tells the opposition that you are ready and will likely win
   c. should avoid using statements of doctors and witnesses that advocate the deserving nature of the client
   d. is most effective if it is no longer than two pages

ANS: b

11. The settlement brochure should include the
   a. personal history of plaintiff
   b. medical history of defendant
   c. pleadings
   d. motions

ANS: a

12. The defense
   a. never proposes a settlement
   b. only reacts to the plaintiff's request for settlement
   c. seldom prepares a settlement brochure
   d. derives no advantage from settlement

ANS: c

13. Preparing for settlement on behalf of an insurance company
    a. is completely different from preparing for settlement on behalf of the plaintiff
    b. is similar to preparing for settlement for the plaintiff with the exception of investigation
    c. requires much less contact with the client
    d. is similar to preparing for settlement for the plaintiff with the exception of the précis and brochure

    ANS: d

14. A pretrial conference
    a. is governed by Rule 13 in the federal rules
    b. is designed to narrow the issues for trial
    c. may not be used to encourage settlement
    d. cannot be used to judicially manage the case

    ANS: b

15. In regard to a pretrial conference, a task the paralegal should leave to the attorney is to
    a. docket reminders of the date of the conference for both attorney and paralegal
    b. see that client has signed all needed authorizations
    c. prepare summaries and gather supporting documents and legal memoranda for the attorney to take to conference
    d. advise client on what a reasonable settlement range will be

    ANS: d

16. A release in the context of settlement is
    a. a document signed by the defendant to release medical or similar records
    b. a document, signed usually by the plaintiff, releasing the defendant from liability
    c. a long complex document setting out the terms of settlement
    d. the judge's certification of the agreement

    ANS: b

17. Federal Rule 41(a)(1) and parallel state rules
    a. permit the plaintiff's application for an order to dismiss an action only if it comes prior to the serving of the answer
    b. permit the application for an order to dismiss an action after the answer is served if both parties stipulate to the dismissal
    c. require the judge to approve the terms of settlement
    d. require a consent decree and order

    ANS: b

18. When an action is dismissed with prejudice, the action
    a. may not be brought again
    b. may be brought again
    c. must be arbitrated
    d. must be mediated

    ANS: a

19. The judge's review and approval is required for the
    a. release
    b. settlement agreement

    c. consent decree and order

    d. stipulation and order for dismissal

ANS: c

20. Mediation

    a. is adversarial

    b. can be voluntary or mandatory

    c. is a formal courtroom process

    d. requires a burden of proof

ANS: b

21. Arbitration

    a. is less formal than mediation

    b. imposes a burden of persuasion

    c. is adversarial

    d. is always voluntary

ANS: b

22. Voluntary arbitration

    a. is controlled by the courts

    b. allows parties to set guidelines

    c. is always binding

    d. is a very formal process

ANS: b

23. If an arbitration decision was obtained by fraud

    a. it may be appealed to the courts

    b. it is dealt with under the Federal Frauds Act

    c. the case is then mediated

    d. there is no recourse

ANS: a

24. Court-annexed arbitration

    a. may end in mediation

    b. may end in a trial de novo

    c. must be requested by parties

    d. is required in all federal cases

ANS: b

25. A trial de novo is a

    a. trial as if no previous hearing or arbitration had been held

    b. trial before a novice judge

    c. form of arbitration

    d. highly publicized trial

ANS: a

26. International business disputes

    a. always go to trial

    b. are negotiated privately because there are no international arbitration rules

    c. are all subject to United Nations Rules
    d. are subject to arbitration clauses in about 80 percent of international business agreements

    ANS: d

27. Rules for mediation arise from
    a. state rules of procedure
    b. Federal Rule 38
    c. the court
    d. the participants

    ANS: d

28. Alternative dispute resolution
    a. is seldom successful
    b. is growing as an alternative to trial
    c. does not work in family disputes
    d. is expensive

    ANS: b

True/False

29. A party's social standing is not involved in the settlement process.

    ANS: False

30. Abilities of opposing attorneys should be researched for trial but are not important in settlement considerations.

    ANS: False

31. Local practice helps determine procedure in pretrial conferences.

    ANS: True

32. LOELs are punitive damages.

    ANS: False

33. The settlement request usually comes from the plaintiff.

    ANS: True

34. A settlement brochure is more effective if it has an emotional impact.

    ANS: True

35. If a plaintiff has not seen a doctor, used home remedies, or missed work, that plaintiff's injury claim is suspect.

    ANS: True

36. The paralegal should keep the insurance adjuster informed.

    ANS: True

37. Pain and suffering is the same as loss of enjoyment of life.

    ANS: False

38. Pain and suffering is an example of exemplary damages.

    ANS: False

39. Future losses are not valid damage claims.

    ANS: False

40. The defense usually prepares a settlement brochure.

    ANS: False

41. A letter may be a sufficient settlement request in small cases.

    ANS: True

42. All witnesses must attend pretrial conferences.

    ANS: False

43. An adjudication on the merits leaves issues that can be brought up at trial.

    ANS: False

44. Because they communicate most closely with clients, paralegals are best equipped to accept offers of settlement.

    ANS: False

45. Discovery is not available in arbitration.

    ANS: False

46. Federal courts discourage ADR.

    ANS: False

47. Arbitration usually takes less time than a trial.

    ANS: True

48. An arbitration hearing is similar to a trial, but more informal.

    ANS: True

49. Arbitration decisions cannot be appealed to the courts.

    ANS: False

50. The standard of proof in arbitration varies.

    ANS: True

51. Mediation focuses on future rather than past conduct.

    ANS: True

52. Mediators must be selected by judges.

    ANS: False

53. There is no burden of persuasion in mediation.

    ANS: True

54. Mediation is not suitable in complex cases.

    ANS: False

55. Verdicts in summary jury trials are binding.

    ANS: False

56. Paralegal tasks for ADR are similar to those for trial.

    ANS: True

57. Paralegals may serve as mediators.

    ANS: True

58. Early case assessment reduces discovery costs.

    ANS: True

59. The focus of a settlement conference is broader than that of a pretrial conference.

    ANS: False

60. A client may be required to attend the pretrial conference.

    ANS: True

Short Answer

61. What are the advantages of settlement over trial?

    ANS: Saves time, trouble, expense, removes uncertainty; reduces adverse publicity and animosity between parties.

62. What are the ethical concerns of a paralegal discussing settlement with a client?

    ANS: A paralegal may not make or accept offers or counsel a client on settlement. Do not reveal harmful or confidential information.

63. List three types of settlement requests from least to most expensive.

    ANS: Settlement letter, précis, brochure.

64. How can a video camera help in preparing for settlement?

    ANS: "Day in the Life" videos are persuasive in establishing documentation of pain and suffering. Videos of friends and relatives regarding an injury's impact on the plaintiff and others are also helpful.

65. Describe the usual setting and participants for a pretrial conference. What is added to the expanded federal pretrial conference process?

    ANS: Judge's chambers; judge and attorneys for both sides, parties may be required to attend. The expanded process includes meetings to help manage the litigation, especially in big cases.

66. Why is it important to have the client sign an authorization for the attorney to settle?

    ANS: It allows the attorney to negotiate in good faith and is required by court decisions and rules.

67. What is court-annexed arbitration?

    ANS: The court controls the process, assigns a case to arbitration, and may try the case if arbitration is not successful.

68. Which of the following are true of arbitration; which are true of mediation?
    a. uses statement of claim
    b. parties reach mutual agreement
    c. burden of persuasion is set
    d. is more adversarial
    e. focuses on future rather than past conduct
    f. can be voluntary or mandatory
    g. less formal

    ANS: Arbitration: a, c, d, f
    Mediation: b, e, f, g

69. Describe med-arb.

    ANS: Alternative dispute resolution that starts as mediation and ends with arbitration of any unsettled issues.

70. How does summary trial lead to settlement?

    ANS: It shows which side may prevail in a full-scale trial, thus encouraging the other side to settle.

CHAPTER ELEVEN: TRIAL PREPARATION AND TRIAL

Multiple Choice

1. A file status sheet is useful in pretrial preparation because it
   a. rates the case as a good case or a bad case
   b. indicates what steps remain to be completed prior to trial

    c. encourages the opponent to settle
    d. brings discovery to a close

    ANS: b

2. A case status sheet shows the
    a. legal team how their case will look to a jury
    b. judge how soon the case will be ready for trial
    c. legal team what is left to be done
    d. opposition how strong your case is

    ANS: c

3. For pretrial preparation, the paralegal needs
    a. to know little about the case
    b. years of experience
    c. to review the file and all summaries carefully
    d. to leave all remaining work to the attorney

    ANS: c

4. In preparing for trial it is best to
    a. subpoena all witnesses needed to prove case
    b. subpoena only the cool or unfriendly witnesses
    c. subpoena only the friendly witnesses
    d. avoid subpoenaing friendly witnesses because they might become irritated.

    ANS: a

5. The federal rule setting out the requirements for service of subpoenas is Rule
    a. 26
    b. 40
    c. 50
    d. 45

    ANS: d

6. Subpoenas need to be reissued if
    a. there is a change of venue
    b. there is a change in the order witnesses will testify
    c. they are challenged
    d. the trial lasts longer than a week

    ANS: a

7. A source of information on a juror that the paralegal should avoid is
    a. juror information sheets
    b. voter registration lists
    c. the juror
    d. juror files kept by other law firms

    ANS: c

8. A juror data sheet is not used for a
    a. summary sheet for the attorney during voir dire
    b. paralegal's checklist to determine what information to gather

c. record of juror experiences related to trial issues

d. checklist for jurors to keep track of evidence during trial

ANS: d

9. The types of audiovisual aids used at trial
   a. are chosen as a matter of personal taste
   b. all cost about the same
   c. can substantially affect how the jury learns and retains information
   d. are chosen primarily for entertainment value

   ANS: c

10. Diagrams for purely illustrative purposes
    a. must be drawn to scale
    b. need not be drawn to scale but must be a fair representation of what is depicted
    c. are generally admissible as evidence
    d. are not worth your time

    ANS: b

11. In preparing a diagram or chart for use in court, it is important to remember that
    a. horizontal wording big enough to see from a distance is best
    b. a paralegal without artistic ability should not attempt such a task
    c. the more complex the diagram, the more help it is
    d. vertical wording breaks the monotony of a diagram and should be used often

    ANS: a

12. A trial notebook
    a. is a brief of legal authority needed at trial
    b. consists of most things an attorney will need at trial, organized for quick access and retrieval
    c. is used for cross examination only
    d. is given to each juror

    ANS: b

13. Trial motions include a motion
    a. for summary judgment
    b. to make more definite and certain
    c. for failure to state a claim
    d. for directed verdict

    ANS: d

14. A motion in limine is a motion
    a. to dismiss
    b. for protection against prejudicial questions and statements
    c. to force a witness to testify
    d. to postpone the trial

    ANS: b

15. Jury instructions
    a. may be drafted in rough by the paralegal
    b. are unique for each case

c.   are seldom necessary
d.   are seldom in dispute

ANS: a

16. A paralegal should avoid
   a.   taking the witness to the courtroom
   b.   talking directly to the witness
   c.   telling the expert to impress the jury with his or her knowledge of the specific terminology in the field
   d.   paying the witness a mileage fee

ANS: c

17. The paralegal can assist in the selection of jurors at trial by
   a.   recording valuable information about each juror on the jury panel chart
   b.   asking questions of the jurors
   c.   making numerous judgments based on body language
   d.   making peremptory challenges

ANS: a

18. A paralegal may be responsible for
   a.   pointing out areas of witness examination missed by the attorney
   b.   deciding when to enter a motion in limine
   c.   voir dire
   d.   the prima facie case

ANS: a

19. Paralegals' trial notes are
   a.   particularly important during direct examination
   b.   a personal record of your experiences
   c.   especially effective when an outline of procedural steps is on the left page and detailed notes of important testimony or evidence on the right
   d.   are seldom necessary because attorneys take their own notes

ANS: c

20. Voir dire is
   a.   jury investigation
   b.   the process of selecting the jury panel
   c.   the process of deciding a verdict
   d.   a trial motion

ANS: b

21. Translating body language
   a.   can be a valuable help in jury selection
   b.   should be done with caution
   c.   is based on science
   d.   should be done by an expert witness

ANS: b

22. If the plaintiff meets the requisite burden of proof at trial
   a.   this is called a prima facie case
   b.   the case is decided in favor of the plaintiff

    c. no more evidence may be presented

    d. no appeals are allowed

ANS: a

23. A juror data sheet

    a. helps determine who is called for jury duty

    b. is filled out by the clerk of court when the jury is selected

    c. is a checklist of information about the trial for jurors

    d. helps the attorney plan for voir dire

ANS: d

24. Demonstrative evidence

    a. can clarify confusing data

    b. should be used in every trial

    c. is too expensive for small trials

    d. is never computerized

ANS: a

25. If the judge for your trial follows a docket list

    a. you can count on a definite trial date

    b. the trial date depends on the rate of completion of other trials

    c. you may select the trial date most convenient for your client

    d. you will have no idea when the trial date will come up.

ANS: b

26. Liquid-crystal display units can be used

    a. to keep track of juror information

    b. to show demonstrative evidence of three-dimensional items

    c. to record trial proceedings

    d. in place of the trial notebook

ANS: b

27. Shadow juries are helpful to

    a. impeach witnesses

    b. review the verdict on appeal

    c. give feedback on the impact of evidence

    d. instruct the jury panel on its responsibilities

ANS: c

28. Shadow juries

    a. are required by Federal Rule 47

    b. can be helpful in preparing the closing argument

    c. are not allowed in federal courts

    d. are allowed only by leave of the court.

ANS: b

True /False

29. Mock juries are ways for inexperienced jurors to practice.

    ANS: False

30. Juror interviews are expensive, but are the most effective means of jury investigation.

    ANS: False

31. Voter registration lists can give you information about jurors.

    ANS: True

32. A motion in limine requests a trial de novo.

    ANS: False

33. In the federal system a motion for a directed verdict is called a motion for judgment as a matter of law.

    ANS: True

34. If a party is dissatisfied with a verdict, the only recourse is appeal.

    ANS: False

35. You can enhance your value to the firm by offering to research and draft memoranda of law.

    ANS: True

36. A primary task of paralegals at trial is keeping track of information.

    ANS: True

37. A judgment notwithstanding the verdict is based on the weight of evidence.

    ANS: True

38. Demonstrative evidence must always be an exact representation.

    ANS: False

39. A good rule of thumb is to use demonstrative evidence whether you think it will help or not.

    ANS: False

40. The appearance of your client is important at a jury trial.

    ANS: True

41. A case status sheet tells the judge whether parties are ready for trial.

    ANS: False

42. Voir dire challenges for cause are unlimited in number.

    ANS: True

43. Subpoenas must be served at least 10 days before trial.

    ANS: True

44. The best practice is to subpoena all witnesses necessary to prove your case.

    ANS: True

45. Service of subpoenas is governed by Federal Rule 45.

    ANS: True

46. Subpoenas may be obtained at the last minute before trial.

    ANS: True

47. A jury survey gives you accurate information on specific jurors.

    ANS: False

48. Jurors can be relied upon to be unbiased and to apply the instructions given by the judge.

    ANS: False

49. It is unethical to research the abilities of the opposing attorney.

    ANS: False

50. Models are the best type of demonstrative evidence if costs are to be kept down.

    ANS: False

51. A trial notebook should be arranged chronologically as issues come up at trial.

    ANS: True

52. A trial notebook should contain all the evidence gathered through discovery.

    ANS: False

53. It is a waste of time to prepare trial motions before trial.

    ANS: False

54. Jury instructions are set by law.

    ANS: False

55. It is unethical to tell a witness how to answer a question at trial.

    ANS: True

56. Findings of fact and conclusions of law state the basis of a judge's decision on a case.

    ANS: True

57. An expert witness should be told all the details of the case.

    ANS: False

58. A paralegal who is called to testify is ethically bound to give answers favorable to his or her client.

    ANS: False

59. Computer technology is helpful in trial preparation, but is not advantageous in the court room.

    ANS: False

Short Answer

60. What do you need to remember about identifying documents on a subpoena duces tecum?

    ANS: They must be described with reasonable certainty, making extensive searches unnecessary. Words such as "every" or "all" are suspect.

61. What can you learn about potential jurors from voter registration lists? Jury surveys?

    ANS: Political party affiliations, where required. Attitudes of a community toward the issues at trial, especially the attitudes of those individuals who match prospective jurors' backgrounds.

62. Besides the jury, who else should be researched before the trial?

    ANS: The judge, opposing counsel, and the community.

63. What factors can help make diagrams effective for use at trial?

    ANS: Simplicity, accuracy, and readability.

64. How can you prepare an expert witness for testimony at trial?

    ANS: Collect and summarize qualifications, provide facts and theories of the case, note expert's suggestions for material needed, guide against defensiveness, jargon, and condescension.

65. What are the grounds for a judgment notwithstanding the verdict (a renewal of the motion for judgment as a matter of law)?

    ANS: The verdict is against the great weight of the evidence, or, as a matter of law, there is only one reasonable conclusion for the verdict.

66. What is the primary type of task for paralegals at trial?

    ANS: This is somewhat subjective, but should be close to the following: Keeping track of information and witnesses to be presented; taking notes of proceedings and impressions.

CHAPTER TWELVE: POST-TRIAL PRACTICE FROM MOTIONS TO APPEAL

Multiple Choice

1. A motion asking that a judgment be set aside because the verdict was contrary to the weight of the evidence is a motion
    a. to dismiss
    b. for a new trial
    c. for judgment as a matter of law
    d. for directed verdict

    ANS: c

2. A motion for JNOV under Rule 50 may be made by
    a. a party if not made before the verdict
    b. the defendant when there were procedural errors
    c. either party's paralegal
    d. the party who previously moved for a directed verdict

    ANS: d

3. A motion asking that judgment be set aside because of procedural or other prejudicial error at trial is a motion
    a. to dismiss
    b. for new trial
    c. for judgment as a matter of law
    d. for directed verdict

    ANS: b

4. Remittitur is a post-trial motion
    a. in which the defendant asks the court to reduce a jury award
    b. in which the plaintiff asks the court to increase a jury award
    c. used only in state courts
    d. is the process used to draw the amount of the jury award from the defendant's wages

    ANS: a

5. Under the federal rules, post-trial motions must be filed within
    a. 5 days after judgment
    b. 10 days after judgment
    c. 20 days after judgment
    d. 30 days after judgment

    ANS: b

6. Federal Rule 54(d) and parallel state rules provide that costs shall be awarded
    a. as determined by the parties
    b. equally
    c. as ordered by the court
    d. only when the bill of costs is included in the damages

    ANS: c

7. A bill of costs does not include
   a. filing fees
   b. witness fees
   c. costs of service of process
   d. attorney's fees

   ANS: d

8. Jewelry is classified as
   a. real property
   b. a fixture
   c. personal property
   d. exempt property

   ANS: c

9. The purpose of a prejudgment remedy is to
   a. prevent the defendant from selling or otherwise disposing of assets to cover an anticipated judgment
   b. hold a deposition so it can be determined what assets are possessed by the defendant
   c. execute on and sell the judgment debtor's property so the judgment can be paid
   d. determine the bill of costs

   ANS: a

10. Garnishment is a procedure used to
    a. attach and sell the property of the judgment creditor
    b. acquire property of the judgment debtor owed to the debtor by a third person
    c. acquire real property of the judgment debtor
    d. acquire intangible property of the judgment debtor

    ANS: b

11. A judgment creditor can locate assets of an uncooperative judgment debtor by means of
    a. additur
    b. postjudgment motions
    c. postjudgment depositions
    d. appellate briefs

    ANS: c

12. A good source for finding information on enforcement of judgments in your state is a
    a. federal book on collections
    b. state book on collections
    c. federal book on remedies
    d. state book on remedies

    ANS: b

13. An example of intangible property is
    a. the royalty rights of an author
    b. a lien
    c. a diamond ring
    d. a fixture on land

    ANS: a

14. Creditor's examinations have the advantage of
    a. flexibility
    b. being inexpensive
    c. reaching a variety of documents
    d. being quick

    ANS: a

15. An example of a self-executing judgment is a
    a. transfer of a deed
    b. payment of $10,000
    c. divorce
    d. return of a painting

    ANS: c

16. Lis pendens is the
    a. record that the plaintiff has asserted a claim against property
    b. process of securing property for the judgment creditor
    c. motion included with the appellate brief
    d. post-trial deposition

    ANS: a

17. Garnishment is
    a. a prejudgment remedy only
    b. a postjudgment remedy only
    c. both a prejudgment and postjudgment remedy
    d. the same as attachment

    ANS: c

18. A lien is
    a. a claim against property
    b. real property
    c. recoverable in the bill of costs
    d. tangible property

    ANS: a

19. Appeals
    a. require the appellate court to retry the case
    b. are most often successful
    c. deal with questions of fact only
    d. deal with questions of law only

    ANS: d

20. An example of a question of fact is:
    a. Was the letter admissible evidence?
    b. Was the road icy the day of the accident?
    c. Were jury instructions proper?
    d. Was the statute constitutional?

    ANS: b

21. If harmless error occurred at trial,
    a. the appeal will be successful
    b. a new trial will be granted
    c. the verdict will stand
    d. the matter will be mediated

    ANS: c

22. Parties are expected to agree on
    a. contents of the appendix to the appellate brief
    b. issues under appeal
    c. questions of law
    d. questions of fact

    ANS: a

23. An example of a question of law is:
    a. Was the contract signed by the defendant?
    b. Did the plaintiff cross the street without looking?
    c. Was the videotape prejudicial evidence?
    d. Did the plaintiff suffer broken bones as a result of the accident?

    ANS: c

24. In federal court the notice of appeal is filed in the
    a. state court
    b. district court
    c. court of appeals
    d. supreme court

    ANS: b

25. On appeal the paralegal cannot
    a. set up an oral argument notebook
    b. keep track of all appellate deadlines
    c. write a rough draft brief
    d. divide the oral argument with the attorney

    ANS: d

26. Grounds for a motion for a new trial include
    a. lis pendens
    b. a judgment proof defendant
    c. excessive or inadequate damages
    d. garnishment

    ANS: c

27. Creditor's examinations
    a. are self-executing
    b. can be requested in a motion in limine
    c. are included in the appellate brief
    d. are post-trial depositions

    ANS: d

28. A judgment debtor secures the amount of the judgment during a stay pending outcome of appeal by posting
    a. a supersedeas bond
    b. a levy
    c. an appeal bond
    d. garnishment

    ANS: a

29. A writ of execution specifies
    a. who has prevailed on appeal
    b. all the assets of a judgment debtor
    c. defendant's property to be sold to satisfy the judgment
    d. the lien on intangible property

    ANS: c

30. When a judgment is entered and recorded, in most jurisdictions, it is good
    a. for one year
    b. for ten years
    c. indefinitely
    d. for the period specified by the court

    ANS: b

True/False

31. If a motion for a new trial is granted, the trial is held in appellate court.

    ANS: False

32. A motion for judgment as a matter of law should be filed if there were procedural errors at trial.

    ANS: False

33. Motions to have a judgment set aside must be filed right after the verdict is read.

    ANS: False

34. Payment of the judgment amount is due within 10 days of the verdict.

    ANS: False

35. Whether Mr. Hart was driving the van at 45 m.p.h. is a subject for appeal.

    ANS: False

36. The clerk of court sends the trial transcript to the appellate court.

    ANS: False

37. Most appeals are unsuccessful.

    ANS: True

38. An experienced paralegal can assume the role of appeals manager.

    ANS: True

39. The jury decides questions of law.

    ANS: False

40. A bill of costs is a list of litigation expenses of the prevailing party.

    ANS: True

41. Receivership secures the amount of judgment pending post-trial motions.

    ANS: False

42. Up to 25 percent of disposable earnings can be garnished.

    ANS: True

43. A notice of lis pendens protects property from being claimed by the judgment creditor.

    ANS: False

44. A judgment-proof defendant is one who has no assets.

    ANS: True

45. Joint tenants have no right of survivorship.

    ANS: False

46. A car is tangible property.

    ANS: True

47. Assets of a judgment debtor that are held by a third party are not available to satisfy that debt.

    ANS: False

48. No property of the judgment debtor is exempt from being used to satisfy the judgment debt.

    ANS: False

49. Postjudgment discovery can help in locating the judgment debtor's assets.

    ANS: True

50. Generally, if an issue is not raised at trial, it cannot be the basis for appeal.

    ANS: True

51. It is unethical for paralegals to draft appellate briefs.

    ANS: False

52. Only the appellant files an appellate brief.

    ANS: False

53. In the federal system, the notice of appeal is filed in the appellate court.

    ANS: False

54. Federal Rules of Appellate Procedure 28, 30, and 32 cover writing appellate briefs.

    ANS: True

55. Colors of covers and page sizes for federal appellate briefs are set by federal rules.

    ANS: True

56. Parties are encouraged to agree on the parts of the trial record to be included in the appendix of the appellate brief.

    ANS: True

57. Since appeals courts decide only questions of law, the facts of the case are not mentioned in appellate briefs.

    ANS: False

Short Answer

58. How may a paralegal assist in post-trial motion practice?

    ANS: by
    a. researching key points of legal authority
    b. reviewing the paralegal's trial notes to pinpoint possible areas for appeal
    c. calendaring time limits in the deadline control system
    d. writing the rough draft motion

59. Name three discovery devices that can be helpful in postjudgment investigations.

    ANS: Interrogatories, production of documents, and depositions (creditor's examination)

60. What are three grounds for a motion for a new trial?

    ANS: Procedural errors, verdict contrary to law, and excessive or inadequate damages.

61. When are plaintiffs allowed to seize defendants' property before a trial?

    ANS: When it is likely that defendant will try to hide or transfer assets to avoid loss.

62. Why is it important to determine a defendant's assets early in a case?

    ANS: If there are no or few assets, the case may not be worth the trouble.

63. Under what circumstances will an appellate judge review evidence?

    ANS: When appeal is on the issue of whether the verdict goes against the weight of the evidence.

64. In what areas is a paralegal's assistance especially effective in appeals practice?

    ANS: Management, research, verifying the record, appellate brief, and oral argument.

TRANSPARENCY MASTERS

TRANSPARENCY MASTERS

1. Exhibit 1.1
2. Exhibit 1.2
3. Exhibit 1.4
4. Exhibit 1.6
5. Exhibit 1.7
6. Checklist—Chapter 2—An Interview Plan
7. Exhibit 2.5
8. Exhibit 2.6
9. Chapter 3—Planning the Investigation
10. Exhibit 3.4
11. Exhibit 3.6
12. Exhibit 3.8
13. Exhibit 3.10
14. Exhibit 4.1
15. Example of Caption, State Court, Party
16. System Checklist for Drafting a Complaint
17. Complaint for Ann Forrester Case
18. Exhibit 4.3
19. Exhibit 5.1
20. Exhibit 5.3
21. Exhibit 5.4
22. Exhibit 5.7
23. Exhibit 5.11
24. Exhibit 5.15
25. Exhibit 6.1
26. Exhibit 6.3
27. Exhibit 6.10
28. Exhibit 6.12
29. Exhibit 6.14
30. Exhibit 6.21
31. Exhibit 7.1
32. Paralegal's Disclosure Checklist
33. Exhibit 7.3
34. Exhibit 7.4
35. Exhibit 7.5
36. Exhibit 8.2
37. Exhibit 8.5
38. Exhibit 8.7
39. Exhibit 8.8
40. Exhibit 9.1
41. Exhibit 9.2
42. Exhibit 9.4
43. Exhibit 9.8
44. Exhibit 10.8
45. Exhibit 10.10
46. Exhibit 10.11
47. Exhibit 11.1
48. Exhibit 11.2
49. Exhibit 11.3
50. Exhibit 11.5
51. Exhibit 12.1
52. Exhibit 12.3
53. Appellate Procedure Checklist
54. Exhibit 12.12
55. Exhibit 12.16

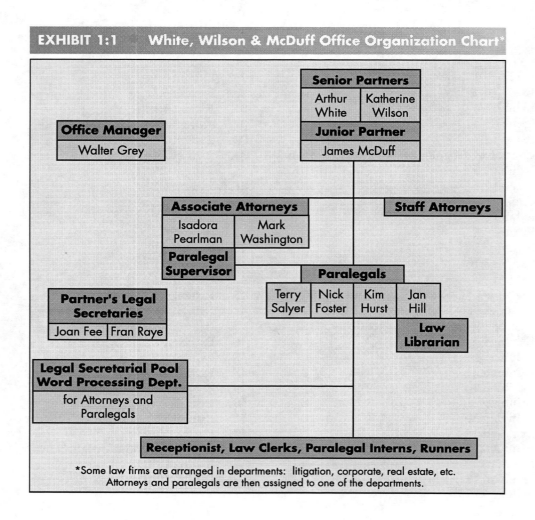

EXHIBIT 1:1   White, Wilson & McDuff Office Organization Chart*

Senior Partners	
Arthur White	Katherine Wilson

Junior Partner
James McDuff

Office Manager
Walter Grey

Associate Attorneys	
Isadora Pearlman	Mark Washington

Staff Attorneys

Paralegal Supervisor

Paralegals			
Terry Salyer	Nick Foster	Kim Hurst	Jan Hill

Partner's Legal Secretaries

Joan Fee	Fran Raye

Law Librarian

Legal Secretarial Pool Word Processing Dept.
for Attorneys and Paralegals

Receptionist, Law Clerks, Paralegal Interns, Runners

*Some law firms are arranged in departments: litigation, corporate, real estate, etc. Attorneys and paralegals are then assigned to one of the departments.

Transparency Master 2

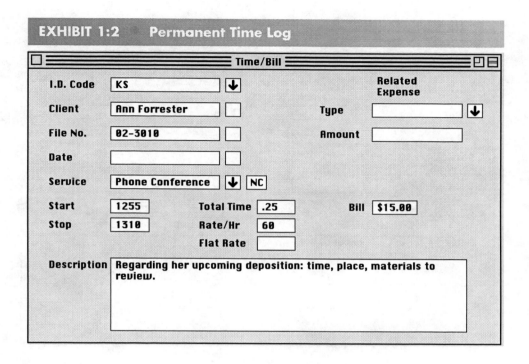

EXHIBIT 1:2   Permanent Time Log

Time/Bill

I.D. Code	KS ⬇
Client	Ann Forrester ☐
File No.	02-3010 ☐
Date	☐
Service	Phone Conference ⬇ NC

Related Expense

Type ⬇

Amount

Start	1255	**Total Time**	.25	**Bill**	$15.00
Stop	1310	**Rate/Hr**	60		
		Flat Rate			

Description Regarding her upcoming deposition: time, place, materials to review.

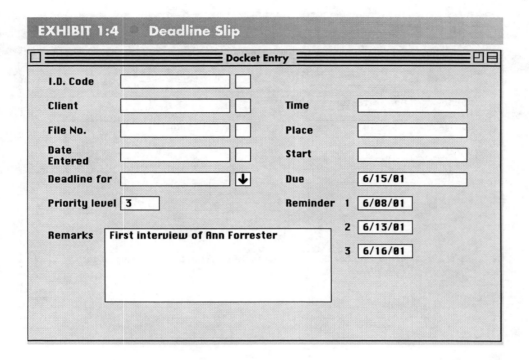

EXHIBIT 1:4 Deadline Slip

Docket Entry

I.D. Code

Client   Time

File No.   Place

Date
Entered   Start

Deadline for   ↓   Due   6/15/01

Priority level 3   Reminder 1 6/08/01

                                                    2 6/13/01
Remarks   First interview of Ann Forrester
                                                    3 6/16/01

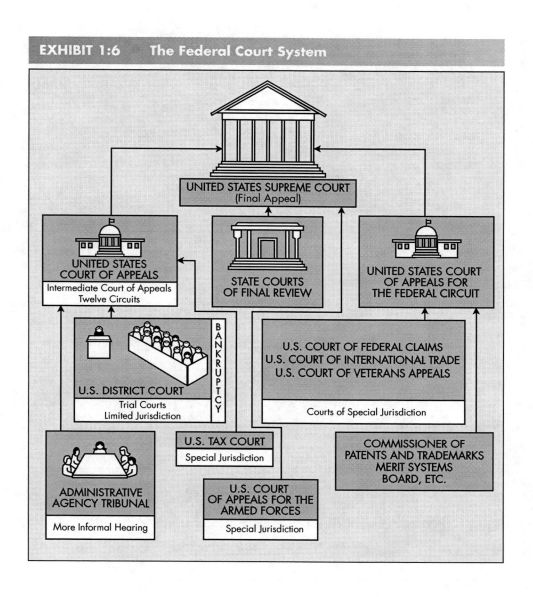

EXHIBIT 1:6   The Federal Court System

UNITED STATES SUPREME COURT
(Final Appeal)

UNITED STATES
COURT OF APPEALS
Intermediate Court of Appeals
Twelve Circuits

STATE COURTS
OF FINAL REVIEW

UNITED STATES COURT
OF APPEALS FOR
THE FEDERAL CIRCUIT

BANKRUPTCY

U.S. DISTRICT COURT
Trial Courts
Limited Jurisdiction

U.S. COURT OF FEDERAL CLAIMS
U.S. COURT OF INTERNATIONAL TRADE
U.S. COURT OF VETERANS APPEALS

Courts of Special Jurisdiction

ADMINISTRATIVE
AGENCY TRIBUNAL
More Informal Hearing

U.S. TAX COURT
Special Jurisdiction

U.S. COURT
OF APPEALS FOR THE
ARMED FORCES
Special Jurisdiction

COMMISSIONER OF
PATENTS AND TRADEMARKS
MERIT SYSTEMS
BOARD, ETC.

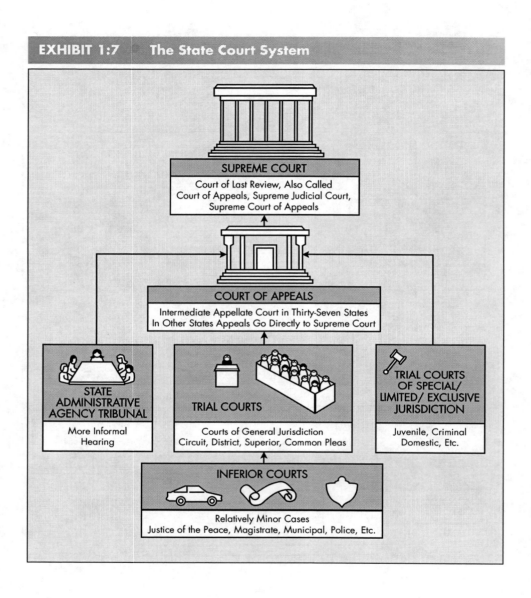

EXHIBIT 1:7   The State Court System

SUPREME COURT

Court of Last Review, Also Called
Court of Appeals, Supreme Judicial Court,
Supreme Court of Appeals

COURT OF APPEALS

Intermediate Appellate Court in Thirty-Seven States
In Other States Appeals Go Directly to Supreme Court

STATE ADMINISTRATIVE AGENCY TRIBUNAL

More Informal Hearing

TRIAL COURTS

Courts of General Jurisdiction
Circuit, District, Superior, Common Pleas

TRIAL COURTS OF SPECIAL/ LIMITED/ EXCLUSIVE JURISDICTION

Juvenile, Criminal Domestic, Etc.

INFERIOR COURTS

Relatively Minor Cases
Justice of the Peace, Magistrate, Municipal, Police, Etc.

A. INTERVIEW PLAN CHECKLIST

Step 1 *Review all available information on the case.*

Step 2 *Locate or develop an appropriate interview form.*

Step 3 *Select a location for the interview.*

Step 4 *Determine what information the client should bring.*

Step 5 *Schedule the interview (tentatively); check with attorney.*

Step 6 *Anticipate and arrange for any special needs.*

Step 7 *Review pertinent ethical and tactical considerations.*

Step 8 *Review recommended interview techniques.*

Step 9 *Prepare orientation and instruction materials for the client.*

Step 10 *Prepare any forms for the client's signature.*

Step 11 *Prepare the interview site.*

EXHIBIT 2:5   Standardized Release Form

WHITE, WILSON & McDUFF
ATTORNEYS AT LAW
FEDERAL PLAZA BUILDING, SUITE 700
THIRD AND MARKET STREETS
LEGALVILLE, COLUMBIA 00000
(111) 555 - 0000

Address

Date

RE: (Name of client, date of birth, Social Security number)

This form authorizes _____ to release to my attorney, White, Wilson & McDuff, or their designated representative, all of the following information about me as indicated (X), and to discuss it, send it, make it available for inspection, or photocopy it as they may request.

( ) All medical and hospital records, including medical history, tests, test results, diagnoses, treatment, x-ray reports, current medical status, prognosis, bills, and any other information designated in the attached letter relevant to treatment occuring from [date], _____ to _____, _____.

( ) Employment records: description of position, length of employment, pay, benefits, absences, performance, accumulated sick leave, etc.

( ) Academic and school records: attendance dates; evaluations; grade performance; psychological, aptitude, and achievement tests; class ranking; teachers, etc.

( ) Military records

( ) All state and federal tax returns for the years _____

( ) Other: _____

_____   _____
Client   Date

_____
Address

EXHIBIT 2:6   Summary Sheet: Initial Interview of Client

File no.   Date opened: Interviewer:

Client: (M) Spouse: (C) Children, ages: (P)Phone:

Party opponent(s):

Date of incident:

Type of Action: Statute of limitations:

Summary of facts of action:

Noteworthy facts related to elements of action:

Noteworthy facts related to possible defenses:

Witnesses:

Summary of injury and treatment to date:

Total medical bills to date:

Summary of business or wage loss:

Total business or wage loss to date:

Evaluation of client as witness:

Other comments:

Things to do:

Planning the Investigation

1. Review the file and other available information.
2. Identify the essential elements of proof as defined by the appropriate substantive law.
3. Identify what facts will be needed to prove each of these elements.
4. Determine what sources, including witnesses, may provide those facts.
5. Record the investigation plan.
6. Consult with the attorney in selecting the most appropriate sources and methods of investigation to be followed.

EXHIBIT 3:4   Request for Medical Records

WHITE, WILSON & McDUFF
ATTORNEYS AT LAW
FEDERAL PLAZA BUILDING, SUITE 700
THIRD AND MARKET STREETS
LEGALVILLE, COLUMBIA 00000
(111) 555-0000

Ms. Betty Noble
Medical Records Librarian
Good Samaritan Hospital
4600 Church Street
Legalville, Columbia 00000

Re: Medical Records of Ms. Ann Forrester

> 1533 Capitol Dr., Legalville, Columbia 00000
> Soc. Sec. No. 123-45-6789
> Birthdate: 4/23/—
> Dates of Care: 2/26/—
> to discharge 3/29/—

Dear Ms. Noble:

The firm of White, Wilson, and McDuff has been retained to represent the above-named individual.

Enclosed is a current Authorization to Release Medical Information executed by our client.

Please send a copy of the following records to me:

(X) Discharge summary
(X) ER and outpatient reports
(X) Patient's chart
(X) History and physical
(X) Operative and pathology reports
(X) X-ray reports
(X) Lab reports
(X) Progress noted by physicians and nurses
(X) Doctors' orders
(X) Consultation reports
(X) Nurses' notes
( ) Alcohol and drug treatment notes
( ) Others

On receipt of the records, our firm will submit reasonable payment for any preparation fee.

Thank you for your assistance.

Sincerely,

Terry Salyer
Paralegal

Enclosure: Authorization to Release Medical Information

Transparency Master 11

WHITE, WILSON & McDUFF
ATTORNEYS AT LAW
FEDERAL PLAZA BUILDING, SUITE 700
THIRD AND MARKET STREETS
LEGALVILLE, COLUMBIA 00000
(111) 555-0000

Albert Meyer, M.D.
Medical Arts Building
4650 Church St.
Legalville, Columbia 00000

Re: Ms. Ann Forrester, Soc. Sec. No. 123-45-6789

Dear Dr. Meyer:

Ms. Forrester has retained this office to represent her regarding injuries sustained from being struck by a van on February 26, ___. Ms. Forrester suffered multiple fractures of the pelvis and left leg, and also had spinal and internal injuries. As a result of these injuries, Ms. Forrester is currently bound to a wheelchair and may not be able to return to work for some time.

To assist Ms. Forrester, we would appreciate it if you would send us a report on the following:

1. Your diagnosis of Ms. Forrester's mental, emotional, and physical injuries
2. Your opinion as to the cause of Ms. Forrester's injuries
3. A description of the treatment given Ms. Forrester
4. Likely degree of pain and discomfort related to such injuries
5. Mental, physical, and emotional limitations as they relate to employment, recreational activities, and enjoyment of life
6. Future treatment needed
7. Prognosis
8. Likelihood of Ms. Forrester being able to return to work. If so, when?

In addition, please send an itemized bill for all your services related to these injuries.

The necessary authorization is enclosed. Upon receipt of your report, this office will promptly pay any preparation fee.

Please keep us informed regarding Ms. Forrester's future visits to your office and any change in condition or prognosis.

Thank you for your cooperation.

Terry Salyer
Paralegal

Enclosed: Authorization to Release Medical Information

cc: Ms. Ann Forrester

Transparency Master 12A

EXHIBIT 3:8   Accident Scene Checklist

1. Nature of area: urban, rural, intersection, highway, school zone, other _____
2. Weather (if at scene soon enough to observe) _____
3. Other conditions: visibility _____
   road surface _____
   lanes _____
   curves _____
   grade _____
   speed limit _____
   other _____

4. Witness   Position to view accident   View, obstructions

   _____   _____   _____

   _____   _____   _____

   _____   _____   _____

5. Possible distractions that might cause inattention _____
6. Measurements of critical distances°
   skid marks _____
   road width _____
   distance vehicle traveled after impact _____
   distance from witness position to scene _____
   other _____
7. Traffic control
   signs _____
   lane markings _____
   other _____
8. Sun or other lighting conditions at time of day accident occurred
   from plaintiff's position _____
   from defendant's position _____
   from witness's position _____
   other _____
9. Temporary conditions
   construction _____
   parked vehicles _____
   other _____
10. Flow of traffic, same time of day, same day of week _____

°A handy formula for converting speed to distance (and vice versa) is mph × 1.5 = ft. per sec.

11. All possible causes of accident _____

_____

12. Evidence of damage

vehicles _____

signs _____

trees _____

buildings _____

other _____

13. Photograph and videotape important items noted above from different angles to show relevant conditions or defects such as a pothole in the street, uneven sidewalk, slippery spots, etc.

14. Carefully note pertinent directions (N, NE, E, SE, S, SW, W, NW) _____

15. Locations of other possible witnesses regularly at the scene

homes _____

businesses _____

joggers _____

dog walkers _____

farm workers _____

maintenance or public works people _____

other _____

16. Other physical evidence relevant to case _____

17. Special needs

expert to view scene _____

professional photographer to capture lighting, angles (good source: International Council of Evidence Photographers) _____

_____

_____

aerial photograph _____

other _____

18. Carefully preserve evidence.

EXHIBIT 3:10   Checklist for Witness Interview

- ☐ **1.** Complete Witness Information Cover Sheet.
- ☐ **2.** Identify taker of statement, time, date, place.
- ☐ **3.** Witness's activity just prior to accident: ☐ location ☐ time ☐ date
  - ☐ witness's activity ☐ view of scene ☐ distance from scene
  - ☐ obstruction ☐ location of plaintiff and defendant
  - ☐ activity of plaintiff ☐ activity of defendant ☐ others present
  - ☐ names ☐ their location ☐ activities
  - ☐ other possible witnesses ☐ others in vehicle
  - ☐ key issue questions
- ☐ **4.** Setting at time of accident:
  - ☐ time ☐ weather ☐ lighting conditions ☐ road conditions
  - ☐ wind ☐ unforeseen obstructions (repair work, children, animals, fallen trees or rocks, etc.)
  - ☐ dangerous conditions
  - ☐ traffic flow ☐ speed limits ☐ traffic signs
  - ☐ school zone ☐ intersection ☐ type of road ☐ hills
  - ☐ curves ☐ shoulders ☐ any unusual or particularly notable activity of parties or others (recklessness, inattentiveness, evidence of influence of alcohol or drugs, etc.)
  - ☐ speed of vehicles ☐ distance between plaintiff and defendant
  - ☐ vehicle window obstructions ☐ other conditions of importance
  - ☐ when witness's attention first drawn to plaintiff and defendant
  - ☐ other key issue questions
- ☐ **5.** The accident:
  - ☐ time ☐ general description of sequence
  - ☐ attempt to evade (sound horn, brake, head for shoulder, etc.)
  - ☐ skidding ☐ sounds of contact
  - ☐ detailed description of what happened to plaintiff and defendant (thrown from car, hit windshield, fell, etc.)
  - ☐ detailed description of what happened to vehicles
  - ☐ exact point of contact ☐ exact position of parties at time of contact ☐ position of other people ☐ opinion as to cause of accident
  - ☐ diagram ☐ other key issue questions
- ☐ **6.** Setting after accident:
  - ☐ witness's description of scene (diagram)
  - ☐ position of plaintiff and defendant ☐ position of vehicles
  - ☐ injuries and damage (persons and property)
  - ☐ description of sequence of events after accident
  - ☐ time of arrival and activity of all emergency personnel
  - ☐ care rendered at scene to injured ☐ other persons and witnesses present after accident, including reporters, photographers, investigators ☐ cleanup activities (name of tow truck)
  - ☐ who, if anyone, made or recorded statements ☐ conversations overheard (parties, witnesses, emergency personnel, etc.)
  - ☐ opinion as to truthfulness and character of parties and witnesses
  - ☐ witness's record of character and honesty ☐ any conversation with any of the parties since accident about accident or injuries
  - ☐ other key issue questions
- ☐ **7.** Record statement and have witness read, sign, and date it.
- ☐ **8.** Check to see if witness made statements about the accident to anyone else. If so, to whom and what kind (oral, written, recorded)?
- ☐ **9.** Assess witness's abilities
  - ☐ voice ☐ sincerity ☐ power of observation ☐ confidence
  - ☐ appearance ☐ appreciation of importance of truthfulness
  - ☐ recognition of evidence, persons, photos, etc. ☐ objectivity
  - ☐ truthfulness ☐ vulnerability to impeachment
  - ☐ willingness to testify ☐ availability for trial

Transparency Master 14

(caption)	STATE OF COLUMBIA CAPITOL COUNTY CIRCUIT COURT MARY E. JOHNSON, Plaintiff v. Civil Action, File No. 00000 ARTHUR HENDRICKS, Defendant JURY TRIAL DEMANDED COMPLAINT FOR NEGLIGENCE

(body)	The Plaintiff states that:
	1. The court has jurisdiction in this matter under Section 403A, Title 23 of the Columbia Revised Statutes.
	2. Plaintiff is a paralegal and resides at 43 South Senate Avenue, Legalville, in Capitol County, Columbia.
	3. Defendant is a baker and lives at 500 Maple Street, Legalville, in Capitol County, Columbia.
	4. Defendant owns and operates the Deli Bakery at 508 Maple Street, Legalville, in Capitol County, Columbia.
	5. On August 23, ____, at said bakery, Defendant sold Plaintiff a chocolate eclair, which was negligently prepared containing pieces of glass.
	6. Plaintiff ate said pastry, receiving the following damage:
	   a. Great pain and suffering
	   b. Internal injuries
	   c. Medical and hospital bills
	   d. Loss of income

(prayer for relief)	WHEREFORE, Plaintiff demands judgment in the amount of ten thousand dollars ($10,000), together with the costs and disbursements of this action. Plaintiff demands trial by jury. _____ Plaintiff's Attorney 407 E. Second Avenue Legalville, Columbia
(verification)	State of Columbia County of Capitol Mary Johnson, on oath, deposes and states that she has read the foregoing complaint and that the matters stated therein are true to the best of her knowledge, information, and belief. _____ Mary Johnson Subscribed and sworn to before me this 12th day of October, ____ _____ Notary Public My commmission expires: ____

Example of Caption: State Court

STATE OF COLUMBIA   CAPITOL COUNTY   CIRCUIT COURT

ANN FORRESTER, Plaintiff

v.   Civil Action, File No. <u>1000</u>

RICHARD HART and
MERCURY PARCEL SERVICE, INC., Defendants

COMPLAINT FOR NEGLIGENCE

Example of Caption: Federal Court

UNITED STATES DISTRICT COURT FOR THE EASTERN DISTRICT
OF COLUMBIA Civil Action, File Number <u>1001</u>

ANN FORRESTER,

                            Plaintiff

v.

RICHARD HART and   COMPLAINT
MERCURY PARCEL SERVICE, INC.,

                        Defendants

Party Caption for Suit by Minor or Person Under Disability

BARRY SMITH,
a minor by his parents and guardians,
SAMUEL and EDNA SMITH,

                                      Plaintiff

        v.
JOHNSON MOTORS, INC.,

                                        Defendant

Party Caption for Suit by Deceased Person

HAROLD WEBER
Executor of the estate of
[(or) Personal Representative for the Estate of]
MARY WEBER,

                                      Plaintiffs

        v.
FRANCIS LONG,

                                      Defendant

Party Caption for Suit by Multiple Parties

SAMUEL HARRIS
     and
IRENE BOND,

                                      Plaintiffs

        v.
EDWARD SUMMER,
SPIKES, INC.,
     and
JOHNSON MANUFACTURING COMPANY, INC.,

                                      Defendants

Party Caption for Subsequent Pleading in Preceding Case

SAMUEL HARRIS, et al.,

                                      Plaintiffs

        v.
EDWARD SUMMER, et al.,

                                        Defendants

System Checklist for Drafting a Complaint

A. PREPARATION

☐ If the complaint is to be filed in state court, consult state rules for differences from the federal rules. Remember that each court may also have its local rules.

☐ Review the file for the names and addresses of the parties, the type of claim, and so on.

☐ Confirm in what court the action should be filed.

☐ Confirm the existence of venue, subject matter jurisdiction, and personal jurisdiction.

☐ Research the necessary elements for each cause of action to be alleged.

☐ Formulate those elements into a legal syllogism to form the body of each count of the complaint. (If A, B, and C exist, then plaintiff is entitled to X.)

☐ Identify the facts needed to support each element of the syllogism.

☐ Identify the appropriate remedies.

☐ Consult with the supervising attorney to confirm all of the preceding points.

☐ Make corrections as the attorney indicates, and do further research or investigation as needed.

☐ Check your system folder for appropriate samples of both federal and state complaints or sections thereof.

☐ Obtain one good copy of a recent complaint for the type of claim or claims to be alleged and for the specific court in which the action is to be filed.

☐ Check local court rules for size of paper, backing sheets, color, and any other requirements.

B. DRAFTING

☐ Draft the caption.

    ☐ Indicate the court (branch, if several branches) and its location.

    ☐ Indicate the parties, the joinder thereof; check spelling and the addresses if included; capacity, real party in interest, and so on. Federal Rule 17(a)(b)(c), 19(1), 20(1); State rule ___; system folder page ___.

    ☐ Indicate the docket or court file number of the action if available, or leave an appropriate space.

    ☐ Indicate the type of complaint (negligence, breach of contract, etc.).

    ☐ Include the references to federal and state rules and forms on drafting. Federal Rule 10(a), Form 1; State Rule ___, Form ___; system folder page ___.

    ☐ Include a demand for jury trial if so instructed.

☐ Draft simple, concise, and direct statements. Avoid repetition and legalese.

☐ Use double spacing; quoted matter should be single spaced.

☐ Draft the jurisdictional allegation, if required, including any monetary amount. Federal Rule 8(a)(1), Form 2; State Rule ___; system folder page ___.

211

☐ Make sure all allegations regarding venue, if required, are included (not necessary in the federal system): location of incident and addresses of parties. State Rule ___; system folder page ___.

☐ Draft the body of the complaint.

    ☐ Include facts to support each element of the claim.

    ☐ Use brief, numbered paragraphs limited to one idea. Federal Rule 10(b); State Rule ___; system folder page ___.

    ☐ Add just enough detail to meet the minimum requirement for fact pleading or for notice pleading, depending on applicable rules. Federal Rule 8(a)(2), 8(e)(1), Forms 3-17; State Rule ___; system folder page ___.

    ☐ Do not state evidence or conclusions.

    ☐ Avoid impertinent, scandalous, or immaterial language. Federal Rule 11, 12(f); State Rule ___.

    ☐ Be truthful; make sure there are provable facts to support a good-faith allegation. Model Rule 3.3(a)(1).

    ☐ State those allegations that are uncertain but have some basis on information and belief.

    ☐ Do not anticipate defenses.

    ☐ Plead hypothetically, in the alternative, and state uncertainty when necessary. Federal Rule 8(e)(2); State Rule ___; system folder page ___.

    ☐ Do not plead the law, except (1) when the action is under a specific statute or administrative rule, or (2) when the action is in one state but relies on the law of another state.

    ☐ List various damages in one paragraph, unless local rules or practice dictates otherwise.

    ☐ Check to see that all separate claims are alleged and all separate counts included. Federal Rule 8(e)(2), 18; State Rule ___; system folder page ___.

    ☐ Check to see that paragraphs flow logically and tell an interesting and easy-to-read story.

    ☐ Choose assertive, persuasive words to evoke sympathy and convey confidence.

    ☐ Check that all incorporations by reference (including exhibits and appendixes) have been accurately stated where needed.

☐ Draft special matters as they arise.

    ☐ Aver the capacity of the parties unless not required by local rules. It is not required in the federal system [Rule 9(a)].

    ☐ Aver the circumstances supporting the allegation of fraud or mistake with particularity [Rule 9(b)].

    ☐ Aver malice, intent, knowledge, or other condition of the mind generally [Rule 9(b)].

    ☐ Aver the performance of all conditions precedent generally [Rule 9(c)]; aver the denial of performance with particularity.

    ☐ Aver that an official document was issued or act done in compliance with the law [Rule 9(d)].

☐ Aver a judgment or decision of domestic or foreign court, administrative tribunal, or of a board of officers without alleging facts showing jurisdiction to render it.

☐ Aver time and place [Rule 9(f)].

☐ Aver specifically any special damages [Rule 9(g)].

☐ Draft the prayer for relief (demand for judgment).

☐ State relief in the alternative when necessary. Federal Rule 8(a)(3);State Rule ___; system folder page ___.

    ☐ damages   ☐ recovery of property

    ☐ injuries   ☐ specific performance   ☐ other

☐ Draft the subscription and see to it that the attorney's address and phone number are included. Federal Rule 11(b); State Rule ___; system folder page ___.

☐ Draft verification if required (not required in federal pleadings). Federal Rule 11(b); State Rule ___; system folder page ___.

☐ Have the client swear to the truthfulness of the complaint and sign it in your presence if you are a notary.

☐ Attach exhibits and appendices.

☐ See that the complaint is typed with sufficient copies.

Complaint for Ann Forrester Case

STATE OF COLUMBIA   CAPITOL COUNTY   CIRCUIT COURT

ANN FORRESTER and
WILLIAM FORRESTER,
   Plaintiffs

Civil Action, File No. <u>1000</u>

   v.

RICHARD HART and
MERCURY PARCEL SERVICE, INC.,
   Defendants   Plaintiff Demands Trial by Jury.

COMPLAINT FOR NEGLIGENCE

The Plaintiffs make the following allegations:

1. The jurisdiction of this court is based on the amount in controversy in this action which is more than $2,500.
2. Plaintiff Ann Forrester is a teacher and homemaker and resides at 1533 Capitol Drive, Legalville, in Capitol County, Columbia.
3. Plaintiff William Forrester is the husband of Ann Forrester and resides with her.
4. Defendant Richard Hart is a driver employed by Defendant Mercury Parcel Service, Inc., and resides at 1223 Penny Lane, Cincinnati, Ohio.
5. Defendant Mercury Parcel Service, Inc., is incorporated in the state of Delaware with its principal place of business located at 603 Stoker St., Cincinnati, Ohio.
6. On February 26, _____, at approximately 7:30 A.M., Plaintiff Ann Forrester was walking across a hilly and partially icy section of Highway 328 in the City of Legalville, County of Capitol, in the State of Columbia.
7. At that time, Defendant Hart was driving a van on behalf of his employer and the owner of the van, Defendant Mercury Parcel Service, Inc.
8. Defendant Hart operated the van negligently by:
   (a) driving the vehicle at an excessive rate of speed under the circumstances;
   (b) failing to exercise a proper lookout;
   (c) failing to exercise adequate control of said vehicle; and
   (d) otherwise failing to exercise due and adequate care under the circumstances.
9. As a direct consequence of the Defendants' negligence, the Plaintiff was struck down by the Defendants' van and seriously injured.
10. Because of said negligence, the Plaintiff suffered fractures of the left leg and hip; damage to the lower spine; torn muscles, tendons, tissue, and nerves; insomnia; paralysis that confines her to a wheelchair; depression; and other maladies, causing her intense pain and great suffering and considerable inconvenience which will continue in the future.
11. As a consequence of the Defendants' negligence and the aforesaid injuries, the Plaintiff has incurred and will incur substantial monetary losses for hospital and medical care, loss of income and benefits, domestic services, and

property damages to her coat and clothing.

WHEREFORE the Plaintiff demands judgment in the amount of seven hundred and fifty thousand dollars ($750,000), together with the costs and disbursements of this action and for such other relief as this court may deem just and proper.

COUNT TWO

12. The Plaintiffs hereby allege and incorporate by reference paragraphs 1 through 9 of Count One.

13. Because of the Defendants' negligence, Plaintiff William Forrester has suffered the loss of consortium with his wife, Ann Forrester, in the amount of twenty thousand dollars ($20,000).

WHEREFORE, Plaintiff William Forrester demands judgment against the Defendants in the sum of twenty thousand dollars ($20,000) and costs and for such other relief as this court may deem just and proper.

Arthur White
White, Wilson & McDuff
Attorneys at Law
Federal Plaza Building
Suite 700
Third and Market Streets
Legalville, Columbia 00000
(111) 555-0000

STATE OF COLUMBIA

SS.

County of Capitol

Ann Forrester and William Forrester, being duly sworn on oath according to law, depose and state that they have read the foregoing complaint and that the matters stated therein are true to the best of their knowledge, information, and belief.

Ann Forrester

William Forrester

Subscribed and sworn to before me this 1st day of October, _____.

Notary Public

My commission expires January 1, _____

EXHIBIT 4:3   Motion for Preliminary Injunction—General Form[6]

[Fed R. Civ. P. 65(a)]

[Title of Court and Cause]

Plaintiffs, _____and _____, move the Court for a preliminary injunction in the above entitled cause enjoining the defendants, and _____and _____, their agents, servants, employees, and attorneys, [and those persons in active concert or participation with them] from

_____

_____

The grounds in support of this motion are as follows:
1. _____
2. _____

Unless restrained _____ and _____will immediately [*state action defendants will take unless restrained*].

Immediate and irreparable injury, loss, and damage will result to the plaintiffs by reason of the threatened action of the defendants, as more particularly appears in the verified complaint filed herein and the attached affidavit of _____. The plaintiffs have no adequate remedy at law.

If this preliminary injunction be granted, the injury, if any, to defendants herein, if final judgment be in their favor, will be inconsiderable and will be adequately indemnified by bond.

[Add if appropriate: Plaintiffs further move the Court that the trial of this action on the merits be advanced and consolidated with the hearing of this motion for preliminary injunction. The grounds in support of consolidation are as follows: *Add matter similar to matter in second paragraph of form in § 5272*].

_____
Attorneys for Plaintiffs

AO 440 (Rev. 5/85)   Summons in a Civil Action

United States District Court

_____ DISTRICT OF _____

ANN FORRESTER and
WILLIAM FORRESTER, Plaintiffs

V.

RICHARD HART and
MERCURY PARCEL, INC., Defendants

SUMMONS IN A CIVIL ACTION

CASE NUMBER:

TO: (Name and Address of Defendant)

Richard Hart
1223 Penny Lane
Cincinnati, OH

YOU ARE HEREBY SUMMONED and required to file with the Clerk of this Court and serve upon

PLAINTIFF'S ATTORNEY (name and address)
Arthur White
White, Wilson & McDuff
Attorneys at Law
Federal Plaza Building, Suite 700
Third and Market Streets
Legalville, Columbia 00000

an answer to the complaint which is herewith served upon you, within _____20_____ days after service of this summons upon you, exclusive of the day of service. If you fail to do so, judgment by default will be taken against you for the relief demanded in the complaint.

J. D. Walterson
_____
CLERK

10/2/--
_____
DATE

_____
BY DEPUTY CLERK

Transparency Master 19B

AO 440 (Rev. 5/85) Summons in a Civil Action

RETURN OF SERVICE

Service of the Summons and Complaint was made by me[1]	DATE
NAME OF SERVER	TITLE

Check one box below to indicate appropriate method of service

☐ Served personally upon the defendant. Place where served : _____
_____

☐ Left copies thereof at the defendant's dwelling house or usual place of abode with a person of suitable age and discretion then residing therein.
Name of person with whom the summons and complaint were left: _____

☐ Returned unexecuted: _____
_____
_____

☐ Other (specify): _____
_____
_____

STATEMENT OF SERVICE FEES

TRAVEL	SERVICES	TOTAL

DECLARATION OF SERVER

I declare under penalty of perjury under the laws of the United States of America that the foregoing information contained in the Return of Service and Statement of Service Fees is true and correct.

Executed on_____   _____
              Date   *Signature of Server*

              _____
                      Address of Server

1) As to who may serve a summons see Rule 4 of the Federal Rules of Civil Procedure.

EXHIBIT 5:3 Notice of Lawsuit and Request for Waiver of Service of Summons

AO 398 (12/93)

NOTICE OF LAWSUIT AND REQUEST FOR
WAIVER OF SERVICE OF SUMMONS

TO: (A)_____

as   (B)_____ of (C) _____

     A lawsuit has been commenced against you (or the entity on whose behalf you are addressed.) A copy of the complaint is attached to this notice. It has been filed in the United States District Court for the

(D) _____ District of _____ and has been assigned docket number (E) _____.

     This is not a formal summons or notification from the court, but rather my request that you sign and return the enclosed waiver of service in order to save the cost of serving you with a judicial summons and an additional copy of the complaint. The cost of service will be avoided if I receive a signed copy of the waiver within (F) _____ days after the date designated below as the date on which this Notice and Request is sent. I enclose a stamped and addressed envelope (or other means of cost-free return) for your use. An extra copy of the waiver is also attached for your records.

     If you comply with this request and return the signed waiver, it will be filed with the court and no summons will be served on you. The action will then proceed as if you had been served on the date the waiver is filed, except that you will not be obligated to answer the complaint before 60 days from the date designated below as the date on which this notice is sent (or before 90 days from that date if your address is not in any judicial district of the United States.)

     If you do not return the signed waiver within the time indicated, I will take appropriate steps to effect formal service in a manner authorized by the Federal Rules of Civil Procedure and will then, to the extent authorized by those Rules, ask the court to require you (or the party on whose behalf you are addressed) to pay the full costs of such service. In that connection, please read the statement concerning the duty of parties to waive the service of the summons, which is set forth at the foot of the waiver form.

     I affirm that this request is being sent to you on behalf of the plaintiff, this _____ day of _____, _____.

_____
Signature of Plaintiff's Attorney
or Unrepresented Plaintiff

A — Name of individual defendant (or name of officer or agent of corporate defendant)
B — Title, or other relationship of individual to corporate defendant
C — Name of corporate defendant, if any
D — District
E — Docket number of action
F — Addressee must be given at least 30 days (60 days if located in foreign country) in which to return waiver

EXHIBIT 5:4   Waiver of Service of Summons

AO 399 (12/93)

WAIVER OF SERVICE OF SUMMONS

TO: _____

(NAME OF PLAINTIFF'S ATTORNEY OR UNREPRESENTED PLAINTIFF)

      I acknowledge receipt of your request that I waive service of a summons in the action of (CAPTION OF ACTION), which is case number (DOCKET NUMBER) in the United States District Court for the _____ District of _____. I have also received a copy of the complaint in the action, two copies of this instrument, and a means by which I can return the signed waiver to you without cost to me.

      I agree to save the cost of service of a summons and an additional copy of the complaint in this lawsuit by not requiring that I (or the entity on whose behalf I am acting) be served with judicial process in the manner provided by Rule 4.

      I (or the entity on whose behalf I am acting) will retain all defenses or objections to the lawsuit or to the jurisdiction or venue of the court except for objections based on a defect in the summons or in the service of the summons.

      I understand that a judgment may be entered against me (or the party on whose behalf I am acting) if an answer or motion under Rule 12 is not served upon you within 60 days after _____, or within 90 days after that date if the request was sent outside the United States.   (DATE REQUEST WAS SENT)

_____   _____

DATE   SIGNATURE

Printed/Typed Name: _____

As _____ of _____

          (TITLE)   (CORPORATE DEFENDANT)

Duty to Avoid Unnecessary Costs of Service of Summons

      Rule 4 of the Federal Rules of Civil Procedure requires certain parties to cooperate in saving unnecessary costs of service of the summons and complaint. A defendant located in the United States who, after being notified of an action and asked by a plaintiff located in the United States to waive service of a summons, fails to do so will be required to bear the cost of such service unless good cause be shown for its failure to sign and return the waiver.

      It is not good cause for a failure to waive service that a party believes that the complaint is unfounded, or that the action has been brought in an improper place or in a court that lacks jurisdiction over the subject matter of the action or over its person or property. A party who waives service of the summons retains all defenses and objections (except any relating to the summons or to the service of the summons), and may later object to the jurisdiction of the court or to the place where the action has been brought.

      A defendant who waives service must within the time specified on the waiver form serve on the plaintiff's attorney (or unrepresented plaintiff) a response to the complaint and must also file a signed copy of the response with the court. If the answer or motion is not served within this time, a default judgment may be taken against that defendant. By waiving service, a defendant is allowed more time to answer than if the summons had been actually served when the request for waiver of service was received.

EXHIBIT 5:7 Affidavit of Service of Summons and Complaint

**UNITED STATES DISTRICT COURT FOR
THE CENTRAL DISTRICT OF COLUMBIA CIVIL ACTION**

File No. _____

_____
Plaintiff

v.

_____
Defendant

Affidavit of Service of Summons and Complaint

I served a copy of the summons and complaint in the above matter by __[type of service]__ at __[time]__ on the ___ day of _____, _____, on

Name _____
Address where served _____

__[signature of process server]_____
Name
Signed and sworn to before me on:

_____
_____

Notary Public
My commission expires on _____

EXHIBIT 5:11   Request for Entry of Default Judgment by Clerk

REQUEST FOR ENTRY OF DEFAULT JUDGMENT BY CLERK WITH SUPPORTING AFFIDAVIT

The Plaintiff in the above entitled action requests the clerk of [*name of court*] to enter judgment by default against the Defendant [*name of defendant*] in the amount of [*state sum*], plus interest at the rate of [*state rate*], and costs.

_____
Attorney for Plaintiff
(Address)
(Phone number)

AFFIDAVIT

State of _____

} ss.

County of _____

[*name of attorney*], being duly sworn, deposes and states:
1. That s/he is the attorney for Plaintiff in the above entitled action.
2. That Defendant's default in this action was entered on [*date default entered*].
3. That the amount due Plaintiff from Defendant is a sum certain in the amount of [*state amount*].
4. That the Defendant is not an infant, incompetant person, or in military service.
5. That the amount indicated is justly owed Plaintiff no part of which has been paid.

_____
Attorney for Plaintiff

[Jurat]
(A brief statement of amount due may be included.)

EXHIBIT 5:15   Motion to Set Aside Default Judgment

THE UNITED STATES DISTRICT COURT FOR THE _____ DISTRICT OF _____

Civil Action, File No. _____

_____,
Plaintiff

v.

MOTION TO SET ASIDE DEFAULT
JUDGMENT (NOTICE OF MOTION)

_____,
Defendant

The Defendant moves the Court for an order to set aside the default judgment entered in the above action on _____, _____, on the grounds that _____

    [date]

_____

_____

_____

Attorney for Defendant
(Address)

EXHIBIT 6:1   Motion to Dismiss Complaint

STATE OF COLUMBIA	CIRCUIT COURT	CAPITOL COUNTY

MARY ANN JAMES,
           Plaintiff

    v.

ALLEN HOWARD,
          Defendant

Civil Action, File No. <u>22222</u>

MOTION TO DISMISS COMPLAINT

Defendant moves the court pursuant to Rule 12 (b)(6) of the Columbia Rules of Civil Procedure to dismiss the action because the complaint fails to state a claim against the Defendant upon which relief can be granted.

                                     _____
James McDuff
Attorney for Defendant
(Address)

EXHIBIT 6:3   Memorandum of Law in Support of Defendant's Motion to Dismiss Complaint

STATE OF COLUMBIA	CIRCUIT COURT	CAPITOL COUNTY

MARY ANN JAMES,

        Plaintiff

    v.   Civil Action, File No. <u>22222</u>

ALLEN HOWARD,

        Defendant

MEMORANDUM OF LAW
IN SUPPORT OF DEFENDANT'S MOTION TO DISMISS COMPLAINT

Defendant argues to the court that the Plaintiff's complaint should be dismissed on the grounds that it does not state a claim against the Defendant on which relief can be granted. In support of said motion, Defendant states the following.

That Plaintiff's complaint does not allege facts in support of a critical element of a claim for negligence. A long-standing precedent in the state of Columbia is the case of *Winthrop v. Walters*, 200 Col. 392, 105 W.W. 63 (1934).* That case established the rule of law that a civil complaint must allege and state facts in support of each element of the cause of action, and that failure to do so made the complaint defective and upheld the lower court's dismissal of the complaint for its failure to state a cause of action.

In the recent case of *Arnold v. Taggie*, 592 Col. 365, 354 S.W.2d 615 (1992)* where the plaintiff failed to allege that the defendant's negligent operation of a van was the cause of plaintiff's injuries, the court held the dismissal of the complaint for failure to state a cause of action was proper.

Plaintiff's complaint in this action does not allege that the Defendant's conduct caused her injuries, nor does it allege any facts to support such a conclusion.

Therefore, Plaintiff's complaint is defective and should be dismissed.

Date _____

                                               _____

                                               James McDuff
                                               Attorney for Defendant
                                               (Address)
                                               (Phone number)

* Citations in this memorandum are fictitious

Transparency Master 27

TYPE	FORM [each answer after "reasonable inquiry" must be accurate and submitted in good faith (Rule 11)]	EFFECT
Deny	Defendant denies the allegations of paragraph ____ of the complaint, or Denied (depending on jurisdiction).	Denies each allegation of that paragraph; any allegation not denied is admitted [Rule 8(d)].
Without knowledge	Defendant is without knowledge or information sufficient to form a belief as to the allegation that (state specific allegation) of paragraph ____ of the complaint.	Works as denial but provides flexibility as more information comes to light. Defendant has burden to make "reasonable inquiry."
Admit in part	As to paragraph ____, defendant admits to operating the van on (date) but denies the balance of the allegations in the paragraph.	Makes the admission specific, but denial of remainder of paragraph avoids having to list and possibly omitting a response to some of the items.
Leave to proof	As to paragraph ____, defendant neither admits or denies but leaves plaintiff to his/her proof.	Works as denial by requiring plaintiff to prove facts at trial.
Own allegation	Defendant denies the allegation in paragraph ____ and alleges (own version of facts).	Gives defendant the opportunity to be free from certain implications of plaintiff's langauge and to state more accurately what happened.
No answer/ conclusion of law	The allegation in paragraph ____ of the complaint improperly states a conclusion of law.	Protects defendant but points out that pleadings are not to allege conclusions of law, just facts in support of the conclusions.
Denial on information and belief	Defendant, on information and belief, denies the allegation in paragraph ____ of the complaint.	Generally used by corporations to deny based on the best information they have at the time from their employees. Permits change if necessary.
Not applicable to defendant	Paragraphs ____ to ____ of the complaint do not apply to this defendant, but insofar as they do refer to, may refer to, or may apply to this defendant, each allegation is denied.	Provides notice that defendant feels the allegation does not apply to this defendant but protects defendant in case it is intended to apply.

EXHIBIT 6:12   Answer and Counterclaim to Forrester Complaint: Notice Pleading

UNITED STATES DISTRICT COURT FOR THE EASTERN DISTRICT OF COLUMBIA

Civil Action, File No. _____

ANN FORRESTER
  and
WILLIAM FORRESTER,

                    Plaintiffs

        v.   DEFENDANTS' ANSWER
                                                    AND COUNTERCLAIM

RICHARD HART
  and
MERCURY PARCEL SERVICE, INC.,

                    Defendants

COUNT I

1. Admitted.
2. Denied that Defendant drove vehicle negligently.
3. Defendant lacks knowledge sufficient to form a belief regarding the truth of the allegation in paragraph 3 of Plaintiff's complaint, and therefore denies same.

FIRST AFFIRMATIVE DEFENSE

Plaintiff was more than 50 percent negligent in causing the accident, and is therefore barred from recovery.

COUNT II

4. No answer required.
5. Denied.

COUNTERCLAIM

On February 26, _____, on Highway 328 in Capitol County, Columbia, Plaintiff Ann Forrester negligently tried to cross the road in front of Defendant's vehicle, causing injury to Defendant Hart.

   As a result of plaintiff's negligence, Defendant Hart suffered lacerations and contusions and lost days of work all to the sum of $2,200.

SECOND COUNTERCLAIM

Defendant Mercury Parcel incorporates by reference the facts as alleged in the first counterclaim and alleges the Plaintiff's negligence caused damage to the defendant's vehicle and required the hiring of an extra employee for one week all to the sum of $4,250.

   WHEREFORE, Defendants request that Plaintiffs' action be dismissed and demand judgment against the Plaintiffs for $2,200 for Defendant Hart and $4,250 for Defendant Mercury Parcel Service, Inc., plus interest and costs.

                                            _____
                                            Attorney for Defendants
                                            (Address)
                                            (Phone number)

EXHIBIT 6:14 Answer and Counterclaim to Forrester Complaint: Code (Fact) Pleading

STATE OF COLUMBIA	CAPITOL COUNTY	CIRCUIT COURT

ANN FORRESTER
  and
WILLIAM FORRESTER,

          Plaintiffs

      v.   Civil Action, File No. _____

RICHARD HART
  and
MERCURY PARCEL SERVICE, INC.,

          Defendants   Jury Trial Demanded

DEFENDANTS' ANSWER, NEW MATTER, AND COUNTERCLAIM

1. Admitted.
2. Admitted.
3. Admitted.
4. Admitted.
5. Admitted.
6. Admitted.
7. Admitted.
8. Denied. Defendant specifically denies negligence in the following areas:
   a. Driving the vehicle at an excessive rate of speed under the circumstances.
   b. Failure to exercise a proper lookout.
   c. Failure to exercise adequate control of vehicle.
   d. Failure to exercise due and adequate care under the circumstances.
9. Admitted in part, denied in part. Defendant admits the Plaintiff was struck by Defendant's van and denies the balance of the allegations in the paragraph.
10. Denied. Defendant, after reasonable investigation, lacks sufficient knowledge to form a belief regarding the truth of Plaintiff's allegation of injuries, and therefore denies same.

11. Denied. Defendant, after reasonable investigation, lacks sufficient knowledge to form a belief as to the truth of Plaintiff's allegation of loss of money, and therefore denies same.

WHEREFORE, Defendants request the Plaintiffs' complaint be dismissed and that judgment be entered for Defendants for their costs and disbursements.

NEW MATTER

12. Defendants incorporate by reference paragraphs 1 through 11 of their answer.
13. Defendant alleges that Plaintiff is more than 50 percent responsible for the accident and resulting injuries and therefore barred from recovery due to the following:
    a. Failing to stop, look, and listen for oncoming traffic prior to stepping onto the highway.
    b. Failing to maintain a lookout for oncoming vehicles while crossing said highway.
    c. Not taking care for her safety and the safety of others in light of the ice on the highway.

WHEREFORE, Defendants request that Plaintiff's complaint be dismissed and that judgment be entered for Defendants for their costs and disbursements.

ANSWER TO COUNT II

14. No response to Plaintiff's paragraph 12 is required.
15. Denied. Defendants specifically deny being negligent or responsible for Plaintiff's alleged injuries. Defendant, after reasonable investigation, lacks suficient knowledge to form a belief regarding the truth of Plaintiff's allegation of loss of consortium of his wife and the amount of the loss.

WEREFORE, Defendants request that Plaintiffs' complaint be dismissed and that judgment be entered for Defendants for their costs and disbursements.

NEW MATTER COUNT II

16. Defendants incorporate by reference paragraphs 12 and 13 of their answer alleging the Plaintiff is more than 50 percent responsible for the accident and is barred from recovery.

WHEREFORE, Defendants request that Plaintiffs' complaint be dismissed and that judgment be entered for Defendants for their costs and disbursements.

DEFENDANTS' COUNTERCLAIM

17. Defendants incorporate by reference paragraphs 1 through 16 of their answer.
18. On February 26, _____, Plaintiff Ann Forrester negligently walked onto Highway 328 in Capitol County, Columbia by failing to take the following precautions:
    a. Stop, listen, and look for oncoming traffic
    b. Maintain a lookout while crossing said highway.
    c. Exercise due care for her own safety and that of others in light of the ice on the highway.
19. As a result of Plaintiff's negligence, Defendant Hart had to take emergency evasive action, unsuccessfully avoiding Plaintiff, and causing his vehicle to leave the road and strike a tree.
20. Because of Plaintiff's negligence, Defendant Hart suffered lacerations to his head and legs, bruises to various parts of his body and head, intense emotional anxiety, insomnia, and substantial pain and suffering.
21. As a further consequence of Plaintiff's negligence and the aforesaid injuries, Defendant Hart has incurred the expense of hospital and medical care, and a loss of income totaling two thousand two hundred dollars ($2,200).

COUNT II

22. Defendants incorporate by reference paragraphs 1 through 21 of their answer.

23. Becaue of Plaintiff Ann Forrester's negligence, Defendant Mercury Postal Service suffered damage to their delivery van and expenses necessitated by a replacement employee for Mr. Hart for one week, totaling four thousand two hundred and fifty dollars ($4,250).

WHEREFORE, Defendants demand judgment against Plaintiff Ann Forrester for Defendant Hart in the amount of $2,200, and for Defendant Mercury Parcel Service in the amount of $4,250, plus their costs and disbursements.

_____
Attorney for Defendants
(Address)
(Phone number)

State of Columbia

        ss.

Capitol _____

Richard Hart, being duly sworn on oath according to law, deposes and states that he has read the foregoing Answer and Counterclaim, and that the matters stated therein are true to the best of his knowledge, information, and belief.

_____
Richard Hart

Subscribed and sworn to before me this _____ day of _____, _____.

_____
Notary Public

My commission expires January 1, _____.

State of Columbia

        ss.

County of Capitol _____

Sandra Franz, being duly sworn on oath according to law deposes and states that she is the president and duly authorized representative of Mercury Parcel Service, Inc., and has read the foregoing Answer and Counterclaim, and that the matters stated therein are true to the best of her knowledge, information, and belief.

_____
Sandra Franz

Subscribed and sworn to before me this _____ day of _____, _____.

My commission expires January 1, _____.

_____
Notary Public

EXHIBIT 6:21   Motion for Summary Judgment by Plaintiff

[FED. R. CIV. P. Rule 56(a)]

[*Title of Court and Cause*]

Plaintiff, by his attorneys and pursuant to Rule 56 of the Federal Rules of Civil Procedure, moves the Court to enter summary judgment for the plaintiff on the ground that there is no genuine issue as to any material fact, and the plaintiff is entitled to judgment as a matter of law.

In support of this motion, plaintiff refers to the record herein including the amended complaint, the answer thereto, the defendants' amendment to the answer, plaintiff's annexed affidavit sworn to the ___ day of _____, _____, and _____.

_____

Attorney for Plaintiff

Address: _____

Transparency Master 31

[Caption and Names of Parties]
1. Pursuant to Fed.R.Civ.P. 26(f), a meeting was held on (date) at (place) and was attended by:
(name) for plaintiff(s)
(name) for defendant(s) (party name)
(name) for defendant(s) (party name)
2. Pre-discovery Disclosures. The parties [have exchanged] [will exchange by (date)] the information required by [Fed.R.Civ.P. 26(a)(1)] [local rule _____].
3. Discovery Plan. The parties jointly propose to the court the following discovery plan: [Use separate paragraphs or subparagraphs as necessary if parties disagree.]
Discovery will be needed on the following subjects: (brief description of subjects on which discovery will be needed)
All discovery commenced in time to be completed by (date) . [Discovery on (issue for early discovery) to be completed by (date) .]
Maximum of _____ interrogatories by each party to any other party. [Responses due _____ days after service.]
Maximum of _____ requests for admission by each party to any other party. [Responses due _____ days after service.]
Maximum of _____ depositions by plaintiff(s) and _____ by defendant(s).Each deposition [other than of _____] limited to maximum of _____ hours unless extended by agreement of parties.
Reports from retained experts under Rule 26(a)(2) due:
  from plaintiff(s) by (date)
  from defendant(s) by (date)
Supplementations under Rule 26(e) due (time(s) or interval(s)).
4. Other Items. [Use separate paragraphs or subparagraphs as necessary if parties disagree.]The parties [request] [do not request] a conference with the court before entry of the scheduling order.
The parties request a pretrial conference in (month and year).
Plaintiff(s) should be allowed until (date) to join additional parties and until (date) to amend the pleadings.
Defendant(s) should be allowed until (date) to join additional parties and until (date) to amend the pleadings.
All potentially dispositive motions should be filed by (date). Settlement [is likely] [is unlikely] [cannot be evaluated prior to (date)] [may be enhanced by use of the following alternative dispute resolution procedure: _____].
Final lists of witnesses and exhibits under Rule 26(a)(3) should be due
  from plaintiff(s) by (date)
  from defendant(s) by (date)
Parties should have _____ days after service of final lists of witnesses and exhibits to list objections under Rule 26(a)(3).
The case should be ready for trial by (date) [and at this time is expected to take approximately (length of time)].[Other matters.]
Date: _____
[Adopted April 22, 1993, effective December 1, 1993.]

I. PARALEGAL'S DISCLOSURE CHECKLIST

☐ Review case file, pleadings, complexity, and so on.
☐ Get date for court scheduling conference/order.
   ☐ Calculate other deadlines based on this date.
   ☐ Modify according to subsequent plan, stipulation, or court order.
☐ Meet with the supervising attorney to determine desired depth and amount of disclosure and discovery needed and any objections to disclosure.
☐ Assist the attorney in arranging the parties' planning meeting
   ☐ Assist at meeting.
   ☐ Draft agreed plan (Exhibit 7:1), stipulations, and objections as directed.
   ☐ Submit the parties' planning report to court if so directed.
☐ Using the investigation plan (Chapter 3) or similar approach, identify, gather, and organize the supporting evidence to be disclosed as set out in Rule 26(a). Remember to include any pertinent electronic data and documents, such as e-mail.
☐ Review each item to be disclosed to raise any concerns about client confidentiality and/or attorney work product. Do this throughout the disclosure and discovery process.
☐ Format materials to be disclosed as directed. They must be written.
   ☐ Include signature line and attorney's address.
☐ Give formatted materials to supervising attorney for final review and signature.
☐ Serve disclosure materials on all parties.
☐ Upon receipt of disclosure materials from the other parties, review these materials carefully to see that all disclosure requirements have been met.
☐ Prepare disclosure of any expert witness, accompanying report, and other materials as set out in Rule 26(a)(2). Review parallel materials from other parties.
☐ Using the pertinent steps outlined above, serve and promptly file with the court all pretrial discovery, including witnesses to be called, exhibits and other evidence described in Rule 26(a)(3). Do at least thirty days before trial.
☐ In consultation with the supervising attorney, prepare any objections to pretrial material disclosed by the other party within fourteen days of its receipt.
☐ Check calendar dates periodically to see whether supplementation of previously submitted disclosure is needed. Supplement as required [Rule 26(e)].
☐ Use a tracking log for all disclosure and discovery.

EXHIBIT 7:3   Checklist for Planning and Drafting Interrogatories

- ☐ Planning the Interrogatories
  - ☐ Have the attorney's directions for the task firmly in mind.
  - ☐ Review the file, especially the pleadings, and all related information discovered to date.
  - ☐ Review the elements of the claim, defense, counterclaim, and so on.
  - ☐ Determine the goals to be accomplished.
    - ☐ Review the pleadings for areas needing more detail or explanation.
    - ☐ Brainstorm on each element of the claim, defense, counterclaim, and so on, to develop useful theories of liability and areas of inquiry.
    - ☐ Determine what must be discovered (witnesses, documents, physical evidence, etc.) and the likely leads to it.
  - ☐ Acquire and read form interrogatories for suggested areas of inquiry, format, and questions.
  - ☐ Organize areas of inquiry by logical topics.
  - ☐ Avoid pitfalls.
    - ☐ Do not try to cover entire areas exhaustively if other methods of discovery are available and better lend themselves to the specific objective.
    - ☐ Keep brief to avoid setting off a paper war.
    - ☐ Avoid forcing the other side to prepare their case.
- ☐ Drafting the Interrogatories
  - ☐ Acquire the civil practice rules for interrogatories and locate samples of interrogatories in the jurisdiction for the particular case.
  - ☐ Draft an introductory paragraph stating to whom the interrogatories are directed, applicable rules, and time required for a reply.
  - ☐ Provide a definition and abbreviation section.
  - ☐ Provide an instruction section so the answer and any objections will be placed in a format most useful to the questioner.
  - ☐ Draft questions that focus on finding out more about the basis for the allegations in the opponent's pleadings.
  - ☐ Draft questions that cover the theories of liability and defenses thereto as they relate to the elements of the offense.
  - ☐ Draft questions calling for opinion and legal and factual contentions [Rule 33(b)].
  - ☐ Draft concluding or summary interrogatories.
  - ☐ Include notice of continuing obligation to update answers.
  - ☐ Provide for attorney's signature and certificate of service.
- ☐ Specific Drafting Techniques
  - ☐ Ask whether the question elicits information that is likely to lead to admissible evidence.
  - ☐ Keep questions concise, precise, and easy to understand.
  - ☐ Avoid excessive questions.
  - ☐ Number questions and sets of questions sequentially.
  - ☐ If the number of interrogatories is limited:
    - ☐ Do not number or letter subdivisions.
    - ☐ Avoid making subtopics conspicuous: avoid "and," "or," "the," semicolons, and colons.
    - ☐ Reduce lists to single word or class.
    - ☐ Ask singular questions that require multiple answers.
    - ☐ Use multiple-choice questions where appropriate.
  - ☐ Use correct verb tense.
  - ☐ Phrase questions to determine if answers are based on firsthand knowledge and if impediments to accuracy exist.
  - ☐ Avoid questions that permit yes or no answers unless more detail is requested.
  - ☐ Phrase questions to restrict evasiveness in the answer.
  - ☐ Proofread carefully prior to submitting to attorney for review.
  - ☐ Final Preparation and Service of Interrogatories
  - ☐ Make all final corrections.
  - ☐ Get attorney's signature.
  - ☐ Prepare copies for each opponent and the court, if the court requires filing.
  - ☐ Serve copies on the opposing attorney by mail or in person.
  - ☐ Execute the certificate of service and file it and the original interrogatories with the court clerk.

WHITE, WILSON & McDUFF
ATTORNEYS AT LAW
FEDERAL PLAZA BUILDING, SUITE 700
THIRD AND MARKET STREETS
LEGALVILLE, COLUMBIA 00000
(111) 555-0000

November 1, _____

Ms. Ann Forrester
1533 Capitol Drive
Legalville, Columbia 00000

Dear Ms. Forrester:

I have enclosed a set of questions called "interrogatories" submitted by the attorney for Mercury Parcel Service. The rules of the court require your full cooperation in answering each of the questions. We are permitted to assist you. Our office has the information to answer questions 1, 2, 8, 9, and 10. We need information from you to draft answers to 3, 4, 5, 6, 7, and 11.

We must have the information and your answers no later than November 15. Failure to return the answers when they are due may be harmful to your case. On receipt of this information and your answers, we will integrate them into our draft and return the answers for your review and verification before a notary public. Should it be necessary to have you come to the office to discuss your answers, we will inform you.

Please begin gathering all the documents and other information needed to answer the questions identified above. When writing answers to the questions, keep the following in mind:

1. Answer all questions completely but concisely.
2. Always be truthful.
3. Do not try to withhold information or be evasive. For example, if asked about witnesses (and you know of three), name all three; or, if you are asked about prior injuries, lawsuits, or criminal convictions, state them with identifying dates, times, location, etc. Any evasiveness is a serious matter and can definitely affect the outcome of the case.
4. Look up all dates, amounts, times, and other information requested.
5. You are not required to make an unreasonable search or incur unreasonable expense. If you do not have access to the information, you are not required to provide it. State any reasons for not answering a question.

After answering the questions, return them in the enclosed envelope.

Thank you for your assistance. If you have questions, please let me know.

Sincerely,

Terry Salyer
Paralegal
White, Wilson & McDuff

Transparency Master 35A

[Case Caption]
DEFENDANT UNITY DELIVERY SERVICES, INC.'S ANSWERS TO PLAINTIFF'S
FIRST SET OF INTERROGATORIES
INTRODUCTION

A. The enclosed responses are intended for and restricted to use in this case only.

B. No enclosed answer should be taken as an admission to the existence of any facts for purposes of trial.

C. [*Others*]

ANSWERS

INTERROGATORY NO. 1

Identify the physician(s) who conducted the company's annually required physical exams of Donald Jordan (defendant driver) and the dates of the last two exams.

ANSWER

Walter P. Hayes, M.D., 1644 W. Endover Ave., South Town, Columbia 11000, phone: (500) 000-0000. Exams were held on June 15, ___ and April 28, ___.

INTERROGATORY NO. 2

State Rodney Robert's (your disclosure material, page 3) qualifications at the time he worked on the van in question, and the dates, hours, and nature of the work performed, and identify any records and documents not previously disclosed that record what was done on the van, including any of Mr. Robert's comments and assessments concerning repairs made or that should be made.

ANSWER

Mr. Roberts worked on the van in question on September 2, ___, for 2.2 hours. He was an apprentice mechanic at that time, having been employed at that job for seven months. He had previous vocational training at Warton County Tech. On September 2, Mr. Roberts gave the van a forty-point safety inspection, changed the oil, and replaced the air filter. A parts department form 3510 reflects any parts ordered by a mechanic for a vehicle. The daily work order form was disclosed previously.

INTERROGATORY NO. 3

What company correspondence exists for the three-year period immediately preceding the accident regarding your policies or proposed notices on driver health and safety?

ANSWER (OBJECTION)

Defendant corporation objects to interrogatory 3 because it is too broad in scope, the burden or expense of the proposed discovery outweighs its likely benefits, and it covers material that is protected by defendant corporation's attorney-client privilege.

INTERROGATORY NO. 4

State defendant driver Donald Jordan's traffic record for the last five years.

ANSWER/OBJECTION

To defendant corporation's knowledge, Mr. Jordan has no violations in the last three years, but objects to interrogatory no. 4 insofar as it requests information that is in the custody of the Columbia Division of Motor Vehicles and is as easily obtainable by plaintiff as it is by defendant.

INTERROGATORY NO. 5

State the number of vans of the same make and model as the van in question purchased by your company in the last three years.

ANSWER (OBJECTION)

Defendant corporation objects to interrogatory no. 5 because the information requested is irrelevant to issues in this action and is not likely to lead to the discovery of admissible evidence.

INTERROGATORY NO. 6

State each fact on which you rely to support your allegation in paragraphs 3 and 4 of your counterclaim that plaintiff assumed the risk of injury and caused the accident in question.

ANSWER

1) Plaintiff was intoxicated at the time of the accident and 2) plaintiff entered the road and thumbed her nose not only at defendant driver, but also at the driver of a vehicle that passed seconds earlier.

Date_____

_____
Barbara J. Lane, CEO
Unity Delivery Service, Inc.

Date_____

_____
Lincoln Case, Attorney
789 Courthouse Square
Legalville, Columbia 00000
Phone: (111) 111-1111

Transparency Master 36A

AO 88 (11/91) Subpoena in a Civil Case

United States District Court

_____ DISTRICT OF _____

V.

SUBPOENA IN A CIVIL CASE

CASE NUMBER:

TO:

☐ YOU ARE COMMANDED to appear in the United States District Court at the place, date, and time specified below to testify in the above case.

PLACE OF TESTIMONY	COURTROOM
	DATE AND TIME

☐ YOU ARE COMMANDED to appear at the place, date, and time specified below to testify at the taking of a deposition in the above case.

PLACE OF DEPOSITION	DATE AND TIME

☐ YOU ARE COMMANDED to produce and permit inspection and copying of the following documents or objects at the place, date, and time specified below (list documents or objects):

PLACE	DATE AND TIME

☐ YOU ARE COMMANDED to permit inspection of the following premises at the date and time specified below.

PREMISES	DATE AND TIME

   Any organization not a party to this suit that is subpoenaed for the taking of a deposition shall designate one or more officers, directors, or managing agents, or other persons who consent to testify on its behalf, and may set forth, for each person designated, the matters on which the person will testify. Federal Rules of Civil Procedure, 30(b) (6).

ISSUING OFFICER SIGNATURE AND TITLE (INDICATE IF ATTORNEY FOR PLAINTIFF OR DEFENDANT)	DATE

ISSUING OFFICER'S NAME, ADDRESS AND PHONE NUMBER

(See Rule 45, Federal Rules of Civil Procedure, Parts C & D on Reverse)

AO 88 (11/91) Subpoena in a Civil Case

PROOF OF SERVICE

	DATE	PLACE
SERVED		

SERVED ON (PRINT NAME)	MANNER OF SERVICE

SERVED BY (PRINT NAME)	TITLE

DECLARATION OF SERVER

I declare under penalty of perjury under the laws of the United States of America that the foregoing information contained in the Proof of Service is true and correct.

Executed on _____
              DATE

SIGNATURE OF SERVER

ADDRESS OF SERVER

_____

Rule 45, Federal Rules of Civil Procedure, Parts C & D:

(c) PROTECTION OF PERSONS SUBJECT TO SUBPOENAS.

(1) A party or an attorney responsible for the issuance and service of a subpoena shall take reasonable steps to avoid imposing undue burden or expense on a person subject to that subpoena. The court on behalf of which the subpoena was issued shall enforce this duty and impose upon the party or attorney in breach of this duty an appropriate sanction, which may include, but is not limited to, lost earnings and a reasonable attorney's fee.

(2)(A) A person commanded to produce and permit inspection and copying of designated books, papers, documents or tangible things, or inspection of premises need not appear in person at the place of production or inspection unless commanded to appear for deposition, hearing or trial.

(B) Subject to paragraph (d)(2) of this rule, a person commanded to produce and permit inspection and copying may, within 14 days after service of the subpoena or before the time specified for compliance if such time is less than 14 days after service, serve upon the party or attorney designated in the subpoena written objection to inspection or copying of any or all of the designated materials or of the premises. If objection is made, the party serving the subpoena shall not be entitled to inspect and copy the materials or inspect the premises except pursuant to an order of the court by which the subpoena was issued. If objection has been made, the party serving the subpoena may, upon notice to the person commanded to produce, move at any time for an order to compel the production. Such an order to compel production shall protect any person who is not a party or an officer of a party from significant expense resulting from the inspection and copying commanded.

(3) (A) On timely motion, the court by which a subpoena was issued shall quash or modify the subpoena if it

(i) fails to allow reasonable time for compliance;
(ii) requires a person who is not a party or an officer of a party to travel to a place more than 100 miles from the place where that person resides, is employed or regularly transacts business in person, except that, subject to the provisions of clause (c)(3)(B)(iii)

of this rule, such a person may in order to attend trial be commanded to travel from any such place within the state in which the trial is held, or

(iii) requires disclosure of privileged or other protected matter and no exception or waiver applies, or

(iv) subjects a person to undue burden.

(B) if a subpoena

(i) requires disclosure of a trade secret or other confidential research, development, or commercial information, or

(ii) requires disclosure of an unretained expert's opinion or information not describing specific events or occurrences in dispute and resulting from the expert's study made not at the request of any party, or

(iii) requires a person who is not a party or an officer of a party to incur substantial expense to travel more than 100 miles to attend trial, the court may, to protect a person subject to or affected by the subpoena, quash or modify the subpoena or, if the party in whose behalf the subpoena is issued shows a substantial need for the testimony or material that cannot be otherwise met without undue hardship and assures that the person to whom the subpoena is addressed will be reasonably compensated, the court may order appearance or production only upon specified conditions.

(d) DUTIES IN RESPONDING TO SUBPOENA.

(1) A person responding to a subpoena to produce documents shall produce them as they are kept in the usual course of business or shall organize and label them to correspond with the categories in the demand.

(2) When information subject to a subpoena is withheld on a claim that it is privileged or subject to protection as trial preparation materials, the claim shall be made expressly and shall be supported by a description of the nature of the documents, communications, or things not produced that is sufficient to enable the demanding party to contest the claim.

Transparency Master 37A

WHITE, WILSON & McDUFF
ATTORNEYS AT LAW
FEDERAL PLAZA BUILDING, SUITE 700
THIRD AND MARKET STREETS
LEGALVILLE, COLUMBIA 00000
(111) 555-0000

Ms. Ann Forrester
1533 Capitol Drive
Legalville, Columbia 00000

November 1, _____

Dear Ms. Forrester:

As we previously discussed, the time has come when you will need to testify about the accident and your injuries at a deposition. We will work with you to prepare for the deposition. Mr. White will be with you and is confident you will do just fine.

The deposition is scheduled for Wednesday, December 2, _____, at 10:00 a.m. in room 202 in the Federal District Court Building at Third and Race Streets. Parking is available at the Municipal Parking facility behind the courthouse. Please be there by 9:30 a.m.

A deposition is an examination of a witness under oath by the opposition and in the presence of a court reporter. The examination is to determine the witness's version of the facts, the evidence in support of those facts, and the location of the evidence and names and addresses of persons having information about the evidence. It is an important stage in the lawsuit because the other side will be evaluating you as a witness, including your appearance, ability to recall facts, truthfulness, etc. Depositions produce evidence that might lead to a settlement of the case. They may also be used at trial to test the consistency and credibility of a witness. Therefore, good preparation on your part is important. It will give you confidence.

In preparing for the deposition, please keep the following in mind:

1. Depositions are occasionally postponed, and if so, you will be informed.
2. Chronologically review the facts of the case up through your current medical status; anticipate questions on dates, times, directions, distances, speeds, weather, clothes, events, injuries, medical treatments, expenses, witnesses, statements, etc. If you do not know distances and the like for sure, reasonable approximations are acceptable. A return to the scene of the accident to check distances, obstructions, and other details before your deposition might be helpful.
3. Be sure you have informed your attorney of all matters about the incident and those that reflect on your own honesty and credibility. Do not allow your attorney to be surprised to your detriment.
4. Expect the opponent's attorney to do most or all of the questioning. Your attorney will object when it is necessary.
5. Dress neatly, be pleasant, and speak up.
6. Listen to each question carefully. If you do not understand the question, *do not guess at its meaning*, simply state you do not understand.
7. Think about your answer; do not blurt out answers. Be cautious of a series of questions in quick succession that intend to lead you to the answer your opponent desires. Answer thoughtfully at your own pace.
8. Above all, tell the truth. You will be under oath and should avoid giving in to the temptation to fill in gaps of information. Do not guess. Should you want to correct an earlier answer, simply indicate your desire to do so. The attorney will assist you.

9. If you are asked, "Did you speak with your attorney about testifying today?" answer "yes." There is nothing wrong with speaking with your attorney about testifying. If the question is, "Did your attorney tell you what to say?" the correct answer is, "He told me to tell the truth." Other than that, your attorney will not tell you what to say.

10. While testifying, it is preferable that you not seek guidance from your attorney. You must answer the question as best you can. If your attorney feels a question is improper, an objection will be stated. An objection is a signal to you to stop answering.

11. A common technique of adverse attorneys is to remain silent after your answer. They frequently do this in the hope that you will feel compelled to add more information. It can be damaging information. Therefore, resist the temptation to add information and to fill silences.

12. Avoid discussing your case and any aspect of your testimony with anyone other than your attorney. Casual conversation about your case can be damaging.

13. You may be asked at the deposition to sketch a diagram of the accident scene. If you try some practice sketches, you should not have any difficulty with this.

14. During the deposition you may be given documents, diagrams, photographs, or other items to identify. Be sure to examine such items carefully to see that they accurately reflect what they intend to reflect before you agree to their accuracy.

15. Be prepared to describe your injuries and medical treatment in detail. Do not exaggerate or understate.

16. Be prepared to discuss any injuries you suffered or claims you made before this accident.

17. Bring any documents that you have been requested to bring.

18. Be prepared to discuss changes such as loss of pay, property damage, and other out-of-pocket expenses.

19. It is not necessary to memorize possible answers and is probably better if you do not.

In summary, you will do the best job at your deposition if you are well prepared, thoughtful, deliberate, and truthful. I will be contacting you soon to set up a time when you and Mr. White can meet to discuss the deposition. Meanwhile, if you have any questions or concerns, please feel free to contact me or Mr. White.

Very truly yours,

Terry Salyer
Paralegal

EXHIBIT 8:7   Page Extracts from Topical (Subject) Deposition Summaries

TOPICAL DEPOSITION SUMMARY

Case: FORRESTER v. MERCURY PARCEL

Case File No. _____

Deponent: Ann Forrester

Date: 12/10/___

Page 1

Attorney: L. Ott

Paralegal: C. Sorenson

TOPIC: INJURIES

Page	Line	Summary	Exhibits/ Notes
38	3	Date of accident 2/26/___ ... she felt sharp pain at point of impact.	
	6	... pain was extreme in hip, lower abdomen, and upper left leg.	
39	1	... she felt nauseated.	
53–54	28–1	Date: 3/10/___ ... after two weeks in hospital the leg felt numb and she could not move it. etc.	

TOPIC: EMPLOYMENT

Page	Line	Summary	Exhibits/ Notes
62	7	... she said she rarely missed work before the accident.	
66	12	... believed she would have been promoted by now to master teacher.	
71	2	... does not see how she can return to teaching with her current disabilities. etc.	

EXHIBIT 8:8   Deposition Digest (Narrative)

DEPOSITION DIGEST (NARRATIVE/TOPICAL)

CASE: Johns v. Brown No. Civ 880050   Page 1
DEPONENT: Catherine Johns

                                                       Atty: H. Ray
DATE: 7/16/01   Plgl: C. Borden

Background

Catherine Johns is 34 years old, residing at 1437 Oak St., Legalville, Columbia, is divorced and has one child, Edward, 10. (pages 1–2)

She has a master's in business administration from Columbia State and her high school diploma from East Legalville H.S. (3)

Employment

She worked for two years after high school for Columbia Foods as a secretary from 1993–95. She has worked for Fairmont Computers as a market analyst from 2000 to the present, earning $30,000 per year. (4–5)

The Accident

On May 3, 2000, Johns was driving to work, proceeding north on Holiday Blvd. in Legalville at 7:40 A.M. She was wearing a seat belt. She drove a 1999 Chevrolet Camaro and was 200 feet from the intersection of Holiday and East Twenty-third St. when defendant, Harold Brown, suddenly backed out of his driveway at 3201 Holiday Blvd. in his 2000 Buick Le Sabre. (9, 32)

Johns "swung car to left" but the back of Brown's car hit hers in the Camaro's left front. (10–11)

Johns' car "lurched" into oncoming traffic lane, crossed lane avoiding car driven by Walter Forth, went up curb and "smashed" into Roy's Hot Dog Stand and stopped. (11–12, 23)

Injuries

Johns hit her head on the steering wheel, breaking her nose and cheekbone. Ligaments in her left knee were severed, and she suffered muscle damage and internal injuries to the stomach lining causing internal bleeding. (14, 27)

Johns was rushed to Mount Sinai Hospital where she was admitted and operated on to correct fractures, stop internal bleeding, and repair ligaments in knee. Minor plastic surgery was performed on her nose by Dr. Kizar on 7/2/00. (15, 28)

One year after accident Johns still needs cane to walk. The fractures have healed satisfactorily but chewing is limited and painful, and one obvious scar remains on her nose. (16, 28–30).

Loss of Employment

(*narrative continues*)

Transparency Master 40

[FED. R. CIV. P. Rule 34]

[Title of Court and Cause]

Plaintiff A_____ B_____ requests defendant C_____ D_____ to respond within _____ days to the following requests:

(1) That defendant produce and permit plaintiff to inspect and to copy each of the following documents:
[Here list the documents either individually or by category and describe each of them.]
[Here state the time, place, and manner of making the inspection and performance of any related acts.]

(2) That defendant produce and permit plaintiff to inspect and to copy, test, or sample each of the following objects:
[Here list the objects either individually or by category and describe each of them.]
[Here state the time, place, and manner of making the inspection and performance of any related acts.]

(3) That defendant permit plaintiff to enter *[here describe property to be entered]* and to inspect and to photograph, test, or sample *[here describe the portion of the real property and the objects to be inspected]*.
[Here state the time, place, and manner of making the inspection and performance of any related acts.]

_____
Attorney for Plaintiff

Address: _____

EXHIBIT 9:2   Example of a Production and Inspection Request Form

UNITED STATES DISTRICT COURT FOR THE EASTERN DISTRICT OF COLUMBIA

ANN FORRESTER,
                Plaintiff
      v.
MERCURY PARCEL SERVICE, INC.,
                Defendant
}
Civil Case, File No. _____

PLAINTIFF'S REQUEST FOR PRODUCTION AND INSPECTION OF DOCUMENTS,
THINGS, AND REAL PROPERTY

According to Rule 34 of the Federal Rules of Civil Procedure, Plaintiff requests Defendant Mercury Parcel Service to respond within thirty days to the following requests:

1. That Defendant produce and permit Plaintiff to inspect and to copy each of the following documents:
   a. The specific rules and regulations of the Interstate Commerce Commission requiring regular safety checks, maintenance, and repair of vehicles used in interstate commerce.
   b. Defendant's file copies of all Form 2010s submitted to the ICC between Feb. _____ and Jan. _____
   c. All Form ICC-2010As recording the regular maintenance and safety checks on van number 23 over the two-year period preceding the accident on February 26, _____.
   d. All Form ICC-2010As for all other Defendant's delivery vehicles over the two years preceding the accident.
   e. All Form ICC-2015s recording complaints and needed repairs and subsequent repairs made to van number 23 for the two years preceding the accident.
   f. All Form ICC-2015s on all other vehicles for the two years preceding the accident.
   g. All photographs or negatives therof that Defendant had taken of the accident scene and the damage to the van. Plaintiff will inspect and copy these items at the office of Plaintiff's attorney on November 1, _____ at 9:00 A.M., or at any other reasonable time and place convenient to counsel in this action.

                                        _____
                                        Arthur White
                                        Attorney for Plaintiff
                                        (address)
                                        (phone number)

Transparency Master 42

EXHIBIT 9:4	Document Production Original Source Log	
New File No.	Description	Source
F-1	Maint. form 20's ____	Merc. Parcel Rm 108 drawer 31 Ralph Johnson
F-2	Maint. form 20's ____	Merc. Parcel Rm 108 Dr. 31 R. Johnson
F-3	Driver Hour Logs ____	Merc. Parcel Rm 108 Dr. 81 Betty Robinson

WHITE, WILSON & McDUFF
ATTORNEYS AT LAW
FEDERAL PLAZA BUILDING, SUITE 700
THIRD AND MARKET STREETS
LEGALVILLE, COLUMBIA 00000
(111) 555-0000

December 15, _____

Ms. Ann Forrester
1533 Capitol Drive
Legalville, Columbia 00000

Dear Ms. Forrester:
You may recall I mentioned in our initial interview the possibility that the other side in this case may request an examination by a doctor of their choosing to confirm the existence and extent of your injuries. Lynn Ott has contacted me to request such an exam.

The exam is scheduled for January 23, _____, at 1:30 in the afternoon. The examining physician is Dr. Melissa Ward, whose office is at 1644 Fountain Drive near exit 103 off I-275 in Legalville. Please make arrangements to be at Dr. Ward's office at the appointed time.

The exam will consist of a routine examination of your injuries, brief strength and movement tests, and a discussion with the doctor about your injuries and disabilities. The exam should last about an hour.

Before going to the examination, you may choose to make a list of your injuries, treatments, pain, disabilities, and current status. A review of your injury diary should help you.

You should cooperate fully in the exam and be sure neither to overstate nor understate the progress of your condition.

Mr. White believes the exam will be beneficial to your case. If you have any concerns, please let me know.

Very truly yours,

Terry Salyer
Paralegal

EXHIBIT 10:8   Settlement Agreement

SETTLEMENT AGREEMENT

[*Name of first party*] of [*address*], hereafter referred to as _____ and [*Name of second party*] of [*address*], hereafter referred to as _____ in order to settle the controversy between them designated as _____ v. _____ civil case file number _____ filed in the [*name of court*] by the dated signatures below, HEREBY AGREE AND INTEND TO BE LEGALLY BOUND BY THE FOLLOWING TERMS:

1. (Here state in detail each term, condition, and covenant agreed to by both parites: amount, time, and terms of payment; nature and extent of releases that will be executed and delivered; when and how the action will be dismissed; how court costs and legal fees will be handled; whether goods or documents will be exchanged or discharged; what collateral, if any, will be used to insure the agreement; and any other items suggested by the attorney.)

(Seal)   (First Party)

Attest _____   by _____
                                                          Party (or duly authorized officer)

                                                          _____
                                                          Address

                                                          Date _____

(Seal)   (Second Party)

Attest _____   by _____
                                                          Party (or duly authorized officer)

                                                          _____
                                                          Address

                                                          Date _____

EXHIBIT 10:10   Stipulation and Consent Decree and Order

(Caption omitted)

STIPULATION AND CONSENT DECREE

The parties to this action, having agreed to settle this case, hereby consent to the entry of the following order.

This order and stipulation shall not be interpreted as an admission of wrongdoing by either party.

THE PARTIES, BY THEIR ATTORNEYS, STIPULATE THAT THIS CASE SHALL BE SETTLED BY CONSENT DECREE AS FOLLOWS:

1. The Defendant, _____, shall pay to the Plaintiff, _____, the agreed upon sum of $_____ for all injuries, pain and suffering, and damages, past, present, and future sustained from [*state accident or other source of claim*] on [*date*]   .

2. The Defendant, _____, shall pay the sum in the following manner: _____.

3. The Plaintiff, _____, shall pay to the Defendant, _____, the sum of $_____, for all damages, past, present, and future, incurred by the Defendant as a consequence of [*restate accident as source of claim*] as alleged in Defendant's counterclaim against Plaintiff.

4. The Defendant shall pay the costs of this action in the sum of $_____

5. The parties will pay their own attorney's fees.

6. At the time of compliance with all terms of the stipulation and decree, the above captioned action shall be dismissed with prejudice.

For Plaintiff,   For Defendant,

_____   _____
Attorney for Plaintiff   Attorney for Defendant

_____   _____
Address   Address
Date _____

(Caption omitted)

ORDER

Having reviewed the above entitled case and the Stipulated Consent Decree freely entered into by both parties to this action as evidenced by the signature of their respective counsel, the Court ORDERS, ADJUDGES, and DECREES that the Stipulation is approved, as set forth and attached hereto, so ordered this _____ day of _____.

_____
Judge, United States District

Court for the _____

District of _____

EXHIBIT 10:11 Settlement Distribution Statement

WHITE, WILSON & McDUFF
ATTORNEYS AT LAW
FEDERAL PLAZA BUILDING, SUITE 700
THIRD AND MARKET STREETS
LEGALVILLE, COLUMBIA 00000
(111) 555-0000

SETTLEMENT DISTRIBUTION STATEMENT

CASE: _____ vs. _____   CLIENT: _____

   Civil Case No. _____

   Court _____

Total Gross Settlement (received from _____) $_____

   Less Attorney's Expenses (Itemized)

      Travel $_____

      Printing $_____

      Doctors' Report Fees $_____

      Medical Records Fees $_____

      Phone Calls $_____

      Court Costs and Filing Fees $_____

      Photocopies $_____

      Others $_____

                      Subtotal $_____ $_____

Less Attorney's Fee (figured by percentage of gross in contingency fee case or by itemized billing entries)

                                          $_____

           Total Net Settlement Due Client $_____

EXHIBIT 11:1   Trial Preparation Checklist

At Least Three Months Prior to Trial

- ☐ If a trial has not yet been set, check with the attorney and file any request or praecipe needed to have trial date set.
- ☐ Calendar the trial date, unless done previously, and check for any scheduling conflicts.
- ☐ Check case status sheet and calendar more frequent updatings right up to trial.
- ☐ Check to see that all required disclosure to date has been completed, including exchange of expert witness names and written report (federal rules).
- ☐ Check time deadline chart and confirm that key dates are calendared and that litigation team members are reminded.
- ☐ Meet with team to assess need for special exhibits and technology at trial.

At Least Six Weeks Prior to Trial

- ☐ Meet with litigation team to review case status and establish countdown work schedule.
- ☐ Review the case status sheet and keep it updated in the file. Inform the attorney of any depositions, discovery, or other steps needing completion or updating.
- ☐ Review the facts of the case to determine if there is a need to amend the pleadings.
  - ☐ Keep the client fully informed. Meet as needed.
  - ☐ Prepare witnesses' statements or witness sheets.
  - ☐ Highlight important facts both for and adverse to client.
- ☐ Review pretrial order to determine if the issues have been narrowed.
  - ☐ List documents, exhibits, and witnesses needed on each point, including refutation of the opponent's key points and evidence.
- ☐ See that legal memoranda have been completed on all questions of law including any likely questions relating to the admissibility of evidence or any motions likely to be made at trial.

At Least Three Weeks Prior to Trial

- ☐ Prepare a list of all witnesses needed; confirm with the attorney and have subpoenas prepared and served.
- ☐ Conduct the jury investigation.
- ☐ Conduct an investigation of the judge, the opposing attorney, and the community if not previously done.
- ☐ Prepare any exhibits, diagrams, audiovisual aids.

At Least One Week Prior to Trial

- ☐ Verify the court date.
- ☐ Complete the trial notebook.
- ☐ Verify service of all subpoenas.
- ☐ Prepare client and witnesses for testimony.
- ☐ Make final arrangements for the following:
  - ☐ Lodging of the client, witnesses, and staff as needed.
  - ☐ Payment of lost wages for witnesses if committed by the attorney.
  - ☐ Transportation of all files, documents, audiovisual equipment, computer terminal, and other items needed at trial.
  - ☐ Petty cash needed for parking, meals, phone calls, and so on.

One Day Before Trial

- ☐ Meet one last time with the trial team.
- ☐ Meet with the client.

Transparency Master 48A

Trial date: Case name and no.:
Client: (plaintiff, defendant)   Defendant:
Attorney: Court:
Paralegal: Date filed:
Date client interviewed: Judge:

PLEADINGS AND MOTIONS ON PLEADINGS

Description	Date filed and served	Response date	Check if met	Hearing date
Complaint				
Motion to dismiss				
Answer and counterclaim				
Motions				
Reply				

Amended pleadings (list)/dates filed/response date

Default: Date: Judgment for default: Date
Jury trial demanded   ☐ yes   ☐ no

INVESTIGATION

Signify investigations to be conducted and witnesses to interview

☐ Done/date:
☐ Done/date:
☐ Done/date:

DISCOVERY

Interrogatories

Plaintiff's	Date served	Due date	Response date served	Motion to object or compel

Defendant's

Depositions (by plaintiff)

Deponent/date	Notice/fee	Subpoena/fee	Location	Court reporter	Done
					☐
					☐
					☐

Depositions (by defendant)

					☐
					☐
					☐

Request for Production of Documents and Things (Plaintiff's)

Describe	Served	Due	Answer/served	Objections/motions	Conducted	Copies delivered
					☐	☐

(Defendant's)

					☐	☐

Request for Mandatory Physical Examination   ☐ yes   ☐ no

Person examined: Date: Physician:

Request for Admissions (Plaintiff's)

Served	Due	Answer/served	Objections/motion to compel	
				☐
				☐
				☐

(Defendant's)

			☐
			☐
			☐

MOTIONS

Describe	Notice	Served	Response	Argued	Result

CASE EVALUATED

Plaintiff's damages: Total:

Other notes:

PRETRIAL CONFERENCE

Date: Judge:

Preparation (describe)	Done
	☐
	☐

Notes on result:

SETTLEMENT

Settlement précis or brochure	☐

Date: Terms:

Releases/settlement agreement	☐
Stipulation, consent decree, order for dismissal	☐
Settlement distribution statement	☐

FINAL PRETRIAL

Witness	Address	Subpoenaed	Fees
Jury Investigation			☐
Preparation of Exhibits and Diagrams			
			☐
			☐

253

Preparation of Trial Notebook (Proof chart, voir dire questions, witness sheets, legal research, motions, jury instructions, etc.) ☐

Preparation of Witnesses, Including Experts ☐

Final Arrangements (Lodging, meals, parking, petty cash, transportation of trial materials) ☐

Trial Date: Verdict/Date: Judgment/Date:

Motions: Served   Reply due   Reply

☐

☐

APPEAL

Notice filed: ☐

Order transcript and preparation of record ☐

File brief: Plaintiff/date   Defendant/date

Oral argument: Date:

Court Decision

Motion for reconsideration: ☐

Bill of costs ☐

EXHIBIT 11:3   Juror Data Sheet

Case: File no: Court: Date:

Attorney: Paralegal:

Juror no. _____ Name: Aliases:

Overall Evaluation: Good _____ Bad _____ ? _____

Place and date of birth: Race: Ethnic group:

Address:

Previous addresses (list most recent first):

Grew up at:

Home phone: Work phone:

Employment (list most recent first):

Occupation: Employer: Address: Phone: Dates:

Present annual income:

Highest level of education completed: Date:

Health:

Marital status: single: married: divorced: widowed: remarried:

Immediate family

    Parents: Age: Occupation/education:

    Where lived most of life: Current address

Spouse: Age: Occupation/education:

Children: Age: Occupation/education:

Grandchildren: Age: Occupation/education:

Juror's political affiliation: Rep ( )   Dem ( )   Ind ( )

Liberal ( )   Middle of road ( )   Conservative ( )

Juror's professional and service associations:

Veteran:

Religious affiliation: Active: Inactive:

Hobbies and activities:

Friends and relatives:

Financial concerns in case:

Relationship to parties:

Prior jury service: Where: When:

Type of case: Verdict: Foreperson:

Previous or current litigation: Plaintiff: Defendant:

Where: When: Type: Outcome:

Close family or friend involved in litigation: Plaintiff: Defendant:

Where: When: Type: Outcome

Prior experiences related to trial and issues: (for example, ever injured in an accident, ever at fault in accident, etc.)

Assessment of opinion on: Issues:

Source of information: Survey: Fellow workers: Other:

Assessment of jury leadership potential and strength of personality:

Source of information:

Record of juror on current panel:

Overall evaluation: Good: Bad: ?:

Explanation:

Additional comments:

EXHIBIT 11:5   Outline of Trial Notebook

Page or tab number   Divisions

Section One: Reference
      1. Table of contents (complete last)
      2. Persons and parties at trial
         a. Court, courtroom, judge, clerks, bailiff: name, phone, office.
         b. Own staff at trial: attorneys, paralegals, others: names, phone numbers, motel, etc.
            (1) Firm's office numbers for assistance
            (2) Client
            (3) Witnesses   Names, addresses, phone numbers, affiliations
            (4) Expert witnesses
            (5) Others
         c. Opponent's staff at trial and witnesses, experts, phone, affiliation, etc.
      3. Case summary: factual and legal issues
      4. Proof chart: elements and proof in case

EXAMPLE OF PROOF CHART

Plaintiff's elements and facts to prove	Source of proof
Negligence:	
Excessive speed	Wit: Schnabel "between 45–50 mph" Statement
	Client: "over 45" deposition p. 26 (Tab____)
	Photo: skidmarks, test. of Officer Timms
Inattentiveness	Hart's test.: "looking at speedometer" deposition p. 35 (Tab____)
Same for defendant's proof	

Section Two: Pleadings and Pretrial
      1. Major pleadings as amended: complaint, answer, defenses (all tabbed and color coded to separate plaintiff's from defendant's with key sections highlighted)
      2. Alternative method: (Simply summarize pleadings stating allegations, admissions, and denials. Highlight remaining issues.)
      3. Any pretrial order could go here

Section Three: Last-Minute Motions
      1. Any remaining pretrial motions with supporting authorities
      2. Authority to oppose any expected last-minute motions by the opposition

Section Four: Voir Dire (Jury Selection)
      1. Jury challenge chart: (usually eighteen to twenty boxes on standard sheet of paper to enter no. and name of each juror, plus attorney's and paralegal's notes on suitability)

2. Profiles of jurors most and least wanted (predetermined by jury investigation)

3. Outline of voir dire questions: (if the attorney is permitted to conduct voir dire—if not, proposed questions for the judge to ask jurors with copies for the judge and opponent. Questions are usually drafted by the attorney or an experienced paralegal with attorney review. There are numerous sources on conducting voir dire.)

4. List grounds and authority for challenges for cause (a challenge for cause is a request to remove a juror for lawful reasons such as inability to be impartial)

5. List of authorities on any anticipated jury issues (including legality of any voir dire questions)

6. Jury panel chart (usually twelve boxes to place names and comments about jurors finally selected to hear the case)

7. Blank loose-leaf sheets to write notes on voir dire or to record any objections

Section Five: Opening Statement

1. Complete text

2. Alternative: outline (both drafted by attorney. Use large orator's type.)

Section Six: Outline of Order of Proof and of Opponent's Proof

Section Seven: Witness Examination

1. Own witnesses: direct examination (tabbed subsections for each witness in the order they will be called by the attorney). Each witness subsection should include:

   a. A synopsis of witness information, whether subpoenaed and interviewed.

   b. An outline or chronological list of the questions that will be asked on direct examination on each critical issue. Use wide margins so notes can be added.

   c. Notations of what exhibits will be introduced by the witness with inserted copies of the exhibits.

   d. Notations inserted on any references to diagrams or other audiovisual aids.

   e. Conflicting testimony of witness (references to prior statements, depositions, interrogatories, admissions)

   f. Questions to rehabilitate witness, especially if harmful cross-examination by opponent is expected

   g. Summaries of any statement, letters, memos, or depositions with key quotations highlighted. Cross-indexed to section containing copy of full statement, deposition transcript, memos, etc.

   h. Copies of subpoena with proof of service

2. Opponent's witnesses: cross-examination (Some attorneys prefer an entirely separate, different colored notebook for dramatic effect.)

   a. Similar structure to item 1 above with emphasis on conflicting and inconsistent statements, testimony, or other impeachment material

   b. Inserted copies of necessary exhibits, criminal records, etc.

Section Eight: Exhibits (sometimes kept as separate book)

    1. Exhibit log

EXAMPLE OF EXHIBIT LOG

Ex. no. (as premarked or as assigned at trial)	Descript. or title of exhibit	Whether introduced, accepted or rejected. Notes.
<u>Own ex.</u> (in order of introduction)	Title	Introduced ( ) Accepted ( ) Rejected ( ) Notes:
P-1 (Plaintiff) <u>Opponent's ex.</u>	Title	Introduced ( ) Accepted ( ) Rejected ( ) Notes:

    2. Each exhibit in expected order of introduction (may be separated by identifying tabs, including exhibit no. if premarked by clerk

    3. Each exhibit section should include:

        a. Exhibit summary sheet paper-clipped to exhibit (includes brief description of exhibit and significance, case file location or code no., witness needed for introduction, foundation, brief statement of authorities on admissibility

        b. Exhibit

            (1) Marked copy for judge, opponent, one for each juror if desired, one for witness section, one for exhibit section

            (2) If oversized, specially indexed to separate container or if cannot be hole punched, place in three-hole plastic envelopes

        c. Place exhibits in box if there are too many for notebook.

    4. List of all audiovisual props and accessories indexed to specially numbered containers if necessary.

Section Nine: Trial Motions and Authorities

(Any motions such as for dismissal or for directed verdict. Reminders to make motions should be placed at chronologically appropriate places and cross-indexed to this section. Consult with the attorney for what and where.)

Section Ten: Jury Instructions (Charge to Jury)

    1. Attorney's copy of all instructions proposed to be read to the jury. (Should contain complete language of instruction, one instruction per page, plus any legal authorities supporting its use. Each should contain a checkoff for given, modified, or refused. Have enough copies for all parties and the judge.)

    2. Opponent's proposed instructions with checkoff

    3. Final copy of instructions read by the judge

    4. If no jury, copy of request for findings of fact and conclusions of law for the judge

Section Eleven: Proposed Plain or Special Issue

(Verdict) (Optional section depending on detail of verdict desired by attorney. Necessary copies for judge and opponent. Section for supporting authorities.)

Section Twelve: Closing Statement
1. Text or outline of closing statement (orator's size print)
2. Props or list of props
3. Notepad for recording items to add as trial progresses

Section Thirteen: Law Section
1. Trial memo or brief covering the law on all significant questions of law concerning the issues, evidence, motions, and other anticipated objections or conflicts
2. Geared to the judge's bench book (legal authority book)
3. Should include points and responses to law likely to be argued by opponent
4. May include concisely typed copy of the Rules of Evidence and pertinent Rules of Procedure with authorities
5. Cross-indexed to relevant sections in notebook

Section Fourteen: To Do, Notes, and Reminders
1. List of items to do before trial in completing notebook, serving subpoenas, gathering exhibits, etc.
2. Reminders of motions to make, whether to poll jury, and others
3. Notepad for items that come up at trial that should be commented on, argued, noted for appeal, etc.

EXHIBIT 12:1   Renewal of Motion for Judgment as a Matter of Law (State: Motion for Judgment Notwithstanding the Verdict)

UNITED STATES DISTRICT COURT

THE _____ DISTRICT OF _____

_____ DIVISION

ABC

    Plaintiff   Civil Action File No._____

    v.

XYZ

    Defendant

RENEWAL OF MOTION FOR JUDGMENT AS MATTER OF LAW

[Plaintiff or Defendant] ABC having, at the close of all the evidence, moved this court for judgment as a matter of law, which motion was denied, and subsequently a verdict was entered for [plaintiff or defendant], [plaintiff or defendant] ABC now renews his/her motion for judgment as a matter of law pursuant to Rule 50(b), Federal Rule of Civil Procedure.

    This motion is made on the grounds that [*state specific grounds for each point*].

    Dated_____

                                  Respectfully submitted,

                                    _____

                                    Attorney

                                    Address:

                                    Phone:

[*Notice*]

Transparency Master 52A

United States District Court

_____ DISTRICT OF _____

_____   **BILL OF COSTS**

V.

_____   Case Number:

Judgment having been entered in the above entitled action on _____ against _____,
                                                    Date

the Clerk is requested to tax the following as costs:

Fees of the Clerk . . . .$ _____

Fees for service of summons and subpoena . . . . _____

Fees of the court reporter for all or any part of the transcript necessarily obtained for use in the case . . . . _____

Fees and disbursements for printing . . . . _____

Fees for witnesses (itemize on reverse side) . . . . _____

Fees for exemplification and copies of papers necessarily obtained for use in the case . . . . _____

Docket fees under 28 U.S.C. 1923 . . . . _____

Costs as shown on Mandate of Court of Appeals . . . . _____

Compensation of interpreters and costs of special interpretation services under 28 U.S.C. 1828 . . . . _____

Other costs (please itemize) . . . . _____

                              TOTAL $ _____

SPECIAL NOTE: Attach to your bill an itemization and documentation for requested costs in all categories.

DECLARATION

I declare under penalty of perjury that the foregoing costs are correct and were necessarily incurred in this action and that the services for which fees have been charged were actually and necessarily performed. A copy of this bill was mailed today with postage prepaid to:

_____.

Signature of Attorney: _____

Name of Attorney: _____

For: _____ Date: _____
        Name of Claiming Party

Costs are taxed in the amount of _____ and included in the judgment.

_____ By: _____ _____
   Clerk of Court   _Deputy Clerk_   _Date_

Transparency Master 52B

WITNESS FEES (computation, cf. 28 U.S.C. 1821 for statutory fees)						
NAME AND RESIDENCE	ATTENDANCE		SUBSISTENCE		MILEAGE		Total Cost Each Witness
	Days	Total Cost	Days	Total Cost	Days	Total Cost	
					TOTAL		

NOTICE

Section 1924, Title 28, U.S. Code (effective September 1, 1948) provides:
"Sec. 1924. Verification of bill of costs."

"Before any bill of costs is taxed, the party claiming any item of cost or disbursement shall attach thereto an affidavit, made by himself or by his duly authorized attorney or agent having knowledge of the facts, that such item is correct and has been necessarily incurred in the case and that the services for which fees have been charged were actually and necessarily performed."

See also Section 1920 of Title 28, which reads in part as follows:
"A bill of costs shall be filed in the case and upon allowance, included in the judgment or decree."

The Federal Rules of Civil Procedure contain the following provisions:
Rule 54 (d)

"Except where express provision therefor is made either in a statute of the United States or in these rules, costs shall be allowed as of course to the prevailing party unless court otherwise directs, but costs against the United States, its officers, and agencies shall be imposed only to the extent permitted by law. Costs may be taxed by the clerk on one day's notice. On motion served within 5 days thereafter, the action of the clerk may be reviewed by the court."

Rule 6 (e)

"Whenever a party has the right or is required to do some act or take some proceedings within a prescribed period after the service of a notice or other paper upon him and the notice or paper is served upon him by mail, 3 days shall be added to the prescribed period."

Rule 58 (In Part)

"Entry of the judgment shall not be delayed for the taxing of costs."

Transparency Master 53A

APPELLATE PROCEDURE CHECKLIST

Appellate procedure is fairly standardized in the federal courts, but it varies among states. Research the applicable state rules and adhere to them. Following is a list of the significant procedural steps and deadlines for the Federal Rules of Appellate Procedure (FRAP).

- ☐ Consult with the attorney for go-ahead on the appeal.
- ☐ Develop a case appeal log for recording compliance with all requirements of the appellate process.
- ☐ File a petition for leave to appeal from *interlocutory order* pursuant to 28 U.S.C. § 1292(b). (Appellee has seven days after service of petition to file opposition, FRAP 5.)
- ☐ For post-trial appeals, verify that a judgment or order has been entered [FRAP 4(a)(7); FRCP 58, 79(a)].
- ☐ Draft a notice of appeal (see following form).
- ☐ File the notice of appeal within thirty days of entry of judgment or order, or within sixty days if the United States or an officer or agency thereof is a party [FRAP 3, 4(a)(1)]. Pay fees.
- ☐ File a bond for the cost of the appeal or a supersedeas bond if the execution of judgment is stayed [FRAP 7 and 8]. Seek stay or injunction pending appeal.
- ☐ File with the court of appeals a statement naming each party represented on appeal by the attorney within ten days after filing the notice of appeal [FRAP 12(b)].
- ☐ Order a transcript of the trial proceedings (pertinent parts or pertinent videotape if so recorded) from the court reporter within ten days after filing the notice of appeal or entry of an order disposing of the last motion such as a motion for a new trial, whichever is later. File a copy of the order with the clerk of district court [FRAP 10(b)(1)]. Unless the entire transcript is ordered, file (within ten days of notice or entry of an order) a statement of issues on appeal. Notify all other parties of the issues on appeal and the parts of the transcript ordered so appellee can designate other parts of the record needed for appeal within ten days of service of the order and statement of the issues. Appellant must order the added parts within the next ten days [FRAP 10(b)(3)]. Parties may stipulate to omit certain parts of the record.
- ☐ See to it that the reporter files a transcript with the clerk of district court within thirty days of the date ordered by appellant [FRAP 11(b)]. See that the record is complete (pleadings, exhibits filed in district court, transcript or parts thereof, and certified copies of docket entries), prepared by the clerk, and submitted by the clerk of court to the court of appeals. Check to see if the record is sent by the clerk. The clerk of the court of appeals will docket the case upon receipt of the notice of appeal and the docket entries (FRAP 12).
- ☐ Send to appellee a designation of the parts of the record to be included in the appendix within ten days of the filing of the record, unless there is an agreement on the contents (FRAP 30) or the alternative method of filing the appendix is chosen [FRAP 30(c)].

- ☐ File all papers with the clerk of the court of appeals by mail addressed to the clerk. Some courts of appeal permit electronic filing. All papers must arrive within the required time limit. Briefs are considered timely if mailed before expiration of the time limit [FRAP 25(a)]. Proof of service should be filed with the papers [FRAP 25(d)].
- ☐ Service on the party or the party's counsel may be personal, by mail, or by commercial carrier.
- ☐ File a motion for extension of time if good cause can be shown [FRAP 26(b)]. The time for filing a notice of appeal may not be extended.
- ☐ Draft the brief and appendix according to the specifications in FRAP 28, 29, 30, and 32.
- ☐ File and serve appellant's brief and appendix within forty days after the date on which the record is filed. If the brief is not filed on time, the appellee may move for dismissal of the appeal. File twenty-five copies of all briefs [FRAP 31].
- ☐ File for an extension of time, if necessary.
- ☐ Note the date that appellee's brief is due. (Appellee has thirty days after receipt of appellant's brief to file and serve brief. [FRAP 31(a)].
- ☐ Check the opponent's brief for accurate statements of fact, case holdings and citations, and accurate recitation of the record.
- ☐ File and serve the appellant's reply brief within fourteen days after service of the appellee's brief [FRAP 31(a)]. Double-check all case citations and citations of the record before filing.
- ☐ Be sure all time limits are on the docket deadline control calendar.
- ☐ Record notice from the clerk of court whether oral argument is to be heard, and if so, the time, place, and duration of each side's oral argument [FRAP 34(b)]. Notify the attorney and see that all deadlines are calendared.
- ☐ Assist in the preparation of oral argument as requested by the attorney. Prepare an oral argument notebook.
- ☐ Arrange delivery of any exhibits to the court set up prior to oral argument, and removal immediately after argument.
- ☐ Attend oral argument to assist the attorney if requested (FRAP 34).
- ☐ Note the receipt of opinion and judgment (FRAP 36) and convey it to the attorney.
- ☐ Submit an itemized and certified bill of costs to the clerk with proof of service within fourteen days after entry of the judgment. Objection to the bill of costs must be filed within ten days of service of the bill [FRAP 39(d)].
- ☐ Draft and file a petition for rehearing if so directed by the attorney. The petition must be filed within fourteen days after entry of the judgment, forty-five days if United States or agency or officer is a party [FRAP 40(a)]. The petition should follow the form prescribed by Rule 32(a) and served according to Rule 31(b).
- ☐ Consider with attorney the filing of a motion to stay the mandate (direction of the Court of Appeals based on the judgment) pending an application to the U.S. Supreme Court for a writ of certiorari [FRAP 41(b)]. The motion must be filed within twenty-one days of the entry of judgment.

Transparency Master 54

EXHIBIT 12:12 Notice of Appeal

FORM 1. NOTICE OF APPEAL TO A COURT OF APPEALS FROM A JUDGMENT OR ORDER OF A DISTRICT COURT

United States District Court for the
_____ District of _____

File Number _____

Plaintiff
v.
Defendant

Notice of Appeal

Notice is hereby given that (here name all parties taking the appeal), (plaintiffs) (defendants) in the above named case,* hereby appeal to the United States Court of Appeals for the _____ Circuit (from the final judgment) (from an order (describing it)) entered in this action on the _____ day of [*date*]

(s) ________________________

Attorney for ________________

Address: __________________

*See Rule 3(c) for permissible ways of identifying appellants.

Transparency Master 55A

| EXHIBIT 12:16 | Sample Appellate Brief |

IN THE UNITED STATES COURT OF APPEALS
FOR THE _____ JUDICIAL CIRCUIT
Case No. _____

_____

_____,
           Appellant
  v.

_____

_____,
          Appellee

On Appeal from the United States District Court for the _____ District of _____

BRIEF AND ARGUMENT OF APPELLANT

(Attorney)_____
(Address)_____
Attorney for_____

(Table of Contents Page)
TABLE OF CONTENTS

Table of Contents i
Table of Authorities Cited ii
Statement of Subject Matter and Appellate Jurisdiction iii
Statement of the Issues iv
Statement of the Case 1
Statement of the Facts 2
Summary of the Argument 6
Argument 13
Conclusion 30

Transparency Master 55B

(Authorities Page)

TABLE OF AUTHORITIES CITED

Cases*   Page

*In alphabetical order. [These cites are fictional for purposes of illustration.]

Abrams v. Pure Manufacturing, Inc.,
500 U.S. 312, 33 L. Ed. 2d 419 (1995)..14, 27, 30

Cardigan v. Kramer,
439 U.S. 712, 30 L. Ed. 2d 108 (1980)..15, 22

Johnson v. Greenwood Supply, Inc.,
732 F.2d 19 (C.A.6, 1981) 15, 18

Wilson v. NLRR Labor Union,
298 F. Supp. 420 (N.D. Columbia, 1993)..25, 26

Rules
FED. R. CIV. P. 26 ....15, 17
FED. R. EVID. 410...16, 17

Statutes
COLO. REV. STAT. § 501 (1976) 28

Treatises
RESTATEMENT OF TORTS § 340 (1952) 28

....

STATEMENT OF JURISDICTION

The basis for subject matter jurisdiction at the district court for the _____ district of _____ is _____.
Appellate jurisdiction for . . .

STATEMENT OF THE ISSUES

The Honorable Walter F. DAVIS, Judge of the Northern District of Columbia, it is asserted made three errors at or following the trial in this case. The errors alleged are stated below:

1. _____

2. _____

3. _____

....

STATEMENT OF THE CASE*
*(FED. R. APP. P. 28(a)(6) "a statement of the case briefly indicating the nature of the case, the course of proceedings, and its disposition in the court below.")

This case is on appeal from the district court's ruling . . .

Transparency Master 55C

STATEMENT OF THE FACTS*
   *(7) a statement of the facts relevant to the issues submitted for review with appropriate references to the record [Rule 28(a)(7).
   In February of __, Ann Forrester, a brilliant and creative teacher and mother of two, was . . .

SUMMARY OF ARGUMENT*
   *[FED. R. APP. P. 28(a)(8)]

ARGUMENT*
   *[FED. R. APP. P. 28(a)(A)(B)].
   I. BECAUSE THE JURY VERDICT WAS CONTRARY TO THE GREAT WEIGHT OF THE EVIDENCE, THE TRIAL COURT ERRED IN DENYING PLAINTIFF'S MOTION FOR JUDGMENT AS A MATTER OF LAW.
   The law on when a motion for judgment as a matter of law is to be granted was reiterated in the recent Supreme Court case of *Abrams v. Pure Manufacturing, Inc.*, 500 U.S. 312, 33 L. Ed. 2d 419 (1995). The court stated the rule to be:
   When the evidence in a case demonstrates . . .

CONCLUSION*
   *(10)a short conclusion stating the precise relief sought [FED. R. APP. P. 28(a)(10)]. Under the rule of law stated in *Abrams v. Pure Manufacturing, Inc.*, the plaintiff must prove . . .

CERTIFICATE OF COMPLIANCE*
   "(11) the certificate of compliance, if required by Rule 32(a)(7)."

APPENDIX

Page of Transcript		Page of Appendix
T–1	Amended Complaint	1
T–3	Answer	4
T–110	Motion for Judgment as a Matter of Law	8
T–19–21	Relevant Testimony of Ms. Forrester	9–11